Whacked Out

Understanding why, achieving wellness

Michele Poff, PhD

Accomplish Publishing

🐝 Accomplish Publishing
www.accomplishcomm.com

2nd Edition

ISBN 978-1-941162-03-3

Acknowledgements

Thank you to my teachers for guiding me, pushing me, and believing in me. Thank you to my editors, Vandoren Wheeler and Amelia Cronan. Thank you to my artist, Karli Norell. Thank you also to all of those who have read previous drafts and offered input and feedback along the way, and those who have stimulated deeper thought and a richer final product with your provocative questions, challenges, and critiques.

Table of Contents

Introduction

Childhood is a critical time in our lives. As we are running around playing, our brains are developing—every single day until somewhere in our 20s. This brain development in childhood lays the foundation for our adult brains, and thus, for our lives as adults. So whatever happens in our childhoods affects us for our entire lives. This is why childhood is so important, and also why our childhoods hold the answers to many of our life challenges.

In childhood, few of us had perfectly nurturing and supportive mothers and fathers.[a] Most of us experienced some degree of stress in our childhoods, and maybe this kind of treatment has been normal in our family for generations, or maybe even since the beginning of time. Neglect can occur in any area of life, including emotional, social, and more, and it is the simple act of not paying attention to or addressing a child's needs in every life area pretty much at all times. Emotional/psychological abuse can happen in three ways: with emotional manipulation such as blame, verbal aggression which is basically attacks, and a homelife with domestic violence, even if we ourselves were not actually the ones getting smacked. Of course, abuse also includes direct physical violence and childhood sexual contact.

As you can see, this definition of neglect and abuse encompasses a lot of the childhood experiences most of us had. In fact, few people can actually say that their childhood home environment did not contain any of these elements. Lucky them!

Environments of neglect and abuse are stressful, and cause stress to the developing child. Traumatic events, where we feel intense horror, helplessness, or ongoing neglect and/or abuse, bring severe stress into anyone's life, especially a child's. So neglect, abuse, and trauma in childhood all create stress, which affects our developing brains and thus brings significant challenges in adulthood.

---

[a] For most of us, our primary caregiver was our mother. This is why the science talks about mothers and their children. However, we know that a child's primary caregiver is also often not the child's mother, for a variety of reasons. Thus, with the exception of "in utero" discussions, mentions of "mother" in this book should be interpreted as "primary caregiver", particularly if that is more accurate for your situation.

Brain Development

The human brain takes many years to fully develop—it doesn't finish developing until our twenties. So when a child develops in an environment of stress, that stress impacts the child's developing brain in unhealthy ways. The stress actually causes the brain to grow improperly! This is because the child's brain adapts to the stress in its environment and shapes around that stress, which distorts the brain as it grows—the brain regions needed for detection of threat and survival grow enlarged, while those needed for functions like thinking, impulse control, and social appropriateness do not grow large enough. This process is fully discussed in Chapter 4.

Not surprisingly, this brings many many problems to our adult lives, including at minimum distorted perceptions and thinking. The thing is, with distorted perceptions and thinking, we don't even realize our perceptions and thinking are distorted because *this* is the way we were taught to think. *This* is what we were taught is appropriate thinking and behavior. So when we see that society's functions lie at odds with our own perceptions and thinking, we generally tend to think the problem rests with *them*.

These types of distortions are just the tip of the iceberg. Other problems can include addiction, substance abuse, weight management problems, relationship difficulties, attention deficits, and even physiological problems such as migraine and cardiovascular issues, to name a few.

Hope

Fortunately, the brain is plastic. That means that it can be reshaped within and by our environments. And that means, that all is not lost. Even if we suffered stress in our childhoods, which resulted in us having some real issues getting through the day as adults, we can heal, at least a little.

Every area of our lives is adversely affected when we are raised in a stressful home environment—every realm of human existence.

With awareness and a bit of effort, we can shift our perceptions and thinking into healthier zones. We can heal in every area of our lives.

In This Book

This book brings you the science on the entire spectrum of stressful childhood environments and healing from them. It provides all of the pieces to the puzzle of why we are the way we are and how to be better humans. The first part articulates the problems that ensue from a stressful childhood environment and also lays out specific behaviors that create a stressful environment. The second part presents healing options in six primary dimensions of the human experience: spiritual, physical, emotional, psychological, social, and intellectual.

In this material, I feel like I've found the pieces to this giant puzzle of life, and when I piece them all together, a whole new picture emerged about, well, about humanity itself. Like a good scout, once I found the trail, I wanted to mark it for others to easily follow. Hence, this book.

I've searched far and wide in the scientific research literature, and I've brought you science from a lot of places to connect the dots and illuminate what it is, precisely, that we seem to need healing from, and to illustrate many ways to move forward into feeling better, happier, more at ease. All of the tools necessary for that transformation are here. This information is not new, as you can see if you peek at the reference list, but this is the first time anyone has brought it all together into one cohesive narrative that outlines causes, effects, and healing paths for our common life struggles. Nearly all of the material here directly represents the science in each respective area. For you scholars out there, this book is basically a giant literature review.

In addition to bringing together causes, effects, and healing strategies all together into one place that you can carry in one hand, which in itself offers a major contribution to the materials currently available on mental wellness, this book also presents a multitude of healing methodologies and strategies within multiple dimensions. Most healing books tend to address only one dimension or perhaps only a single facet of one dimension—and those books are incredibly important because they will provide much deeper and richer information on that single phenomenon than I can provide here, given the breadth of information this book contains. I hope this book spurs you on to find others that call to you and enable you to learn more deeply about these areas and more.

If you do any of the things this book suggests, you will feel a little better; your anxiety will ease a little. The more of these strategies you work with, the better you will feel.

A Couple of Disclaimers
Ultimately, this book is about healing from our childhood stress. Most of us can cross the threshold into mental wellness with the tools in this book, especially if we are starting from a place of being able to function well in society. Not everyone,

however, can. For some of us, our early experiences misshaped our brains in ways that cannot be recovered or healed very much at all. But even in these circumstances, this book can help, and applying the options presented can help every individual improve their lives, even if only just a little.

Also, as a responsible scholar, I should point out that I am a social scientist, with a background in Communication. That is a sister discipline to psychology, but I am not a neuroscientist or a psychologist. Only a couple of elements of this book come from my home discipline. So no, I am not a bona fide expert in these other fields. However, as a scholar, I am comfortable reading through the scientific research in any field. I have painstakingly reviewed the science as it pertains to this topic and present it to you here, hopefully clearly, cogently, and accurately.

As professionals, we're not supposed to dabble in areas where we lack specific expertise. No one is an expert in all of these fields, so it makes sense that no one has yet tried to bring together material from multiple disciplines to help make sense of this one major life phenomenon. I'm not an expert in all of these fields either by any means, but I'm willing to take a risk by digging into research fields far from my own in order to help make sense of this major mystery in the human condition: Why the heck are we all so whacked out and how do we get better? For sure there are people better qualified than I am to write this kind of book—but they don't seem to be doing it, so I'm giving it my best shot.

The Journey

This book will take you on a journey of discovery of your inner self and others through the objective eyes of science, and offer dozens of options for improving your self and your life. It will give you great awareness about what happened to you and why you have the struggles you do. It will build your understanding of your self, and it carves a path to greater peace and happiness.

Most of these options don't really require you to *do* anything—just shift your thinking a smidge and look at things a bit differently, behave a bit differently. These small efforts will help you feel a lot better and make your life easier in every single way large and small. All of your relationships will improve. You can clear the fog that prevents you from moving further forward. You will be a healthier person, a better person.

If you happen to be in a bit of a critical stage at the moment and are looking for some immediate relief, I recommend Chapter 6 Spirituality, the tapping portion of

Chapter 8 Emotional Intelligence, and/or either the self-esteem portion of Chapter 9 Psychology or Chapter 10 Social Relationships, whichever speaks to you.

The Reason

Why should you go through the trouble to read this book, build your self-understanding and take steps to heal?

When we grew up in homes with neglect and abuse as a way of life, we didn't get the message that we're lovable or worthy of much. But we are! You are worthy of love and you are a valuable human being. The less you feel that way at this moment, the more this book can help you!

You deserve to have a better life. Those in your life deserve to have a better you.

You're worth it.

So let's go! I will take you there.

I.   The Whacking Out

This first section presents the problems of our unwellness. It traces this phenomenon from its roots, the stress in our childhood home environments, to the effects of this kind of environment on our brain development and the issues we have as adults because of this kind of background.

This section begins with a chapter on the adult life consequences of unwellness, which covers the areas of our lives affected. As you will see, issues with addiction, migraine, anxiety, poor stress management, difficult relationships, low self-worth, distorted thinking, and suicide are just the beginning of this discussion. Certainly, you will see yourself or some people you know here. The science here is from psychology and neuroscience.

Chapter 2 discusses how we manage the challenges that severe stress brings. There are healthy and unhealthy ways to cope with our stressful or difficult experiences. The healthy strategies include reflecting on the trauma in a positive light and finding a way to incorporate it into a healthy worldview. Unhealthy strategies include blame, runaway thinking, and logical fallacies. Since we all have difficult experiences in this life, you will certainly recognize your own coping behaviors in this chapter and learn more about what healthy coping strategies look like. The science: psychology.

In chapter 3 we look at the underlying causes of most of our mental unwellness: a stressful childhood home environment. This chapter carefully outlines behaviors that damage us as we grow and develop. A lot of these behaviors are commonplace in a lot of our homes, probably since about the beginning of time. Everyone will identify some of these experiences as their own, and many of us have experienced all of these behaviors in our childhoods and then, consequently, also as adults. The science: psychology, communication.

Chapter 4 takes us through the impacts on our brains as they develop in a stressful home. This chapter demonstrates the kind of brain warping that literally occurs when a child develops in an environment of stress. Here, I walk you through the specific neural processes and effects of being mistreated in childhood. The science: neuroscience, neuropsychiatry, psychology.

A chapter specifically on Post-traumatic Stress Disorder (PTSD) follows and completes this section. I have included this information since PTSD is a common condition many of us live with, and it wreaks havoc in our lives. We can get PTSD in childhood from a traumatic event, and if we do, we cannot expect to magically heal from it by adulthood. Instead, we carry this childhood-onset PTSD with us through life until it's treated and healed. We can also get PTSD from extremely stressful adult experiences. This chapter tells you everything you want to know about PTSD. The science: neuroscience, neuropsychiatry, psychology.

Together, this section presents the entire explanation of the brain warp: what misshapes our brains, how that brain warping makes our lives so difficult, and how we manage our lives despite being whacked out.

1. Life Consequences of Unwellness

Stress in the childhood home comes in many forms. It can be verbal, psychological, emotional, physical, or sexual abuse, or it can be neglect or trauma. Neglect is inattention, and can occur in any facet of our lives—emotional, social, and more. Trauma can come from just about any source that made us feel intense helplessness or horror, and also results from ongoing stress in the childhood home.

When our home lives contain manipulation, aggression, abuse, domestic violence, or any kind of neglect as normal everyday occurrences, this creates a stressful home environment and is considered child maltreatment. Just because a child is not smacked around or touched inappropriately does not mean the child grows in a healthy environment. In fact, psychological maltreatment may be at the "core of child maltreatment".[1] Unfortunately, this characterizes the home lives most of us grew up in, at least to some extent, as you will see. Additionally, any sort of trauma is another kind of stress that some of us are forced to grapple with.

Growing up in a home with significant stress brings adult implications that are not pretty. We could suffer from addiction, substance abuse, anxiety, poor weight management, poor anger control, depression, relationship challenges, physiological problems such as migraine, and the list goes on, as this chapter will detail.

Neuroscience shows us that these issues are part of our lives because as we were growing up, our brains didn't have a chance to grow normally and healthily. Instead, our brains adapted to and molded around the stress we were exposed to and experienced. I will detail those neurological processes for you in upcoming chapters. Here, I want to talk about the aspects of our adult lives that are challenged when we come from a stressful childhood home environment.

The effects of severe stress endured in childhood can easily last a lifetime, and likely will if not treated. Research does *not* suggest that people ever "outgrow" the conditions caused by childhood stress. Rather, we take all of that yucky stuff into every facet of our lives for our entire lives unless and until we treat it.

Everything in the body and mind is interconnected. All of our functions are affected by developing in a stressful environment. Resulting from this kind of childhood stress, people find themselves in this vicious cycle for most or perhaps all of their lives, with tragic effects to both the individual and society. Because this kind of childhood home setting is so "normal" in the world, most people in the world are running around spewing their distortions and extending their own experiences of neglect and abuse in the ways they treat most of those with whom they come into contact. Tremendous pain and suffering, a lot of interpersonal tension and anxiety at every level and in every type of interaction, and even high health care costs result.

Traumatic events are especially harmful to a developing child, carrying tremendous stress. A great determinant of how deeply exposure to a trauma will affect a child depends on where the child was developmentally when the trauma occurred.[2] The younger the child, the worse the effects. Also, the more frequently a trauma is endured, the more damaging to the child's brain.

When the stress a child experiences occurs early and often, it is deeply detrimental to that person's life now and in the future because these are critical developmental stages. In a stressful home, the stress begins possibly even before birth and continues throughout the child's developmental stages—it's not like it starts randomly, or ever stops. So you can bet that someone raised in a home like this, who was exposed to significant stress in every stage of development, will definitely suffer from some of the issues detailed in this chapter.

Unhealthy home environments do not create healthy children. Unhealthy children do not become healthy adults. Most unwell people learn to function in society, for sure, and may even learn how to come across as healthy and mentally well, having developed some sense of what that is supposed to look like and demonstrating appropriate behavior at times. But that is all a thin veneer. Trouble brews not far beneath the surface.

Life Areas Affected

A stressful childhood environment wreaks havoc on our adult lives in many forms. We have challenges in nearly every aspect of life:

- Behavioral
- Physiological
- Emotional

- Stress management
- Relationships
- Identity
- Cognitive
- Suicide

All of these challenges and difficulties result directly from a brain that did not develop properly as a result of stress in the childhood home, as upcoming chapters will illustrate.

Here are some examples of how these issues manifest within our lives, with greater detail to follow in the remainder of this chapter:

Behavioral Issues
- Substance abuse
- Addiction
- General high-risk behavior

Physiological Issues
- Migraines
- Cardiovascular issues
- Inflammation of all kinds
- Sleep abnormalities
- Anything the doctors can't explain

Emotional Disturbances
- Anxiety
- Depression
- Regulating emotions in general

Stress Management
- More sensitive to stress (more easily stressed out)
- Greater chance of developing PTSD, partly due to higher sensitivity to stress

Relationship Difficulties
- Mistreat others
- Low or no empathy for others
- Impaired or distorted perceptions cause relationship problems

- Relationship anxiety
- Interpersonal violence

Identity Issues
- Perception of lack of value
- Low self-worth
- Negative self-perception
- Negative beliefs about one's own power and abilities
- Poor adult emotional and somatic functioning

Cognitive Disturbances
- Distortions
- ADD / ADHD

Suicidality
- Increased risk of suicide

These are the areas of our lives affected by a stressful childhood.

Behavioral Issues

Kids from stressful homes have a lot of problems in their adult life. Many of those problems remain internal, in their ways of thinking and in their perceptions. But our problems do not stay internal to us, silently locked within our minds and our psyches. Rather, we express our anxieties in our behaviors. People abused as kids tend toward high-risk behavior such as continued violence, addiction, sexual promiscuity and heavy gambling.[2-5]

Substance Abuse

Substance abuse is a real problem for many adults from stressful childhood environments. Some research has found that those who witnessed violence, those who were physically or sexually abused, and those with family members suffering from substance abuse (including alcohol) were more likely to abuse substances as adults.[6] Increased risk of substance abuse is also connected with PTSD. Abuse of substances, including alcohol, can reduce the size of the hippocampus, which often occurs in adults with PTSD or histories of childhood abuse.[7-9]

Substance abuse may be related to PTSD, as the self-medication can soothe the anxiety and pain resulting from PTSD. One study found that psychoactive substances reduce negative emotions and feelings.[10] Because these substances reduce the negative feelings and emotions, the person feels compelled to continue seeking and using the substance. Other research has found that people continue abusing alcohol because it helps them reduce stress.[11]

Other Harmful Behaviors

Adults stressed out as kids tend to engage in other self-destructive behaviors as well. Gambling is another problem, and is associated with family violence.[12] Also, since many adults tend to continue negative coping strategies, learned behaviors, and even experiences that reflect early childhood traumas, we tend to repeat our traumas—voluntarily—in our adult lives.

A lot of adults traumatized in their own families don't take good care of themselves in terms of hygiene, rest, and protection, even though they may acutely respond to others' needs. A certain level of self-care is often lacking.

People who suffered sexual abuse might have distorted attitudes toward themselves and sex: They have more negative views about their sexuality[13] and show lower levels of power, particularly interpersonal power, in their sexual relationships. Thus, they may choose to submit to their partner's perceived wishes, voiced or unvoiced, more often than appropriate for a healthy relationship, even when this submission comes at the cost of their own wishes and well-being.

More troublingly, it's not only ourselves that we continue to harm. Those who suffered childhood sexual abuse also tend to be sexually aggressive toward women and children.[14]

Continued Trauma Exposure

Childhood physical and sexual mistreatment have been correlated with higher risk of exposing oneself to additional traumatic events as adults.[2-5] Such exposure to traumatic events (e.g. combat, assault, accidents) is related to psychopathologies that follow the exposure.[15] So, the trauma endured early in life predisposes people to finding more traumatic events for themselves in their adult lives, and these later traumatic events can bring on psychopathologies in their own right. As a result, stressful and traumatizing childhood experiences can influence later psychological symptoms: The early experiences manifest as direct symptoms later in life, or they make symptoms more likely to appear after the person has been exposed to a later trauma.[15]

Physiological Issues

It's not enough that mistreated kids suffer internal distortions and those accompanying life challenges in their adult lives, unfortunately. Chronically stressed and traumatized children can also develop adult physiological conditions at a higher-than-average rate. This includes much higher risks of serious conditions such as heart disease, emphysema, chronic bronchitis, stroke, diabetes, bone fractures, and cancer.[16] A long list of physiological conditions found related to childhood mistreatment follows shortly.

Other problems, such as high stress sensitivity and vulnerability to sleeping and eating disorders, also plague people with stressful backgrounds. They have an impaired ability to relax and sleep peacefully. Also, their behavioral impulsiveness tends to strengthen the pathways to eating disorders. These disturbances cause negative health consequences: chronic pain, cardiovascular issues, migraines, headaches, strokes, inflammatory issues, lower back pain, and fibromyalgia. Also, their chemical messengers shape the body's response to strife, contributing to slow wound healing,[17,18] as well as both emotional and behavioral challenges to normal development.[19]

Neurological and emotional problems manifest as physical pain, psychosomatic conditions, and heart-related problems. There is a long list of physical conditions, primarily in the digestive and cardiovascular systems, that result from childhood stress.

Children with PTSD show changes in cardiovascular functioning. Normal heart rate for kids is 84 beats per minute (bpm).[20,21] A lot of kids in one PTSD-related study, 84%, had resting tachycardia, which is a higher resting heart rate at more than 94 bpm. Forty percent of the kids in this study had resting heart rates at over 100 bpm.

Some of the childhood or adult physiological conditions associated with childhood stress include:

- Chronic lower back pain[22]
- Bone fractures
- Chronic bronchitis
- Cancer
- Cardiopulmonary issues
- Cardiovascular issues
- Diabetes

- Eating disorders
- Emphysema
- Elevated cortisol in stressful situations,[23] associated with higher rates of heart disease[24]
- Fibromyalgia[25]
- Headaches
- Inflammatory issues
- Irritable Bowel Syndrome (IBS)
- Migraines
  - Linked to stroke[26]
- Chronic pelvic pain (from sexual abuse)
- Stroke
- Sleep disturbances
  - Results from stress and the body's resulting hypervigilance, which prevents relaxation and ultimately, sleep
  - Causes immune and neuroendocrine system weakening
  - Can exacerbate depression and PTSD symptoms
- Three kinds of sleep disorders:
  - Insomnia: inability to fall or stay asleep. Often related to stress and depression.
  - Hypersomnia: excessive daytime sleepiness. Often associated with sleep apnea.
  - Parasomnia: unusual sleep behaviors including sleep walking, nightmares, and teeth grinding

This list does not cover the somatization concerns—those physical conditions for which no medical diagnosis can be identified—which also tend to result from overly stressful childhoods.

This is not to say, of course, that experiencing these conditions always falls on the heels of childhood mistreatment, but rather, these conditions have been associated with childhood mistreatment in child and adult patients. If you experience one or more of these conditions and you had a neglectful, abusive and/or traumatic childhood, the two experiences could well be related.

Emotional Disturbances

The research on long-term emotional effects of severe childhood stress isn't pretty. Mistreated kids are four times more likely to suffer from depression[27] and anxiety.[28] Reduced left brain hemisphere growth, caused by childhood stress, increases this risk of depression. Mistreated kids are also more likely to show behaviors connected with anxiety disorder, panic disorder, and obsessive-compulsive disorder (OCD). Those sexually abused as kids are five times more likely to suffer from anxiety disorders.[29,30] Again, the graver the mistreatment, the worse the resulting conditions expected.

Long-term stress or a severe traumatic event can impair a person's ability to regulate emotions. This kind of impairment can lead to a host of quite severe problems including chronic self-destructive behavior, a sense of hopelessness about the future, dissociative episodes, and somatization.[31-34]

Anger and Aggression

Childhood mistreatment can also result in difficulty with managing more specific emotions, especially anger. Anger is a common feeling that comes up with adults abused as kids. They often feel uncontrollable anger or strong irritability. Their anger can be turned inward, as self-blame, self-hatred, and depression, or outward, as young victims become perpetrators themselves in childhood and/or adulthood.[35,36] Turned outward, sometimes those abused in childhood will fight, bully, or exhibit other aggressive behaviors, though these specific kinds of issues tend to be connected with sexual abuse. Common explanations for this aggressive behavior in children include a desire to receive attention, a cry for help, or an external display of the child's internal distress for being abused. Regardless of the specific cause, these aggressive behaviors leave the child or even the adult even more isolated and shunned—who wants to be around that?[37]

Depression

Another common and severe emotional consequence of childhood mistreatment is adult depression. Depression results from critical judgments of one's own emotional state and includes a sense of guilt or shame. Those with depression or dysphoria (meaning general unhappy and unwell feelings) tend toward a way of thinking that emphasizes their own personal flaws. These patterns of negative self-thought become habitual ways of thinking, and the person then suffers from low self-esteem. The person becomes captivated by the negative feelings and negative self-perception, rendering that person incapable of controlling their mental experiences, which results in a continued state of rumination. This creates an unhealthy and unproductive psychological and emotional cycle. Depression is most commonly reported by those who have been abused and specifically molested as children.[13]

Depression and anxiety in people with stressful childhoods also link to other issues, such as isolation, spiritual loss, a sense of ineffectiveness, and hopelessness. These conditions negatively influence self-esteem and can easily make the person self-neglectful. These people can also develop a pervasive sense of hopelessness. Stressed out kids withdraw unto themselves, so they don't ever develop proper relationships with others. This isolates these kids, which in turn gives them less opportunity to cope with their emotions and experiences. Growing up in this way, emotionally and socially isolated, makes the child deficient in relationship skills, in turn isolating them as adults.

Emotional Expression and Empathy
When kids are exposed to interpersonal trauma early in life, this trauma misshapes their developing brains and impacts their social learning development, including the ability to be self-reflective, have empathy for others, and regulate emotions.[38-40]

In addition to poorly regulating their emotions, they are also less able to properly express their emotions.[41] This leads to challenges with emotional awareness, social isolation, and an inability to form meaningful relationships. On the receiving end, they have difficulty identifying the emotions of others, in turn leading to a lack of empathy and also further isolation. Indeed, when you're raised by someone who doesn't care about your emotions or the emotional responses they themselves engender except to the extent to ensure you suffer sufficiently, you don't learn sensitivity to others' emotions and instead, you learn to treat others in the same calloused way. Obviously, if you want to get along with other people and form meaningful relationships, this perception and behavior need adjusting, and empathy must be developed.

Indeed, none of these are problems that vanish by themselves.

Stress Management
Traumatic experiences early in life cause increased sensitivity to stress later in life—stress affects these people more quickly and deeply than it does most people. This stress sensitivity makes the adult more susceptible to psychiatric conditions

including PTSD.[42,43] This PTSD development can be brought on by both the heightened sensitivity to developing PTSD, as well as distorted perceptions that unknowingly put the person in stressful situations which bring about PTSD onset.

People's core sense of self is primarily defined by their ability to regulate their own internal states and how well they can predict and regulate their responses to stress.[44] When they are deficient in these areas, they know it, and their sense of self suffers. This awareness of deficiency becomes even more harmful to the individual's sense of self—they can't handle their own internal states or deal with stress well, resulting in a lower-than-healthy sense of self, and exacerbating this already low sense of self, the knowledge of these deficiencies makes them feel even more inadequate. Poor internal regulation and the knowledge of this fuel a downward spiral.

Their significant problems with self-regulation most clearly appear in their experience of even minor objective stressors as overwhelming. An example is someone who easily becomes overwhelmed and breaks into hysterics at relatively minor stressors such as a very minor vehicle "fender bender" or an upsetting piece of mail.

Adults stressed out as kids didn't get appropriate modeling for dealing with the stressors of everyday life—they weren't shown how to manage stress productively and effectively, so they often can't make clear decisions and aren't equipped to handle life's emotional aspects in healthy ways. The result is a perpetual cycle that contributes to bad adult-level decision-making, stress, violence, depression, and high-risk behaviors.

Trauma experienced in childhood causes very poor mental and physical responses to stressors in both children and adults with stressful childhoods. These poor stress responses include difficulties in regulating their emotions, which in turn brings a greater tendency for self-destructive behaviors such as anger, addiction, eating disorders, suicidality, and serious medical conditions.[16,45,46] They manage overwhelming distress with self-destructive behaviors such as self-injury, substance use, eating disorders, and suicide attempts.[16,47,48] They also have difficulty with anxiety and sexual impulses, depression, somatization, interpersonal sensitivity, physical problems, and higher hospitalization rates.[45,49-51] This poor self-regulation may also appear as a low ability to focus on relevant stimuli, attentional problems, and an inability to inhibit action upon arousal—uncontrollable behavior. The problems with attention and stimulus discrimination may explain the fact that PTSD and

Attentional Deficit Hyperactivity Disorder (ADHD) often appear together in trauma-tized kids, such as sexually abused girls.[52]

Relational Issues

Certainly, with some of the above issues going on inside of the adult with a his-tory of stress, there are bound to be issues in communicating appropriately with others as well. The social and behavioral damage may be even more difficult to repair than the cognitive damage. But there are ways and there is hope.

Poor Interpretation of Others' Mental States

Some research explains that early trauma slows down the development of social learning.[38] Our mentalization capacity allows us to interpret the intentional men-tal states of others, generally by accurately perceiving and interpreting their nonverbal cues. It is damaged in those of us with stressful childhoods. In other words, those among us neglected and wounded as children are pretty much oblivious to the nonverbal cues others send off about what they are experienc-ing as they interact with us. This is a tragic oversight. We are not picking up on cues of anger, frustration, hurt, fear, or anything else in other people's nonver-bal messages, so we're not paying much attention to those states in the other person as we interact with them and as they respond to our communication be-haviors. Communication research suggests that communication is as much as 93% nonverbal and that emotional states are largely communicated nonver-bally.[53] So, in not recognizing the communication messages present in nonverbal cues, including messages about emotional states at the moment, those of us mistreated as kids are missing a huge chunk of each message received, rendering us likely to respond inappropriately and possibly callously since we are missing the emotional impacts of our messages to the other person.

Inappropriate Communication Responses

A very interesting and important point to be critically aware of is that early stress arousal changes how we process and respond to incoming information.

Early life stress causes a shift in the brain's responses. When we receive a stim-ulus, as in a communication message from another person, we are supposed to process it in the prefrontal cortex, in the front, where executive functions lie, and experience an even, thoughtful response to the input. Instead, in those mis-treated as kids, our response occurs in the posterior cortical and subcortical structures of our brain, in the back, which yields a more rapid, automatic, and instinctual response behavior—a knee-jerk, self-protective response. This is an (inappropriate) activation of the body's survival response in response to incoming information. When this is activated, the process of mentalization—thoughtfully processing the cues received—significantly decreases or disappears completely.

This lack of thoughtful processing significantly harms interpersonal situations which require thoughtful processing for accurate interpretation of complex verbal and nonverbal cues.[54] Processing input in the back of the brain rather than in the front as appropriate means that neutral input is perceived as an attack that demands a self-protective response. Instead of processing stimuli properly, by consciously and thoughtfully processing the cues from other people in our worlds, we process social stimuli in the parts of the brain responsible for survival and self-protection. We no longer have the capacity to perceive our worlds accurately and process reasonably; instead we feel our survival response activated and react quickly and inappropriately as if to threat. Defensive anyone? "Chip on your shoulder"? Feeling attacked? Clearly, when we respond to communication messages as if they are threats to us, generally by returning the perceived attack, this has detrimental effects on our relationships.

Difficult Relationship Behavior
Childhood mistreatment has been found to result in many unfortunate psychological conditions that enter into our adult relationships. These include, in part, insecure attachment (see Chapter 4), difficulty trusting others, and much higher rates of revictimization later in life.[55-57] In these ways also, childhood mistreatment makes it difficult to form healthy adult relationships.

We all tend to put ourselves in environments that we find comfortable because they fit with the models we developed in our upbringing. For those of us who grew and developed in stressful environments, this means we seek environments of stress and in turn, revictimizing relationships.

Emotional Detachment
Adults with stressful childhoods tend to have difficulty with intimacy and detach from their emotional experiences. This emotional detachment then interferes with their ability to detect danger and set boundaries. If we are not connected with our emotional experiences, we don't accurately assess our own emotional experiences and we can't accurately assess our fear response—or maybe our fear response doesn't work properly in the first place, having been distorted early on. In any case,

it's difficult for us to see when others are mistreating us since that condition is so our norm, which makes boundary setting really difficult. Also, it could be that trying to set boundaries early in life only brought on further abuse, since abusers don't like being told *no*, which really alters our sense of when it's okay to step in and protect ourselves.

People with stressful childhoods cannot set appropriate boundaries in their interpersonal relationships and emotional experiences. For adults stressed out as kids, our meters of when we need to protect ourselves are a bit off. Our ability to detect signs of threats in our own bodies, such as increased heart rate and other responses, may also be significantly impaired. This makes it easy to put ourselves in legitimately dangerous situations without realizing the danger we are in.

Mistreated children who develop PTSD also tend to have internal models of relationships as exploitive, dangerous, and hurtful, which in turn increases the risk of revictimization since these qualities become viewed as typical of relationships and we tend to get involved in relationships with these characteristics. Perhaps we seek these sorts of relationships in the first place, or worse, perhaps we turn our relationships into this because this is how we believe relationships are supposed to function.

Adhering to Poor Models
Unfortunately, when you were conditioned to be with other people in an environment where people were unkind to you, you tend to have some real challenges interacting with people in a healthy way. Part of this problem lies in the construction of your relational models as stressful and harmful. This means that the models you built for what relationships are supposed to look like and how they're supposed to make you feel are based on the painful relationships you had during your formative years. As a result, we seek future relationships that reflect and reinforce those models. In other words, we look for the same kind of stressful and harmful relationships in our adult lives that we were raised with. In this way, we continue to subject ourselves to stress and harm as adults.

A lot of adults traumatized in childhood home environments often repeat the same family patterns in their own relationships, alternating between roles of victim or persecutor, often justifying their behavior to themselves and others with feelings of betrayal and helplessness.

Poor Emotional Management

Abused people use projective identification, attributing their own most despised characteristics to others, then acting (more like attacking) as if the other person has these characteristics. At the same time, they can't see these characteristics as their own.[71] For example, an abused mother may blame her daughter for behaviors she herself is guilty of and punish her daughter for that inappropriate behavior, while at the same time lacking the ability to recognize the offensive behavior as her own. Of course, this can be very confusing to those in this person's life, and even to the individual experiencing this.

A lot of abused and neglected people also suffer from poor management of emotional and impulse control including aggression against self and others, and uncertainty about other people's reliability and predictability. This explains distrust, suspiciousness, problems with intimacy, aggressiveness, and social isolation many people with these histories show.

Those mistreated in childhood never formed proper caregiver attachments and therefore tend to experience social anxiety disorder. Also known as social phobia, this is avoiding certain situations because these people fear criticism or feel negatively judged and critiqued by others. Thus, many who suffer from this condition tend to be reclusive. They also experience more depression and feelings of persecution.

Interpersonal Violence

Interpersonal violence often falls on the heels of childhood mistreatment. Indeed, mistreated and especially traumatized kids often tend to seek violent relationships as adults.

Early childhood abuse correlates with violence in adult relationships,[58,59] both as victims and as perpetrators. Men abused in early life were twice as likely to be abused or assaulted as adults than those who were not abused.[60] Women abused as children were more likely to be in a romantic relationship with a violent partner, and more likely to engage in risky sexual behavior that increases the risk of sexual assault.[61] Many mistreated people tend to find themselves in situations similar to their abuse. It's called "repetition compulsion",[62] and most of these patterns do not occur at the conscious level, but they are similar to the abuse patterns the adult endured as a child and then repeated in adulthood. People who repeat trauma tend to bring suffering to themselves and to those around them. This is essentially a reenactment of past experiences, but the child-hood victim now becomes either victim or perpetrator as an adult.

Entrenched Behaviors
When people are abused as kids, they tend to believe the world works this way and expect abuse as a way of life. Mistreated children feel helpless in the midst of their caregivers' violence and subsequent "love". In response, they try to make up for their abusers' poor behavior by adjusting their own and when that doesn't work, they blame themselves. When the violence—psychological, emotional, verbal, physical, or sexual—occurs in adult life, as expected, these people revert to traits learned as children in abusive situations. Coping behaviors learned as children re-surface, and responses learned as children become part of the response in the pre-sent moment—not thoughtful adult responses. They may withdraw, avoid, and numb with drugs or alcohol. In this way, temporary states become permanent traits.[63]

Socially, people mistreated as children have a really hard time. Their interactions tend to be abusive and it's hard for them to form healthy relationships. As victims, they might get used to the abuse and deny that it is occurring. They may see them-selves as powerless, attributing power as outside of themselves, and feel hopeless, depressed, and hold a sense of helplessness.[64] It is also possible that these victims internalize the shameful behavior and believe they brought it on themselves, and defend their abuser. This is very common when the abuser is an emotional manip-ulator, who survives on ensuring their victims feel the sting of blame for the abuser's own actions. The impacts are devastating to the victim's psychological and emotional well-being, and serve and support the abuser. Victims are often cut off, either by the self or the abuser, from a social network that would help pull them out of the abusive cycle, allowing the abuse to continue unchallenged.

These people can develop further problems, including disorganized and disoriented attachment patterns,[65,66] which in themselves can bring an increased risk of PTSD and a predisposition to interpersonal violence.[67]

Risks of Repeated Abuse
Victims of early abuse are very susceptible to repeated abuse. This can be explained in part by the distortions in the relational models abused people develop as a result of their early abusive relationships. They form their concepts, or models, of what relationships are supposed to look like and feel like within the context of abusive relationships, so seek adult relationships that fit those models. Additionally,

negative beliefs about the self and a variety of posttraumatic perceptions and thinking patterns develop. The person can feel damaged, unacceptable, and inadequate, leading them straight into relationships where they are treated in these ways so they can reinforce these self-perceptions. In fact, revictimization is a constant finding in abused individuals: Rape victims are more likely to be raped again, and sexually abused kids are more likely to become prostitutes.[68]

Relational Anxiety

When a child expects nurturance but instead receives rejection, pain, hostility, cruelty and abandonment, the child learns to associate normal stimuli with pain, fear, and anxiety. They may have even learned to associate all relationships with anxiety, since they had a lot of anxiety and other negative feelings in their early relationships.

People mistreated as kids may avoid intimacy or closeness all together and restrict their own ability to form fulfilling and supportive relationships.[69-71] Based on their explosive backgrounds, they are overwhelmed with the sense that the world is a harmful, dangerous place, and struggle with crippling fears, catastrophizing, somatization and revictimization.[55-57] With these perceptions of the world and the people in it, it is no wonder that getting into relationships is a difficult, even threatening idea, better to be avoided.

Relationships and PTSD

A lot of research has found connections between PTSD symptoms and intimate relationship struggles, as well as physical and psychological aggression within intimate partnerships.[72] PTSD sufferers struggle in a lot of ways in life, and having peaceful, gentle, and mutually respectful fulfilling relationships isn't really the norm for them. With PTSD, anxiety is a way of life, and of course we bring that intense stress into our most intimate relationships. Some research has found that PTSD-related aggression can also be responsible for anger, physiological reactions, and social problem-solving deficiencies.[73-75] These traits can affect all of our interpersonal interactions, our most intimate relationships surely not excepted.

Relational Satisfaction

Participating in satisfying interpersonal relationships is an important piece of a person's perceived quality of life. When we continue to suffer from problems in achieving satisfying interpersonal relationships, this contributes significantly to struggles in leading satisfying lives.

Close relationships have been repeatedly shown to help individuals heal from many kinds of conditions, physical as well as mental/emotional. Loads of research shows that people heal faster from surgeries and other major health conditions such as heart attacks and strokes when they have the presence and support of loved ones as opposed to when they do not—and this is beyond the comprehension of modern science.

Without these loving and supportive relationships in our lives, we continue to suffer in many ways. When we can't participate in meaningful interpersonal relationships, this is quite problematic because we need competent social relationships to recover from traumatic experiences.[76] This becomes a catch-22: The abused individual cannot appropriately participate in interpersonal relationships because of their traumatic experiences, yet it is the very participation within these relationships that helps one recover from those traumatic experiences.

When you learned about how relationships work within harmful relationships, it makes perfect sense that you continue to seek these kinds of harmful relationships throughout your life until you learn differently. When our models of relationships were constructed to incorporate trauma, abuse, cruelty, mistreatment, pain and suffering, we naturally seek future relationships with those elements—these are the structures of relationships that were built for us, so we seek future relationships that fit within this structure. It's small wonder that we have difficult adult relationships and difficulty forming healthy adult relationships.

Identity Issues

Mistreated kids get the message that they are not worthy of being treated well. Emotional abuse and neglect can very directly communicate to the child that he lacks value. Understandably, this creates low self-worth and a set of negative beliefs about himself and his own personal power and abilities.[15]

For abused and neglected children, and many adults with histories of abuse and neglect, it's hard for them to feel that they know themselves well. They also feel uncertain about their own place among other people and don't view their bodies positively.

These kids also suffer from blaming themselves, blaming others, extending violence toward others, and pretending some things didn't actually happen. As adults, abused children also develop a negative self-perception and they mistreat others.[77]

Cognitive Disturbances

Childhood stress also impacts how we grapple with information. For starters, faulty thinking leads to feelings of guilt and shame, and creates challenges involving self-esteem, worthiness, intimacy, control, and trust.[78]

Things also get weird in how our psyches form, causing incongruent behavioral juxtapositions—contradictory behaviors existing at the same time—that can be really hard to understand. This happens because the human psyche organizes itself around the trauma. It incorporates traumatized thinking and develops it alongside healthy thinking. This can result in high levels of competence and interpersonal sensitivity on the one hand, coupled with interpersonal cruelty, self-hatred, and lack of self-care on the other.[79] This means that it's very possible and even likely that a person's self-view includes only her positive qualities, which allows this person to believe herself to be genuinely good and kind, and actually others' model of that person may also include only those positive attributes. Yet the damaging qualities exist as well, confusing a lot of people who are trying to decide whether or not to have or continue a relationship with this person who is often kind and gentle, yet quick to calloused cruelty.

Thinking processes are disturbed in abused people. The stress can cause a lack of proper communication between the left and right hemispheres of the brain, which is related to attentional disorders including attention deficit disorder (ADD) and attention deficit hyperactive disorder (ADHD). The stress can also cause forgetfulness about past information and forgetfulness about past disturbing experiences.[80] Further, these people may not be able to put together a cohesive narrative[40]—sometimes people remember parts of experiences and fill in the blanks with invented material in efforts to achieve a logical story, the whole time believing their entire story is accurate.

More severe issues also result from just emotional neglect all by itself, as researchers have found a link with borderline personality disorder. In this research, people definitely having this condition remembered both their mothers and fathers as having been significantly less caring and more controlling than the people on the borderline of this condition. Thus, this provides additional support for theories that borderline pathology can develop from biparental failure to attend to a child's full array of needs.[81]

In fact, those with histories of early abuse and neglect have been repeatedly found to suffer from profound and pervasive psychiatric problems.[45]

In graver situations, those with complex PTSD, a person's entire system of meaning can wind up with distortions. These distortions bring a sense of hopelessness and despair about this person's life and future. PTSD sufferers often feel that others do not understand their experiences, which further contributes to increased distress and increases the sufferer's risk for developing conditions such as depression. When you're suffering terribly from something that happened to you and feel that no one understands, this is a very isolating and lonely experience. It is an easy road to depression from here.

The Mayo Clinic website offers some clear information on mental wellness. They have drawn from the Diagnostic and Statistical Manual of Mental Disorders (DSM-5),[82] *the* resource for mental health diagnoses, and summarized some of the most common problems people with mental health challenges face. The list of mental illness categories is not short, and it's not always easy to identify yourself or others in this rather vague list.[83] However, the same website also offers a list of personality disorders with specific characteristics, which is quite useful in helping to identify your own or others' distortions in thinking and behavior. It's not necessary to have all symptoms and signs of a personality disorder for a diagnosis of this personality disorder, and it's common to have characteristics from more than one personality disorder.

Personality Disorders

Cluster A: Characterized by eccentric or odd thinking or behavior

Paranoid personality disorder

- Pervasive suspicion and distrust of others and their motives - Unjustified belief that others are trying to deceive or harm you - Unjustified suspicion of others' trustworthiness or loyalty	- Unjustified, recurrent suspicion of spouse's infidelity - Angry or hostile reactions to perceived insults or slights - Tendency to hold grudges
- Hesitation to confide in others for fear they will use the information against you	- Perception of nonthreatening situations or innocent remarks as personal attacks or insults

Schizotypal personality disorder

- Odd thinking, beliefs, speech, dress, or behavior - Peculiar perceptual experiences, such as hearing someone whisper your name	- Indifferent, inappropriate, or suspicious responses - "Magical thinking" -- that you can influence people and events with your thoughts

29

- Flat emotions or inappropriate emotional responses	- Perception that certain casual events have hidden meaning just for you

Schizoid personality disorder

- Appearance of coldness or indifference - Limited range of emotional expression - Inability to take pleasure in most activities	- Inability to perceive normal social cues - Little or no interest in sexual activity - Preference for being alone; lack of interest in social or personal relationships

Cluster B: Characterized by overly emotional, dramatic, or unpredictable thinking or behavior

Antisocial personality disorder

- Disregard for the needs or feelings of others - Disregard for the safety of self or others - Recurrent legal problems - Common violation of others' rights - Aggressive, often violent behavior	- Persistent lying, conning, using aliases, stealing - Impulsive behavior - Consistent irresponsible behavior - Lack of remorse

Borderline personality disorder

- Intense, frequent anger displays - Fragile or unstable self-image - Intense and unstable relationships - Mood swings, often as reaction to interpersonal stress	- Suicidal behavior or self-injury threats - Intense fear of being alone or abandoned - Pervasive feelings of emptiness - Impulsive, risky behavior, like unsafe sex, gambling, or binge eating

Histrionic personality disorder

- Impulsive, risky behavior, like unsafe sex, gambling, or binge eating - Fragile or unstable self-image - Speaks dramatically with strong opinions and few facts or details to support them - Easily influenced by others	- Thinks relationships are closer than they actually are - Shallow, quickly changing emotions - Excessive concern with physical appearance

Narcissistic personality disorder

- Belief you're special and more important than others - Fantasies about success, power, and attractiveness - Exaggeration of talents or achievements - Unreasonable expectation of advantages and favors; often takes advantage of others	- Failure to recognize others' feelings and needs - Expectation of constant admiration and praise - Arrogance - Envious of others or belief they envy you

Cluster C: Characterized by anxious, fearful thinking or behavior

Avoidant personality disorder

- Fear of embarrassment, ridicule, or disapproval
- Feeling inferior, inadequate, or unattractive
- Avoidance of work activities requiring interpersonal contact

- Socially inhibited, timid and isolated, avoids new activities or meeting strangers
- Extreme shyness in personal relationships and social situations
- Too sensitive to criticism or rejection

Dependent personality disorder

- Feeling the need to be taken care of; excessive dependence
- Tolerance of poor or abusive treatment when other options are available
- Fear of fending for yourself if left alone, self-care
- Lack of self-confidence, requiring excessive advice and reassurance from others even for small decisions

- Difficulty starting or conducting projects along due to lack of self-confidence
- Difficulty disagreeing with others for fear of disapproval
- Urgent need to start a new close relationship when one has ended
- Clingy or submissive behavior

Obsessive-compulsive personality disorder
(Different from obsessive-compulsive disorder, a type of anxiety disorder)

- Preoccupation with orderliness, rules, and details
- Rigid with morality, ethics, and values
- Desire to be in control of others, tasks, and situations; inability to delegate
- Neglect of friends and enjoyable activities due to excessive commitment to work or a project

- Inability to discard worthless or broken objects
- Stubborn and rigid
- Tight, miserly control over spending and budgeting
- Extreme perfectionism resulting in distress when perfection is not achieved, such as inability to complete a project due to failure to meet own strict standards

In a nutshell, this is the list of personality disorders along with their representative characteristics.[84] When left untreated, they can not only cause significant problems in the person's life, but can also get worse.

Suicide

The enduring pain of childhood mistreatment can linger into adulthood, causing negative impacts on the adult's life and increasing the risk of suicide even years after the trauma(s) occurred.[85] Substance abuse, depression, and anxiety are all related to suicide and suicidal behaviors.[86,87]

Victims of childhood mistreatment have a two-to-five-time greater risk of attempting or committing suicide than non-mistreated kids. Therefore, childhood abuse is strongly correlated with suicidality.[88,89] Substance abuse and depression are associated with a three-to-five time greater risk of suicide.

Impacts of Emotional and Psychological Neglect and Abuse

Children need nurturing and supportive environments to achieve normal developmental milestones.[15] Therefore, the absence of nurturance and support may thwart development. This ultimately leads to poor self-care and fewer healthy behaviors for that person,[15] along with a host of additional adult problems. Indeed, this kind of early abuse and neglect—"merely" emotional and psychological—have often been associated with profound and pervasive psychiatric problems.[45]

Additional consequences of childhood emotional and psychological mistreatment are many. They include increased anxiety, depression, PTSD, physical symptoms, and a higher risk of trauma exposure throughout life.[2-5,15] Emotional abuse alone has been associated with higher depression levels,[90-92] suicidality,[90] low self-esteem,[93] and personality disorders.[94] Psychological/verbal abuse on its own has been repeatedly found to predict negative mood.[15,95]

Some studies have examined the impacts of neglect and emotional/psychological abuse in very specific situations. In and of themselves, emotional and psychological abuse and neglect predict adult psychopathology including PTSD symptoms, even without having experienced a traumatic event.[15] These are subtler forms of trauma than physical or sexual abuse or specific traumatic events—yet they still predict physical, anxiety, and depressive symptoms as well as lifetime trauma exposure, even among highly functioning adult women, and in the absence of more severe kinds of mistreatment. Emotional abuse in itself has been found to correlate with poor body image and sexual dysfunction in male college students.[96] Research specific to men and their daughters has found that paternal psychological abuse is a significant predictor of anxiety, depression, interpersonal sensitivity, and dissociation in women.[90] Indeed, the whole "Daddy issue" assertion is a very real phenomenon, and it's no joke. Men can really mess up their daughters without ever laying a finger on them.

Further, emotional mistreatment in childhood can bring on the same kinds of adult health problems as physical and sexual mistreatment. Interestingly, emotional and psychological abuse appears to lead to the same kinds of long-term problems that physical and sexual abuse do. Researchers have found evidence that high *emotional* stress in childhood can lead that adult to seek healthcare for symptoms common to *physical and sexual* abuse.[15] These problems can manifest both directly and indirectly. Directly, they appear through increased anxiety and other psychological issues, therefore also harming physical and psychological health. They can also manifest indirectly in a few ways: poor self-care and thus increased exposure to further mistreatment, and lowering the tolerance threshold which leads people to seek healthcare for their symptoms sooner than most, bringing physical health concerns and treatment.[15] In sum, researchers have found a strong relationship between childhood emotional mistreatment and adult emotional/physical health.[15]

Clearly from this little bit of research, it is not enough to not hit or have sexual contact with children in order for the child to grow healthily and well. The child's emotional and psychological environment must also be healthy, or that child will suffer adult consequences that parallel the consequences from physical and sexual misconduct.

Affected Neurological Processes and Related Consequences

The neuroscience of what happens with childhood stress will be explored in depth in an upcoming chapter. For now, it is enough to know that childhood mistreatment affects our developing brains in unfortunate ways. Certain neurological processes cause clusters of the kinds of issues noted above. Some research has identified specific brain processes affected by childhood stress that can lead to the above challenges.

The Limbic System

The limbic system sits in the middle of our brains. It consists of several brain regions including the amygdala and hippocampus, which will be discussed later. It's also key to our emotions, motivation, learning, and memory, and significantly influences our nervous system.

When a brain develops under stress, the limbic system, including the HPA axis, becomes hyperexcitable—there's too much activity there. The now-hyperexcitable limbic system leads not only to anxiety and depression, but also to panic disorders and PTSD.

With PTSD, additional conditions are common: depression, anxiety disorders, somatization disorders (physical problems with mental/emotional causes), substance abuse, and personality disorders (psychosis).[97,98] When PTSD exists, 84% of the time it is accompanied by a second or even a third condition, with PTSD sufferers eight times more likely to suffer from three or more connected conditions than those without PTSD.[99] The most common co-existing conditions along with PTSD are alcohol abuse (52%) and major depressive disorder (48%).[100] It's very common that in advanced PTSD, as the mind tries to erase the trauma from memory in order to protect and heal, cognition and memory are damaged.

Brain Hemisphere Consequences
Effects of abuse and neglect are long term, and impact the individual well into adulthood. Some of these effects include reduced left brain hemisphere growth, which increases the risk of developing depression.[264] The left and right brain hemispheres may not communicate properly, which is related to attentional disorders including ADD and ADHD. All of these affect how a person responds to situations, other people, and themselves, and can negatively impact productivity, adaptability, and societal integration. These conditions interfere with happiness and can lead to higher suicide risk.

Brain Stem Functioning
Post-traumatic Stress Disorder (PTSD) causes abnormal brain stem functioning (in the catecholamine systems, for those interested) which is tied to changes in central nervous system development and alarm reactions (fight or flight).[101] This abnormal brain stem functioning can bring anxiety, sleep abnormalities, heightened startle response and impairments in our ability to accurately assess threat, and issues with cardiovascular functioning.

Conclusion
This chapter has presented some bad news—the distortions and challenges on every level, the problems we develop, and the suffering we continue to perpetuate unconsciously and unwittingly for ourselves and for those in our lives. This chapter has presented the psychology science on what happens to our psyches as a result of being raised in a stressful home and how that impacts our lives as adults.

We develop distortions in virtually every aspect of our thinking, emotional regulation, behavioral health, and relationship types. Our psyches get constructed incorporating trauma, which splits the planes of our psyches from each other as we develop instead of allowing those planes to work in harmony as we grow and learn.

This causes problems of every conceivable type. Our inner distortions and continued constant emotional and cognitive suffering manifest as physical ailments, poor thinking and behavior, and relational discord. Many people with mental health disorders believe themselves to be normal, so avoid treatment out of shame or fear.

Our scattered and distorted psyches keep us from living satisfying, fulfilling lives. Instead we are caught in an endless state of anxiety throughout our adult lives, in every facet of those lives. This doesn't change until we consciously make some changes.

2. Coping: Living with Difficult Experiences

When we have been through a difficult experience or a tremendously stressful situation, that experience stays with us for a while. It affects us. If the experience was terribly bad, traumatizing, we are thrust into a super-anxious headspace which can create a great deal of difficulty just coping with everyday life events. Our difficulty at coping with our traumas and stressors leads us to indulge in behaviors that numb the pain—drug consumption, unhealthy dietary choices, other dangerous lifestyle behaviors such as gambling and excessive shopping, in addition to more severe self-damaging behaviors.

There are certain things we as adults do in order to try to live with the difficult experiences and the effects of those difficult experiences on our lives. These things we do are called *coping strategies*. We have many to choose from!

Some coping strategies are healthy and they help us put the difficult experience behind us, so it no longer affects our well-being or our lives. These positive coping strategies help us heal and grow.

Most coping strategies are not healthy though. This kind prevents us from moving forward into healing, and pushes us to continue to turn to numbing agents in order to feel better. These negative coping strategies keep the stress-inducing event or situation alive within us and in turn, this causes many distortions and problems in our lives.

Coping Strategies

Science has identified several kinds of coping strategies that humans engage in following a difficult or stressful event, some healthy and others unhealthy. I've presented them here, clustering the unhealthy strategies into loose categories:

Healthy coping:

- Positive Reflection
- Reconciling the Trauma

Unhealthy coping:

- Blame
- Runaway thinking
- Logical Fallacies

Healthy Coping

Two approaches have been identified to help move past a stressful or difficult ex-perience. These two approaches operate together. They consist of positive reflec-tion, and reconciling the trauma.

Healthy Coping: Positive Reflection

Positive reflection is a primary coping strategy to help you move past the stress-inducing event in a positive and healthy way. This positive reflection consists of four steps:

- Putting into perspective
- Planning
- Positive reappraisal
- Acceptance

Putting into perspective is the first step. Here, you view the situation and event from an objective perspective. Try to remove yourself from the sequence of events and observe what happened as if you're an outsider. This helps you gain a proper perspective on what actually happened, with the distortion of trauma and intense emotions removed from the scenario. This then also helps you see the level of your emotional involvement in the situation.

The second step is *planning.* Here, as suggested, you make a plan for how you in-tend to move forward in a healthy way. For example, you might plan to attend events despite the expected presence of the person causing the stress and further, you might plan to keep your distance from her or him by simply walking away whenever s/he comes within a certain distance. Another kind of planning might be to talk to someone about the event, either a professional or perhaps personally confronting the person causing the stress. These are all kinds of plans you might engage in to help yourself heal from the difficult event.

In *positive reappraisal,* you look at the situation in a positive light. You identify the lessons in the struggles, and see how your life is better because of the stress-induc-ing event. Here, you answer the questions what did you gain? what did you learn?

and how is your life better now than before? Your gains might be along the lines of internal strength and fortitude, increased intuition, stronger boundaries, closer re-lationships with certain people, eliminating certain toxic relationships, that sort of thing. However your life is better because of the event, that is what you identify here.

Finally, in *acceptance*, you simply accept the event as something that happened in your life and is now part of who you are. It is with you now. You incorporate it as best you can, learn from it, grow from it, and have empathy for others experiencing it. You can talk about it as if it happened to someone else, because the event no longer has an emotional hold on you. It is, simply, a fact of your life. This is ac-ceptance.

This series of steps is the best way to move past a stress-inducing event in your life, be it large or small. This method will help you heal and grow, putting the pain be-hind you and enriching your life.

Healthy Coping: Reconciling the Trauma

When trauma happens to us, we don't know what to do with it. We are surprised, thrown off base, and our world is upside down. We don't know how to match what just occurred with our view and understanding of the world and our place in it.

One theory from psychology, the social cognitive theory of PTSD, says that people engage in one of three cognitive processes to reconcile their traumatic experiences within themselves. These include assimilation, accommodation, and overaccom-modation. Of these, accommodation is healthy, while assimilation and overaccom-modation are unhealthy.

In *assimilation*, we modify our perception of what happened to fit with how we already think. This is damaging. We see this in rape victims that blame themselves for the attack, which they do because they have an already set belief that the world is a just place or that bad things happen to bad people and because of this social fairness, the violation had to have been their own fault somehow. The experience of the rape doesn't fit with these pre-existing beliefs, so they modify the memory to make the experience fit.

Accommodation happens when we alter existing belief structures to incorporate new information.[102-104] This is a healthy and in fact a critical process to help in a healthy recovery from stressful events and the healthiest of the three responses in order to facilitate healing. The rape victim from above recognizes that the world is not always a just place, and certain behaviors are not a good idea when safety is a concern. So, leaving your glass of water on the bar while you went to the bathroom was not a good idea since someone slipped a roofie into it and then did horrible things to you, and walking home alone at a late hour with a false sense of security can be equally dangerous. We got hurt by operating on our old view of the world, so we adjust our view of the world to incorporate the new information.

In *overaccommodation*, we exaggerate the views of the world that are unhelpful.[105] This is a damaging perspective. An example of this is believing that no one can be trusted or that the world is generally dangerous. This is a bit like overgeneralizing, and believing that all people who share certain physical characteristics behave in the same way. For example, overaccommodation tells you to never walk alone at any hour, to never order a drink in a bar or perhaps to never enter a bar in the first place, and everyone that shares the ethnic background of someone who hurt you is equally as dangerous as your attacker. The event needs to be put properly into perspective without overreacting to it.

One psychological treatment found to help with this process of accommodation, without assimilation and without crossing into overaccommodation, is known as cognitive processing therapy (CPT). This approach is widely supported within the psychology research as an effective treatment for complex PTSD.

Unhealthy Coping

Some strategies we use to get through the day require us to engage in some distortions in our perspectives. These are known as cognitive distortions. Cognitive distortions are thought patterns, or ways of thinking, that are usually exaggerated and irrational. They also cause a cycle of psychopathological states including anxiety.[106]

Cognitive distortions are a distorted thought pattern or mental formation. They are an intentionally distorted view of the current stressor that come to light when the user wants to deny responsibility for their own behavior in the current situation. The intentionality of this distortion can be conscious or unconscious. Either way, the perception of the current situation is distorted by past stress in similar situations. In turn, these distortions help the person behave however they want without taking responsibility for his or her own behavior.

Of course, taking responsibility for one's own behavior falls directly within the job of a conscience, so refusing to take responsibility for behaviors by using cognitive distortions is not an act of conscience.

These distortions can become thinking habits. Feelings in current situations can trigger feelings from past situations and in turn, also trigger the responses to those past stressors. That is, we may respond to the same kind of stressor as an adult as we did as kids—withdrawing, blaming, and numbing possibly with drugs like alcohol. This is how temporary states become personality traits.[63]

A state is a temporary condition, like a mood, and a trait is a permanent personality characteristic. So, when someone experiences the same mood, or state, enough times in response to a certain kind of stimulus, that way of behaving becomes a permanent, embedded personality characteristic. What was a temporary condition as a kid has become a permanent, embedded personality characteristic as an adult.

So if you learned to cope with certain stressors with anger as a kid, then as an adult, you will also use anger as your default for coping with similar stressors, regardless of whether an angry response is an appropriate or distorted response for the current situation. Thus, how we once behaved in response to a certain difficult stimulus has incorporated itself into our characters, into our personality, and even into our identity. We live our lives within these distortions. Through these distortions, we see the world and we move through it, define our expectations of self and other, and live out our beliefs about what is and what is not appropriate behavior in given situations (short answer: what is considered appropriate through a distorted set of lenses is very most likely not appropriate, at all). These distortions are a normal response to a difficult or stressful childhood environment; for healing, they just need to be identified and worked out in order to live life on a healthy plane of reality.

People abused as kids come to expect abuse as a way of life—they feel helpless in the environment of their caregivers' violence and consequent "love", so try to compensate for the caregivers' poor behavior by adjusting their own—in unhealthy ways. When they can't adjust their own behavior to make the abuse stop, they blame themselves. Then when they find themselves in violent situations again as adults, they revert back to the same coping behaviors they learned as abused kids.

People mistreated as children tend toward the more negative coping strategies.[107] In turn, engaging in these negative coping strategies causes more emotional issues and interferes with the person's ability to handle certain situations. Also, using these negative coping strategies is more likely to bring about anger, anxiety, and depression. Some of these misdirected coping strategies actually severely threaten the person's overall health.[108]

Unhealthy Coping: Blame

In an effort to grapple with many different types of harmful coping strategies, I have created loose classifications, the first of which is blame.

The blame category consists of five behaviors:

- Self-blame
- Other-blame
- Denial
- Minimization
- Perpetrator attachment

Self-blame

Self-blame is the condition or habit of blaming the self. This can be for the event's occurrence, as in "I shouldn't have talked back when she said that; it's my fault she attacked me." This self-blame can also become habit-forming, and the person copes with many of life's stressors by blaming the self. Clearly, the individual is not culpable for the behaviors of others, and this practice of blaming the self for others' behaviors can easily lead to deep depression.

Other-blame

The behavior of other blame is to blame other people for the stress one experiences. This blame can be from event itself, such as "I was walking to your house when I got attacked so it's your fault I got attacked," or it can be a habitual behavior whenever any of life's stressors befall that person, such as twisting current situations to find a way to always make it a favorite scapegoat's fault.

Life has stressors in it for each and every one of us. Blaming other people for our own situations and the events in our own lives is not a healthy behavior. This practice prevents us from taking responsibility for our own lives and from moving forward into a place of mental health, not to mention the abuse it brings to the person being perpetually blamed. In fact, blame has been identified as a common thread in all varieties of mental illness.[109] And furthermore, interestingly, the Chinese recognize blame as an impediment to growth with their proverb, "He who blames others has a long way to go on his journey. He who blames himself is halfway there. He who blames no one has arrived."

Denial
In denial, you pretend an event never happened or deny the impact of the consequences of the event. Everything is fine and you are just fine. Your wife is not verbally abusive, your husband only hit you because he was drunk but normally he's a nice guy, your kid does not have a drug problem, your daughter was not violated. Here in denial, you have a fine excuse for not ever even facing the situation, let alone addressing it, because there is nothing wrong in the first place.

Denial keeps you in difficult and stress-inducing situations because you pretend you're not in that difficult situation. This is a very powerful tool for allowing abuse to continue—if you admit it, you have to do something about it, and that is uncomfortable, so it's better to just pretend it's not there. You get to avoid change. Such is the power of denial. Consequently, denial inhibits personal growth.

Denial can be very powerful. Denial keeps smiles plastered on faces and a sense of pervasive righteousness in one's own version of mental health and wellness, which conveniently allows them to take responsibility for resolving any problems because there are no problems to resolve. Denial helps maintain relationships with unwell individuals—permitting the perpetuation of abuse—and break relationships with well individuals who dare identify the unwellness.

Denial is the main driver to inaction—since there is nothing to resolve, no action is necessary or desired; it says, "There is no problem requiring attention. If you think action is necessary and call on us to perform such action, you are the problem, and the changes you want are a product of *your* distorted perceptions." In this way, denial helps perpetuate abuse in families and other relationships, in part by eliminating those not in denial from the equation. Indeed, denial can be extremely powerful as it constructs a protective space for abuse to continue and proliferate.

Minimization
Minimization is similar to denial but instead of pretending it's not there at all, you pretend it's not nearly so bad as it actually is or was. The victim "minimizes" the abuse patterns by denying events ever occurred, in whole or in part. They ignore the full reality of the situation, the emotions the abusive situation generated, and the consequences. They might even rationalize the situation, in this way defending

the perpetrator. They downplay the emotional consequences of the trauma. This is commonly related to feelings of guilt.

This is an easy route to take when your abuser is a close family member, because who wants to admit that they have a mother or partner who abuses them? Yes your husband hit you, but only in the arm. Yes your wife gets abusive, but only when she's had a bad day. Yes you had a car accident and were arrested because you had been drinking, but your blood alcohol content was only 1 point over the legal limit. Yes your boss blew up at you, again, but he'd just gotten some bad news on a case. When we minimize the gravity of the offense, we allow ourselves to continue to pretend the situation is not nearly so bad as it actually is, which in turn allows us to simply be able to stay in those situations. This is why minimization is harmful and prevents us from moving forward.

There are a couple of ways that victims minimize the situation. First, they can be manipulated by the abuser into feeling worthless and helpless, and second, the abuser may create a situation that blames the victim.[110] These make the victim feel responsible and to blame for the abuse. No one likes feeling at fault, so downplaying the emotional significance of abuse helps lessen the guilt associated with it.

Examples of minimization include the perpetrator saying something then claiming they were only joking or teasing, even if what was said was emotionally harmful or hurtful to the victim. Another example is convincing the victim that she in some way had the mistreatment coming as a consequence for something she did, a punishment—she deserved it.

Minimization can also actually happen as a cognitive distortion, as a way to avoid acknowledging negative emotions by minimizing or outright denying them, so people don't have to deal with them.[111] This can also reduce the significance of the events that create the emotions—if the event was not such a big deal as the victim has perceived it, then the victim is overreacting and shouldn't feel so offended. Minimization also allows the abused and abuser to avoid any confrontation because if the victim successfully minimizes the significance of the traumatic event, they don't have to confront the perpetrator. In the victim's mind, this prevents more emotional damage.

Minimization also works to help the victim reduce the anxiety, stress, and depression that comes along with being mistreated. If the abused person emotionally ignores the situation, or perceives it in a way that reduces its emotional impact on his life, that reduces his risk of developing depression or anxiety as a result of the event. This also lessens the emotional severity of the situation and allows him to cope with it satisfactorily. This all works to help preserve the victim's self-esteem to some degree, by not perceiving themselves as victimized to the extent that they are actually being victimized. For example, a woman wants to go home after a long day but her abusive husband wants to stay out, so after he presses her into submission, she simply calls for a glass of wine, effectively minimizing the abuse by numbing its emotional impact with her alcohol.

These aren't healthy strategies, and can work to maintain the cycle of abuse, perhaps for a lifetime. In fact, abuse can even worsen over time under such minimization conditions.

Perpetrator attachment

Perpetrator attachment is an interesting phenomenon by which we humans, and children in particular, get attached to the person who is hurting us. We tend to seek greater attachment when confronted with danger and in the absence of someone healthy to turn to for comfort and emotional support, the perpetrator of the abuse may be the only choice.[13,69]

Both children and adults can develop emotional ties with those who beat, threaten, and harass them. This leads us to not only stay with them but also to defend them and their behavior. An abused spouse may yearn for her abuser, and make excuses for his behavior.

Central to all of these relationship types is captivity and the absence of external emotional support, so isolation. Abused people cater to the abusers' demands and live their lives around those demands. Reinforcement patterns exist, such as the abused spouse enduring a cycle of extreme terror followed by reconciliation. Negative reinforcement strengthens the abused-abuser attachment. In the middle of an abuse episode, the victim dissociates—goes elsewhere in his mind for a few moments—thus emotionally numbing from the trauma. Depression, self-blame, and feelings of helplessness may ensue.

There are three phases to this cycle: The first is the buildup of tension. The second is the battering. The third phase includes loving respite, which is characterized by physical comfort/contact, forgiveness and reconciliation. The violence, then, whether verbal, emotional, physical or otherwise, is preceded by excitement and followed by peace. This cycle reinforces the individuals' attachment. Memories of the abuse are dissociated and state-dependent, and all but forgotten until the next round of abuse. In the meantime, however, this unhealthy attachment interferes with proper judgment and decision-making regarding the relationship, which in turn creates love and longing in the victim for the abuser.

When the victim also has PTSD, the victim's distortion of the perpetrator is even greater.[70] That is, the PTSD sufferer may adopt the perpetrator's belief system in an effort to manage the overwhelming trauma—she may internalize the view the perpetrator is telling her in order to justify the abuse. She may also attribute a great deal of power to the perpetrator and become preoccupied with that relationship. Or, she may become preoccupied with thoughts of revenge and retaliation.

In addition to this phenomenon occurring between captor and hostage, you may have seen this with abused married people who defend their spouses' every abusive move.

These distortions are painful, so we may respond to these types of distortions by numbing. Numbing usually involves some sort of consumption to excess, including substance abuse.

Unhealthy Coping: Runaway Thinking

This category consists of behaviors that let our minds get carried away. The runaway thinking category consists of another five behaviors:

- Rumination
- Catastrophizing
- Hypervigilance
- Dissociation
- Amnesia

Rumination

Rumination is neurotic reflection. When we engage in rumination, we keep replaying the stress-inducing event over and over and over in our minds.[112] Every time we replay it, we relive the horror. Every time we relive the horror, we suffer from it all over again. This thinking pattern is a terrible habit for some people, as it keeps them in anxiety and misery from a single event in the past.

The neurotic reflection means they can't view the situation objectively. They also don't have the perspective to understand that past experiences led to the same or similar current emotional state, so they can't see that the current state has a solution (partly by making different choices at an earlier point).

People feel threatened by their emotional state.[113] The emotional state feels inescapable, consuming the individual. People can't get out of their emotions so they can't see them objectively or apply proper analytical models to them. Therefore, people are driven by those emotions.

There are three kinds of rumination:

- Victimization. The victim dwells on the perceived injustice.
- Magnification. The victim feels upset, angry, or experiences another difficult emotion. Some things are dramatized, so rash decisions are made.
- Chaos. Thoughts are not linear and jump from one idea to the next without adequate consideration of any of them. This may lead the person to withdraw from the situation and avoid it.

People with different stressful experiences tend to ruminate a bit differently. People who were sexually abused are more likely to ruminate on sadness.[114] People traumatized in childhood tend to repeat the events of their childhoods in their adult lives and ruminate over what happened.[112] Abuse and rumination are connected to depression and dysphoria, which means negative moods and an unhealthy level of self-focusing.[113] Rumination has also been linked to victimization.[114] The victimization leads to either dysphoria or back to rumination, but either way, ends up in depression.

Catastrophizing
In catastrophizing, we convince ourselves that the worst possible scenario will be the certain outcome to a given situation, and flip out in fear of that outcome. Catastrophizing generally keeps us in fear of the future, and sometimes that fear can cause paralysis in the present.

Hypervigilance
Hypervigilance is a heightened awareness for threat. A hypervigilant state is one constantly on the lookout for danger, expecting and anticipating it around every corner. This is a state of high anxiety—constantly on the lookout for and preparing for attack. Going through life in a state of hypervigilance cannot result in healing, as it maintains the fear state. The hypervigilant individual may be unable to function in a nurturing environment.

A child that is rejected early in life may learn more anxiety in relationships, and they may also show hypervigilance to any sign of potential abandonment, disapproval, decreased attention and interest, and ultimate rejection. People with attachment anxiety have a distortion of themselves and their worlds that lead them to exaggerate how they see potential threats, perceive themselves negatively, and hold more pessimistic beliefs about the world they are a part of.[115,116] They also react to stress with an exaggerated response, and tend to worry in ways that amplify their stress and the stressor.[116] Also, people with attachment anxiety tend to access negative emotions and memories. As a result, it is clear that anxiety-based behaviors may lead to these people not being able to form healthy adult relationships. This inability to form healthy adult relationships in turn creates a cycle of chronic stress.

Dissociation

Dissociation is a sort of advanced unhealthy coping strategy, meaning not everyone gets to this phase, thankfully. It is typically related to physical and/or sexual abuse, and PTSD. A dissociating person mentally and emotionally removes herself from a situation, which of course inhibits her ability to deal practically with that situation. Trauma impacts attention and can lead to a separation of outer experiences and bodily sensation, as opposed to a mindful and conscious engagement in everyday life.[71,117] It can make the individual be physically present someplace and at the same time, feel entirely disconnected and realms away from that place internally. This is a rough explanation of dissociation.

The dissociation sufferer can feel like a shell of a person, going through the motions, completely separate, disconnected even from themselves and the life they are living on a day-to-day, moment-to-moment basis. They may feel a bit like an avatar in a video game, absent emotion and desire on the one hand and living a mechanical life doing what is expected of them, while on the other, their inner world is entirely someplace else, rife with anxiety, turmoil, chaos, lack of understanding and lack of desire for anything. It is like they are two people—an inner, and an outer.

Dissociation may also affect the ability to retain information.[80] The dissociating child is less able to hold memories of events, and in this convenient forgetfulness, dissociates himself from the abuse. This may be a strategy that abused children employ and that helps create an attachment with an abusive caregiver: If the child's brain can pretend the caregiver's negative emotions and experiences didn't happen, the child is still free to attach to the caregiver.[118] The abuse is still present however, and the child may suffer flashbacks or nightmares, or perhaps even develop dissociative identity disorder (DID), where different personalities form.

Dissociation can also result in the individual feeling a sense of responsibility for the traumatic event, accompanied by great feelings of shame and guilt which contribute to the individual feeling helpless, ineffective, damaged, and undesirable to others.[70,71] These people may feel that others can't understand them, and have difficulty taking responsibility for their behaviors.[70,80,119]

Amnesia
Finally, amnesia is, of course, forgetting. You forget the episode, forget certain details about it, forget similar episodes, just forget. Indeed, one way to cope with a difficult experience is to simply forget it ever happened.

Clearly, lodging something very stressful deep into your psyche and locking it up in there will not result in a healthy healing process from that event. Amnesia to the trauma triggers hyperarousal, an exacerbated fight-or-flight response, and a simple inability to cope with life's stressors.

Engaging in these types of thinking patterns can also result in a run to numb with overconsumption.

Unhealthy Coping: Logical Fallacies
The mind is a powerful tool, and can work its way into justifying behaviors as well as it wants to. Not all justification strategies actually result in sound, logical positioning.

A host of twisted logic tactics, termed logical fallacies, can be used to argue a point and defend a position, even when extremely distorted. The danger of employing logical fallacies is that it keeps the user from healing and moving forward because the user justifies his or her current position and thus, sees no reason to budge from it. They distort the situation's impact and its consequences, and the ability to properly evaluate the situation in the first place. In an abusive relationship, these fallacies keep the abused person in that abusive situation and offer excuses to not move beyond it.

These fallacies are not new by any means—they have pretty much been around since the beginning of when people started making points. Here are some common logical fallacies, though this list is by no means exhaustive:

Logical Fallacies

APPEAL TO IGNORANCE: Because something can't be proven false, it must be true, and the reverse, because something can't be proven true, it must be false. An example is to dismiss science and its findings: Because science cannot unequivocally prove things, they don't really know.

SLIPPERY SLOPE: A first step will lead to other, inevitable events in a series. For example, when someone uses marijuana, they will also eventually shoot heroin.

FALSE DICHOTOMY: Either/or thinking; alternatives are overlooked. "Either you do this for me or you don't love me."

HASTY GENERALIZATION: Forming conclusions based on a single case. Overgeneralizations are applied to all cases we encounter. An example is upon hearing someone express a bit of knowledge, that person is classified as a know-it-all, conceited, and self-aggrandizing, allowing you to discount and ignore everything that person says, ever. Another is to observe a positive action by someone, an abusive husband remaining congenial with his wife's sister after he has destroyed their relationship, for example, and using this as a framework to believe this person is good in all ways and can be trusted.

QUESTIONABLE ANALOGIES: Comparisons between two things that may not be related or shouldn't be compared to each other. An example is to claim that one's assertiveness makes another feel "exactly like" hostile and abusive communicators make people feel. This logic renders harsh punishment (abuse) to the assertive person as justifiable and wholly appropriate.

ALL OR NOTHING: An event or situation is either this or that, with no other alternatives available. If something is less than perfect, it is a failure. An example is identifying one's human imperfections and using them as grounds to classify the entire person as a failure. Another is to hold the sentiment of either loving someone with your whole heart, or not at all.

MENTAL FILTER: When a single negative detail is identified and focused on, amplifying the negative aspects and possibly ignoring positive ones. This is a terrific manipulation tool— identify an individual's shortcoming, real or imagined, then hammer on that, complain about it, show how hurt one is by it, endlessly and repetitively, until the manipulator's targets reject that person.

DISCOUNTING THE POSITIVES: Where someone has decided that any positive aspects of a situation are irrelevant, and therefore discredited. An example may be construing a legitimate apology as a manipulation attempt, so rather than serving to build bridges, it is construed to create further distance and allow continued mistreatment.

RED HERRING: This is a diversion tactic designed to lead the victim to a false conclusion. An example is, when confronted with inappropriate behavior, a manipulative husband starts harping on, or complimenting, his wife about anything he thinks will work at the moment to divert the focus from his inappropriateness. He may ask "How do you like those diamonds I just bought you, huh? Nice eh?" or "It would be great if you could pay a little more attention to the kids' homework. Baxter got a B- on his math test. I thought you were helping him with that?"

These fallacies are favored by those with thinking and perception distortions, and those with emotional problems tend to use some or all of them as a way of thinking in their daily life and particularly in their view toward a difficult, abusive or otherwise negative situation they may be in. They also apply to all types of arguments.

Conclusion

We pack around a great deal of inner turmoil from the stresses and traumas we have experienced throughout our lives, and we humans have to figure out a way to get through the day. So we develop strategies to cope. Some of these strategies are healthy, such as reflection, while we also develop many unhealthy coping strategies, including blaming, rumination, minimization, and even dissociation. Relying on the range of unhealthy coping mechanisms only furthers the anxiety we experience and prevents us from true healing. Instead, the best thing we can hope for is a healthy reflection on the abuse, traumas, and stressors, observing how it made us feel, then developing a healthy perspective toward it, enabling us to move past it. Section II will say more about this.

3. The Stressful Environment Defined

Thus far, we have taken a very close look at the results of growing up in a stressful home environment. We have seen the harmful implications to every aspect of our lives and how our thinking is affected. In this chapter, we take a very close look at the specific kinds of behaviors that create this stress in the childhood home. You may be surprised to find that these behaviors are not nearly as severe as you might think but rather, represent the daily life experience for a lot of us.

When we get ourselves into trouble as adults, when we have an extremely difficult, stressful experience, we know it. We don't feel the same afterward, and we know that particular event caused our current anxiety and discomfort. This can be any kind of horror or super stressful experience—maybe a physical attack of some sort, an unexpected important loss, a narrow escape, or somehow being near or involved in something horrible, for example. Sometimes, traumatic events create clear stressors.

But not all difficult, stressful experiences are so crystal clear when they are occurring or have occurred. Sometimes, sophisticated mistreatment infiltrates our psyches at deep levels, slowly, over time, and we have no idea that it is occurring or has occurred. This can happen to us as adults for sure, and it can also happen to us as children, of course.

When it happens to us as kids, we develop no sense of the world operating in any other way. This becomes our normal, our view of how the world works. This kind of environment sets our expectations for the environments we will seek out and create in our futures, whether we know it or not, no matter how much these kinds of environments continue to bring us pain and suffering.

When physical abuse and sexual mistreatment occur in a childhood home, the child can be expected to experience some developmental problems. This is not new information, fortunately.

But there are other kinds of mistreatment that more commonly occur behind the closed doors of our world's family homes. In many families, these behaviors have been passed down from generation to generation to generation, often taught by our elders as "how to" raise children. In truth, many behaviors common to raising the children of our world's families can be classified as neglectful and/or emotionally abusive through one of the three channels of emotional abuse: emotional manipulation, verbal aggression, and/or a violent environment. These behaviors create a stressful environment for a developing child, in turn causing the child's brain to develop in distorted ways, which we will soon see, and consequently resulting in a whole lot of life problems for the adult that grew up in that environment, as we have just discussed.

The stressful home environment has some types and degrees of neglect and/or abuse present. The abuse can be physical or sexual, and as we know those types of abuse to be deeply damaging, they are not the focus of this chapter. This chapter focuses on the very subtle behaviors that are nearly impossible to identify especially as they are occurring, but that cause deep damage over time especially to a child whose brain is developing under these conditions. So, this chapter focuses on defining neglect, and on defining the three types of emotional abuse: emotional manipulation, verbal aggression, and a violent environment. These represent some kinds of stress in a child's home that bring a whole lot of havoc to that child's entire life.

Neglect

Neglect is simply inattention and/or inaction. It is not tending to a child's needs in any area of life. The most common areas of a child's life that require attention for the child's proper development include:

- Emotional
- Social
- Cognitive
- Educational
- Physical
- Medical

Examples of neglect include:

- Letting the child be hurt or cry without comforting it
- Not giving the child enough chances for
  - Social interaction
  - Cognitive/thinking tasks

- o   Proper emotional expression
- Letting the child fall behind in school without parental help
- Letting the child go hungry
- Not tending to the child's medical needs
- Not giving the child enough opportunities to interact with its environment in various circumstances and conditions

Like most things, neglect is not dichotomous—either/or. It is not a situation that either exists or does not. Rather, it exists on a spectrum from no neglect through moderate neglect to extreme neglect. Cases of extreme neglect are pretty easy to identify—the child is suffering considerably and developmental milestones are not being reached, and the state may step in on the child's behalf. But cases of more moderate neglect are far less obvious. In fact, moderate neglect might just be one of those family behaviors passed down through the wisdoms of our ancestors. Let's see!

The Parental Bonding Instrument (PBI)

In 1979, researchers developed an instrument to measure parental neglect. This instrument is called the Parental Bonding Instrument (PBI). It is a questionnaire of 25 questions. You respond to the complete questionnaire one time each for your mother and your father, keeping in mind how you felt they treated you prior to the age of 16 years. Through your responses to these questions, this instrument measures the amount of emotional neglect you experienced growing up.

The instrument measures two dimensions

Care ——— Rejection

Overprotection / Control ——— Autonomy

Falling short in either and especially both of these areas means the caregiver did not adequately meet the child's developing needs, which constitutes neglect.

Both dimensions are important to the development of anxiety, depression, and schizophrenia. So if you experienced neglect in either or especially both of these areas, and you experience anxiety, depression, and/or schizophrenia, the two could very well be related.

Here is the Parental Bonding Instrument (PBI).

MOTHER FORM

This questionnaire lists various attitudes and behaviors of parents. As you remember your MOTHER in your first 16 years would you place a tick in the most appropriate box next to each question.

	Very Like	Moder-ately Like	Moder-ately Unlike	Very Unlike
1. Spoke to me in a warm and friendly voice.	☐	☐	☐	☐
2. Did not help me as much as I needed.	☐	☐	☐	☐
3. Let me do those things I liked doing.	☐	☐	☐	☐
4. Seemed emotionally cold to me.	☐	☐	☐	☐
5. Appeared to understand my problems and worries.	☐	☐	☐	☐
6. Was affectionate to me.	☐	☐	☐	☐
7. Liked me to make my own decisions.	☐	☐	☐	☐
8. Did not want me to grow up.	☐	☐	☐	☐
9. Tried to control everything I did.	☐	☐	☐	☐
10. Invaded my privacy.	☐	☐	☐	☐
11. Enjoyed talking things over with me.	☐	☐	☐	☐
12. Frequently smiled at me.	☐	☐	☐	☐
13. Tended to baby me.	☐	☐	☐	☐
14. Did not seem to understand what I needed or wanted.	☐	☐	☐	☐
15. Let me decide things for myself.	☐	☐	☐	☐
16. Made me feel I wasn't wanted.	☐	☐	☐	☐
17. Could make me feel better when I was up-set.	☐	☐	☐	☐
18. Did not talk with me very much.	☐	☐	☐	☐
19. Tried to make me feel dependent on her/him.	☐	☐	☐	☐
20. Felt I could not look after myself unless she/he was around.	☐	☐	☐	☐
21. Gave me as much freedom as I wanted.	☐	☐	☐	☐
22. Let me go out as often as I wanted.	☐	☐	☐	☐
23. Was overprotective of me.	☐	☐	☐	☐
24. Did not praise me.	☐	☐	☐	☐
25. Let me dress in any way I pleased.	☐	☐	☐	☐

FATHER FORM

This questionnaire lists various attitudes and behaviors of parents. As you remember your FATHER in your first 16 years would you place a tick in the most appropriate box next to each question.

	Very Like	Moderately Like	Moderately Unlike	Very Unlike
1. Spoke to me in a warm and friendly voice.	☐	☐	☐	☐
2. Did not help me as much as I needed.	☐	☐	☐	☐
3. Let me do those things I liked doing.	☐	☐	☐	☐
4. Seemed emotionally cold to me.	☐	☐	☐	☐
5. Appeared to understand my problems and worries.	☐	☐	☐	☐
6. Was affectionate to me.	☐	☐	☐	☐
7. Liked me to make my own decisions.	☐	☐	☐	☐
8. Did not want me to grow up.	☐	☐	☐	☐
9. Tried to control everything I did.	☐	☐	☐	☐
10. Invaded my privacy.	☐	☐	☐	☐
11. Enjoyed talking things over with me.	☐	☐	☐	☐
12. Frequently smiled at me.	☐	☐	☐	☐
13. Tended to baby me.	☐	☐	☐	☐
14. Did not seem to understand what I needed or wanted.	☐	☐	☐	☐
15. Let me decide things for myself.	☐	☐	☐	☐
16. Made me feel I wasn't wanted.	☐	☐	☐	☐
17. Could make me feel better when I was upset.	☐	☐	☐	☐
18. Did not talk with me very much.	☐	☐	☐	☐
19. Tried to make me feel dependent on her/him.	☐	☐	☐	☐
20. Felt I could not look after myself unless she/he was around.	☐	☐	☐	☐
21. Gave me as much freedom as I wanted.	☐	☐	☐	☐
22. Let me go out as often as I wanted.	☐	☐	☐	☐
23. Was overprotective of me.	☐	☐	☐	☐
24. Did not praise me.	☐	☐	☐	☐
25. Let me dress in any way I pleased.	☐	☐	☐	☐

After filling out these forms, you score each item according to the given scale, noting that items are scored differently.

Care	
Items: 1, 5, 6, 11, 12, 17	Very like = 3 Moderately like = 2 Moderately unlike = 1 Very unlike = 0
Items: 2, 4, 14, 16, 18, 24	Very unlike = 3 Moderately unlike = 2 Moderately like = 1 Very like = 0
Overprotection	
Items: 8, 9, 10, 13, 19, 20, 23	Very like = 3 Moderately like = 2 Moderately unlike = 1 Very unlike = 0
Items: 3, 7, 15, 21, 22, 25	Very unlike = 3 Moderately unlike = 2 Moderately like = 1 Very like = 0

Once you have a score for each parent on each dimension (two scores for each parent: one for care, and one for overprotection), you use the following chart to determine the degree of care and overprotection. As you can see below, for mothers, a care score of 27+ and a protection score of 13.5+ equates to "high" scores, while for fathers a care score of 24+ and a protection score of 12.5+ means assignment to "high" score categories.

Parental bonding quadrants

Based on their scores, parents can be "assigned" to one of four quadrants based on these cut-off scores:
   -    Mothers: *care* score of 27.0 and *protection* score of 13.5.
   -    Fathers: *care* score of 24.0 and *protection* score of 12.5.

High care + high protection = affectionate constraint
High care + low protection = optimal parenting
Low care + high protection = affectionless control
Low care + low protection = neglectful parenting

After you assess whether your parents scored high or low on each scale, you can see which of the four quadrants they fit into: affectionate constraint, affectionless control, optimal parenting, or neglectful parenting.

As you can see, "optimal parenting" results from scores high in care and low in protection. By contrast, "neglectful parenting" is identified by scores low in care and also low in protection.

So, low scores on this instrument indicate neglect.

This matters because neglect prevents the child's brain from developing properly and prevents mother-child attachment, as we will explore in detail in the next chapter. This brings its own set of difficulties in relationships.

Emotional Abuse
Emotional abuse comes in three varieties: emotional manipulation, verbal aggression, and a violent environment.

Researchers have defined emotional abuse as psychological maltreatment and non-physical aggression.[15] Emotional manipulation aims to mess with your mind in order to get you to feel a certain way so you will do certain things the manipulator wants. Therefore, manipulation is certainly a type of psychological maltreatment. Verbal aggression is certainly a type of non-physical aggression, so both fall within emotional abuse. A violent environment can also constitute emotional abuse. This section explores these three deeply harmful dynamics within the overarching category of emotional abuse.

Emotional Manipulation
Simply ignoring a child's emotional needs qualifies as neglect and in itself causes a great deal of harm to the developing child, as we have just discussed. A step more deeply damaging is actual emotional abuse. One of the most insidious forms of emotional abuse is emotional manipulation. This is devastatingly stress-inducing for the developing child.

When you grew up with a parent or caregiver who exhibited a lot of the following behaviors, you most likely grew up in a stressful environment, possibly with an abusive parent. The more of these characteristics that parent exhibited, the more abusive they were. They created a hostile environment for you, and an unhealthy place for you to develop and grow.

People who abuse others, especially children, and most especially their own children, are really not okay in the head. Healthy people don't do this. Only the mentally unwell resort to these tactics. These people are what psychologist George Simon calls "disturbed characters".[109,120] His use of the term "character" suggests that these behaviors define this individual, as in, their core character is disturbed. Indeed, only disturbed people would behave in these highly manipulative ways.

Before we can talk about what it means to have grown up in a stressful or abusive environment, we need to take a moment to identify what a stressful or abusive environment looks like. We can do that first by looking at the characteristics of manipulative abusive people. If your primary caregiver fit with these characteristics, well, you know you can conclude that your homelife was unwell, and consequently, you've got some distorted structures to straighten out for yourself.

Purposes of Manipulation

Simon explains that abusive people—disturbed characters—use several methods for manipulation and control.[109,120] They use these methods to protect themselves from anxiety when they probably "should" be feeling shame or guilt about their behavior. They don't use these tactics to protect themselves from emotional pain, guilt or shame, the way that most people use defense mechanisms. Instead, the disturbed characters in our lives use these behaviors specifically and intentionally to ensure that they get what they want, at another's expense. They use them to manipulate and control others, and to strengthen their resolve against accepting or internalizing social norms.

These tactics are methods that disturbed, mentally unwell people use to keep on doing whatever they want, despite society's rules against their behaviors. Because they use these techniques regularly and often, as a way of life really, they don't develop proper guilt or shame about their inappropriate behavior. These techniques allow them to avoid taking responsibility for their own behavior and to manipulate and control others. Simon points out it is important to remember that when the disturbed character engages in one of these techniques, that person is actually fighting at that moment in two ways: They are fighting against the values or standards they know that other people want them to internalize or adopt, which are the healthy, socially appropriate ones that they so adamantly and persistently reject. They are also fighting to overcome resistance in other people so they can get their way. These are incredibly aggressive behaviors, though they may not appear so on the surface—making them even more insidious.

By using these tactics, these unwell, disturbed people are especially good at hiding their aggressive intentions while simultaneously putting others on the defensive, which confuses their targets and causes them to retreat. As a result of this toppling of their targets, these tactics increase the possibility that the manipulators will get their way and will gain the advantage over their victims. Sometimes they use just one tactic, though more often a skilled manipulator will throw so many of them at you at once that you might not realize how badly you've been manipulated until it's too late. Sometimes they just keep on adding on tactics until they win, pulling out whatever they have to in order to get you to bend to their will.

It's not possible to include all techniques and tactics that disturbed people employ to run their worlds like the little tyrants they are, but below are some of the most common ones, as articulated by Simon.[109,120]

Types of Manipulation

CATASTROPHIZING: This is another kind of minimization. Disturbed people will also catastrophize, or inflate the situation to an absurd level in order to reduce the significance of their actual offense and make the accuser feel petty for even suggesting it. This also plays into a neurotic's highly conscientious nature. "Oh right, I am soo bad. There's not a darn thing I do right in this world" or "Oh yes, I have cheated on you at least one hundred times. Didn't you know? All those times I said I was in night school, I was meeting lovers. Yes that's how I got my degree!"

LYING: It's not always easy to recognize at the moment, but later, when the facts don't line up, the lying becomes clear. These personalities lie in subtle, covert ways, but aggressive disturbed characters lie frequently and readily, sometimes just for fun, and sometimes when the truth would serve them just as well. They also lie by omission and by distortion, either withholding a significant amount of the truth or distorting essential elements of the truth to keep you from clarity. Deliberate vagueness is a favorite manipulator tactic. Some people get out of responsibility for something by implying it was the idea and actions of the other person present, not themselves at all, that is responsible for the wrongdoing.

DENIAL: This type of denial is refusing to admit they've done something harmful or hurtful when clearly they have. It invites the victim to feel unjustified in confronting them and gives the aggressor permission to keep doing it. An example may be to flat deny having said something that was indeed said: "I didn't say that," "That's not what I said."

SELECTIVE INATTENTION / SELECTIVE ATTENTION: Aggressors actively ignore the warnings, pleas, and wishes of others, and refuse to give any attention to anything that might get in the way of reaching their goal and achieving their manipulative purpose. They're often fully aware of what they're doing and blurt something similar to "I don't want to hear it!" This allows the aggressor to resist submitting to paying attention to you or changing in the way you want them to. Some kids diagnosed with attention deficits are actually using this tactic to avoid responsibility. The manipulator may literally stomp out of the room in a confrontation situation when anyone else speaks, pop her head back in for a second to blurt

---

something, then leave again without giving anyone a chance to speak. If you try to say something as she walks away, she keeps talking, not giving you a chance to speak.

RATIONALIZATION: This is an excuse the aggressor makes for engaging in behavior they know to be inappropriate or harmful. It's excuses and justifications. Here, a manipulator may come up with and express a perception, that she claims was her understanding of the issue, in which her behavior was reasonable and rational. "I thought you meant this! If you didn't mean this then why did you say that? Of course I wouldn't have done that if you had been clearer about what you meant," or "why didn't you say so?"

DIVERSION: Here, the aggressor changes the subject, dodges the issue, or throws a curve. Your attention is redirected. Manipulators use distraction and diversion to keep the focus from them and their behavior, get us off track, and keep themselves free to pursue their self-serving hidden agendas. This can be subtle. A manipulator's expertise here lies in bringing up something entirely unrelated that you did wrong, at least in their eyes. It works to keep you on the defensive. "Well what about when you did this, huh??"

EVASION: Here, the manipulator tries to avoid being cornered on something by offering rambling, irrelevant responses to direct questions or trying to skirt issues. Vagueness is one subtle form of evasion. The manipulator may express something partially related or completely off topic, usually accompanied by blame for that behavior. A response such as "well you did (something completely irrelevant)!" would fit here.

COVERT INTIMIDATION: Aggressors often threaten their victims in efforts to keep them anxious, apprehensive, and in the submissive position. They might intimidate their victims with veiled threats. A disturbed man may tell his wife, "I don't know why you would want to hang out with your sister. She's not good for you or our family," while the wife knows, based on past fights, that she will face his wrath (abuse) if she insists on seeing her sister.

GUILT-TRIPPING: This is one of this aggressive character's two favorite weapons (with shaming). It's a special intimidation tactic. Aggressive people know that other types of people, especially neurotics, have very different consciences than they do, and they know that these consciences include levels of guilt and shame that the aggressor doesn't share—it's legitimate guilt and shame, and much deeper than their own. The more conscientious the victim, the more effective guilt is as a weapon. It's very easy for a manipulator to use this tactic on a person with a healthy level of conscience: The mere suggestion that a conscientious person doesn't care enough, is too selfish etc. is usually enough to make that victim feel really bad. Indeed, a manipulative mother may often accuse you of being entirely selfish every single time you don't fully cater to her wishes or read her mind about what she might want in a certain situation. "What's the matter with you?" or again, "I can't believe you're so selfish."

SHAMING: Shaming involves using subtle sarcasm and put-downs to increase fear and self-doubt in others. Aggressive people use this to make others feel inadequate or unworthy. It works to make the victim continue to feel personally inadequate, in turn allowing the aggressor to maintain dominance. These disturbed characters are experts at using this tactic in subtle ways, sometimes just with a tone of voice or a brief glance. Rhetorical comments, subtle sarcasm, and other techniques can lead the victim to feel ashamed of themselves. When the aggressive character is a parent and the victim is their child, it doesn't take much. Some mothers are experts at this tactic as well, drawing up our flaws and even our successes to make us feel bad for them: "I don't know that word. I didn't go to graduate school" in a snotty tone, in response to using a vocabulary item she was unfamiliar with, attempting to make us feel bad for our good education—our success.

PLAYING THE VICTIM: Here, the aggressor portrays themselves as a victim of circumstance or someone else's behavior. The goal is to gain sympathy or evoke compassion, and thereby get something from the other person. These disturbed characters know that those of us with less calloused and hostile personalities don't like to see others suffer, so this tactic is simple and very effective. Convince your victim you're suffering in some way, and they'll want to relieve your distress. With a whimper and feigned hurt, a manipulative mother can get others to do anything for her at all costs to them. "This restaurant is disgusting and I would never eat anything here. I don't like Thai food. What's the matter with you? Can't you go someplace I like too? There's nothing for me to eat here."

VILIFYING THE VICTIM: This is often used together with playing the victim role. This tactic makes it look like the aggressor is only responding to aggression (i.e. defending himself) initiated by the victim. It allows the aggressor to put the victim on the defensive. This is a powerful way to put someone on the defensive while simultaneously masking their own aggressive intent and behavior. Encountering a refusal to cater to a manipulative mother's continued abusive manipulation, she may vilify you to anyone who will listen, causing them to not want anything to do with you. In response to others confronting her on her horrible behavior, she responds with, "Do you know what she did??"

PLAYING THE SERVANT: Here, the self-serving agenda is cloaked in service to a nobler cause. They pretend to be working hard on someone else's behalf, but hide their own ambition, desire for power, and quest for dominance over others. They may offer their time to a charitable cause or ailing neighbor to make them look like generous and kind-hearted people, for example, in order to cultivate a perception of themselves as generous and kind-hearted—and gain manipulation power. Some manipulators do many things to benefit others, often innocent others in need of assistance such as children and the elderly or alone. Then those people see her as "good", so when she opposes someone, that person is automatically "bad".

SEDUCTION: These aggressive personalities are great at charming, praising, flattering, or overtly supporting others to get them to lower their defenses and surrender their trust and loyalty. These aggressors realize that people need approval, reassurance, and a sense of value, so appearing to attend to these needs is a magnificent way to gain power over others. Imagine someone who uses charm and support, but only insofar as it serves her agenda. For example, she will cook for the entire family and be sure to cook the favorite foods for some people though ignoring the needs of others, and she will ensure the children have foods they are not allergic to or do not violate doctors' orders—at least while their parents are present and watching. This allows her to gain their good graces and thus, subject them to her manipulation.

PROJECTING/EXTERNALIZING BLAME (BLAMING OTHERS OR SCAPEGOATING): Disturbed characters are always looking for a way to shift the blame for their own aggressive behavior. They're skilled at finding scapegoats, and expert at doing so in ways that are subtle and difficult to detect. The willingness to blame another person for your own aggressive behavior is in itself an act of abuse. Thus, this very behavior is aggressive. Some people can never take responsibility for their own behavior, not ever, and can never actually apologize for any harm they cause. They know only blame: "It's your fault," "You're the one who owes me an apology," "I didn't do anything. You did everything."

FEIGNING INNOCENCE: This occurs when the manipulator tries to convince you that any harm was unintentional, or they didn't actually do what they're accused of having done. This is designed to make you question your own judgment and indeed your own sanity. This can come in subtle looks of surprise or indignation when confronted with an issue, all aimed to have you second-guess yourself in your justification for calling them out on their behavior. One way this can manifest is by refusing to acknowledge someone whatsoever in a boldly passive-aggressive act, then in their own defense when confronted, they say "I didn't even say anything!" Another line is "I didn't do anything!" in response to any accusation of harm she has inflicted. She deftly turns it all into the accuser's fault.

FEIGNING IGNORANCE OR CONFUSION: This is closely related to feigning innocence. It's when the manipulator acts like s/he doesn't know what you're talking about or is confused about an important issue you're trying to bring up. It's the manipulator's way of getting you to question your sanity by "playing dumb." This is a feature of all disturbed characters, and is very effective in veiling their malevolent intentions. Disturbed characters, particularly the aggressive personalities, are very goal-oriented and agenda-driven, and use tactics in conscious, calculated and deliberate ways. They may say they don't know what you're talking about or had no idea why what they did was offensive to you, but it's important that you not buy into the idea that they're not fully aware of what they're doing. One aggressor will literally say, "I don't know what you're talking about," and another will flat say, "You're lying."

BULLYING: One favorite tactic of aggressive characters is bullying. This is to explicitly threaten or brow-beat someone into giving them what they want, using fear as a terrorizing weapon. The target knows that if they do not submit, much worse things will follow. Disturbed people use bullying to get others to submit, and at the same time, to resist submitting to appropriate social standards in any way. Directly after they've bullied their target into submission, they are often in a normal or even jovial mood. "You will change your behavior or I will take everything you love away from you. You think for a second I won't? Try me."

BRANDISHING ANGER: This is a form of bullying. A deliberate display of anger can be a very calculated and very effective tool for coercion, intimidation, and manipulation. Aggressive personalities use overt anger displays for intimidation and manipulation. They may not actually be angry to start with; they just want what they want and get mad when they don't get it. Sometimes a very effective strategy to shock another person into submission is brandishing sufficient emotional intensity and rage. An aggressor will go from sweet to furious in a split second when she is called out on anything.

GIVING ASSENT: Manipulators can pretend to agree or give in on an issue when they feel cornered and their usual tactics aren't working. In this situation, they will say about anything, but they don't really mean it. They use this tactic to disarm their targets while still resisting social standards. The disturbed husband tells his wife, "Sure we can see your sister, any time! Of course!" Then when it comes time to schedule, different manipulation strategies come out to ensure that meeting never occurs.

POSTURING: All disturbed characters need to maintain the one-up position, so they are frequently posturing to ensure that superior position. They're good at throwing others onto the defensive, then "challenging" the legitimacy of others' outrage toward them. Posturing keeps the disturbed character with the upper hand, but stands in the way of the person accepting or valuing any authoritative guidance or even new information. "Ya, that's a good job you got yourself there. Everyone needs to know how trees grow... [chuckle, sigh, minimizing nonverbal cues]... What? I said it's important stuff!"

HYPERVIGILANCE: This is excessive suspicion and critique of others' behavior. Here, the disturbed person constantly questions others' behaviors, even with small things. They look for "evidence" that someone doesn't like them or is out to get them. This constant suspicion prevents the disturbed person from developing a balanced sense of trust. They don't know how to trust others or how to earn others' trust.

CONNING AND CONTRACTING: The disturbed person will often try to win allies or make others believe he supports an effort by "making deals." These deals they make usually violate accepted social norms. By making these sorts of deals, they reject opportunities to develop strength of character or to stand on principle.

GETTING OUT OF GUILT OR SHAME ON A "TECHNICALITY": The most disturbed people will focus attention on a few small, unessential details, especially when confronted about their poor behavior. They will focus on you getting one word wrong when repeating something they said while ignoring the harsh reality of the overall message. Sometimes they do this to make you think they're as innocent as you are or that they're victims of the system. They will complain for hours about how the police officer "totally exaggerated" about how fast they were driving, while completely ignoring the fact that they were speeding in a school zone and endangering children. This focus on the technicalities while ignoring the bigger picture is an effective tool for lying and deceit. Disturbed people use this to keep the focus off of their wrongdoing and also to resist internalizing the necessary social standards and controls.

FALSE CONCESSIONING: This tactic is a little like giving assent. Here, the disturbed character will admit small things or concede a small point when confronted. In this way, they appear open, honest, forthcoming, and contrite, at least a little, while they still do not genuinely accept the important issues. Disturbed people usually combine this tactic with another one such as distortion, evasion, or lying in order to hide and solidify their insistence against society's principles and standards that they're still battling against. "Yeah, you're right. I came home a little late last night" he may admit, without addressing the accusation that he had been involved in inappropriate behavior.

LEVELING: Here, the disturbed character tries to "level the playing field" and strengthen his position with someone when he finds himself in a "one-down" position. Leveling usually comes in two forms: 1) setting himself up as someone of equal stature to the higher-level person, and 2) trying to equate his own integrity, character, values etc. with someone else's, especially someone with a more developed or mature character. For example, a wife suggests to her disturbed-character husband that they visit her sister who has advanced degrees and lives in an enviable home. He responds with "your sister thinks she knows everything and she thinks she's better than us. Why would you want to go there? Are you starting to think like *her* now?" Here, he implies that he and her sister are of equal character standing, and the wife is being "uppity" for wanting to visit her sister. This can easily get the wife to retreat, even though this means he is cutting her off from her family.

MANIPULATION BY INSINUATION: Using insinuation and subtle suggestions about what they want other people to think, disturbed characters calculate their words carefully, intending to mislead. If they are called out on their game, they can easily say, "I didn't say that", which puts the target on the defensive and casts them as totally misrepresenting things.

These are the most common tactics used by disturbed, manipulative characters to manipulate and control others, and they're not always easy to recognize, especially at the moment in which they're occurring. Aggressive manipulators employ these tactics slickly, subtly and adeptly. If you're dealing with someone that shows these characteristics, you'll need to rely on a heightened gut-level sensitivity to avoid being manipulated.[109]

Dr. Simon points out that the act of blaming, which in itself is an act of abuse, occurs within all types of mental illness.[109] Depending on how many other of the above behaviors were present in your young world and to what extent, your home environment may have been moderately or highly abusive and/or stressful. Either way, chances are good that you developed a small mountain of anxieties as well as distorted perceptions of reality as a result of that kind of upbringing. There are some real, and detrimental, emotional, mental, and even physical effects of having been raised in that kind of environment.

Identification and Awareness
It's very important to realize that when someone uses these tactics frequently, you know what kind of character you're dealing with (a disturbed one). Also, because these tactics are both tools of manipulating others and manifestations of resistance to change, you also know that this person will engage in their problematic behaviors again (and again, and again…). Things will not ever be any different, so you can give up on that fantasy. Nothing will change unless and until they decide to stop fighting and start accepting socially appropriate—and mentally healthy—behavior. But as long as they're engaging in these tactics, it's clear that they have zero intention of changing, regardless of what they may tell you.[109]

If you see one or both of your parents, or another family member, spouse, romantic partner, roommate, friend, business partner, supervisor, coworker, or anyone else in your world in this list of characteristics, you really do need to keep reading this book—and you're the reason I wrote it! Taken together, these behaviors are deeply abusive, and when it's your parent that exhibits them, these manipulation tactics twist you into developing heaps of anxiety and a really distorted view of the world and the people in it, including yourself. You can't possibly develop internal serenity or a normal perception of yourself or life at large when you were raised by someone like this. But it's okay! All is not lost. The first step to making things better is identifying the problem, and that's what we've just done, so progress is occurring right under our noses, and already!

Implications
The above are common behaviors used by emotional manipulators, particularly aggressive ones. Physical abuse of course didn't make the list; yet, I have read that where physical abuse exists, mental and emotional abuse does too. So if you were

physically beaten, you likely experienced at least some of the above treatments as well.

These disturbed characters use emotional manipulation to control their worlds and the people in them—if a parent exhibited these behaviors, that means it's their children they're looking to control. In any case, a home environment with a parent, especially a mother, exhibiting these behaviors is going to bring us a whole slew of problems throughout our lives until we do something to straighten ourselves out.

Verbal Aggression

In addition to or in lieu of the above list of tactics for emotional manipulation, communicators can also use a range of communication patterns intended to inflict emotional and other internal damage. These patterns are combative. For some people, every interaction is an opportunity to try to dominate the other person, stopping at nothing in efforts to achieve that perceived victory. If people can't win an interpersonal interaction based on the merits of their argument, they resort to attacking the person.

Communication scientists have explored interpersonal dynamics for many decades, and some of this work has focused on the area of violent versus nonviolent communication tactics. The violent kind, of course, does a great deal of harm to the recipient. Researchers call this violent communication aggressive, and define it as follows:

> An interpersonal behavior may be considered aggressive it if applies force physically or symbolically in order, minimally, to dominate and perhaps damage or, maximally, to defeat and perhaps destroy the locus of attack. The locus of attack in interpersonal communication can be a person's body, material possessions, self-concept, position on topics of communication, or behavior (p. 158.)[121]

Let us go through this definition more slowly. Physical force involves the use of the body to apply force. Examples include striking or hitting someone or something. Symbolic force means using words or other nonverbal behaviors, e.g. gestures or tone of voice, toward someone or something.

This definition also suggests that this kind of force is used to dominate and defeat someone or something ("the locus of attack is defeated"). This target can be another person's body, possessions, self-concept, or positions on controversial issues.

67

As an example, Brittany is trying to get Joshua to loan her his car. She might shake him and say "give me the keys or I'll slap you!" This qualifies as physical force. She might attack his self-esteem by cursing at him or calling names—profanity or ridicule. She might threaten the relationship with something like "loan me your car now or I'm dumping you." These compliance-seeking tactics are classified as symbolic force because their aim is to attack the person or things of the other person.

Whether a communication behavior is considered constructive or destructive depends basically on whether it's perceived in that way by either of the participants or an onlooker. Aggressive communication is always destructive.[122]

Hostility

Hostility is definitely within the realm of destructive symbolic aggression. We see it when messages are used to express irritability, negativity, resentment, and suspicion. Irritability means having a quick temper, little patience, moodiness, and exasperation when something goes wrong. Negativism here is defined as excessive pessimism about outcomes that others support, refusing to cooperate, and being antagonistic toward authority, rules, and social conventions. Resentment means expressing jealousy and hatred and brooding about real or imagined slights, which causes anger to develop. Suspicion is the distrust of others and believing they want to harm you.

Further, hostility has been defined as "an attitude, a dislike of a particular person, object or issue, accompanied by desire to see this target injured or even destroyed" (p. 265).[123] When we see these behaviors emerge, the communicator using them is resorting to hostile tactics.

Extremely hostile individuals see themselves as being persecuted by others ("people want to be mean to me"), see their world as mean ("People like doing things that upset me"), and view themselves as more aggressive than most ("I'm a better fighter than most people").

Even hostile people aren't hostile all the time. Certain situations, such as fear of losing a job, might keep hostility from being expressed.

A fair amount of research has examined whether hostility and aggressiveness are simply states of being that people can transfer into and out of at will or depending on a certain situation, or whether they are more character or personality traits of the individual, present all the time. Researchers have concluded that hostility and aggressiveness can persist over many years and is a stable trait. Because it's an actual character or personality trait, it doesn't go away when situations change. If people are hostile in youth, that's a good predictor of how hostile and aggressive they'll be later in life.

A subset of hostility is verbal aggressiveness. This is a "tendency to attack the self-concepts of individuals instead of or in addition to their positions on topics of communication" (p. 164);[121] (p. 61).[124] Verbal aggression is when people direct their attack on the person's self-concept ("You're such a liar!").

There are broad domains of self-concept attack and more specific ones. The broader ones include attacks on group membership ("your family is a bunch of jerks"), personal failings ("and let's not forget about all those businesses you ran into the ground"), and relational failings ("and I can count your divorces on only two hands!").[122]

More specific types of verbally aggressive behavior include:[122]

COMPETENCE ATTACKS: Verbal attacks on someone's ability to do something. "You can't do anything right."
CHARACTER ATTACKS: Attacks on someone's character. "You're selfish" or "you're crazy."
TEASING AND RIDICULE: This is a more playful form of aggression. When our target gets offended, we brush it off with "we were only kidding! You're so sensitive!" But it can inflict psychological harm and damage, classifying it in the verbally aggressive category. There are affectionate and aggressive varieties of teasing.
AFFECTIONATE TEASING: Affection shows relational endearment, increases endearment, and strengthens relationships. It acts as an inside joke, bringing people closer together.
AGGRESSIVE TEASING: Teasing turns aggressive when it's not fun anymore for the person on the receiving end, and causes pain instead of pleasure, sometimes concealed with shallow chuckles by the recipient. It is used to cause pain and hurt. It is often used to express anger regarding a specific issue in the relationship or express discontent with a partner or the relationship in general: "It would be a good idea for you to finally use your map!" in a mocking tone, clearly intended to hurt by pointing out the other's shortcomings and poor sense of direction.
RIDICULE: Using words or deeds to evoke condescending laughter at another. Kids use teasing and ridicule all the time.
MALEDICTIONS: Wishing someone harm. "Drop dead."
THREATS: Explicitly suggesting the intention to inflict pain (physical or psychological), injury, or other type of hurt. "Don't make me slap you." Or "I'll destroy your favorite thing if I have to."
NONVERBAL VERBAL AGGRESSION. NONVERBAL EMBLEMS: These are aggressive gestures and other behaviors such as flipping the middle finger, gritting one's teeth, crinkling

your nose, sticking out your tongue, making a fist and shaking it in front of them, using your thumb and forefinger to form the letter L on your forehead for "loser", etc.

PERSONALITY ATTACKS: Attacks on the personality. "He's a timid fool."

NEGATIVE COMPARISON: Putting you down with a comparison of someone better. "Wow your friend is much better at that than you are."

ATTACKING THE TARGET'S SIGNIFICANT OTHERS: Attacks on their family members. "Your sister is so full of herself. How do you stand to be around her? She's always right and she knows everything. What an idiot."

DISCONFIRMATION: "Ghosting" someone. Ignoring them or behaving as if they don't exist.

Verbal aggressiveness can be caused by any of several sources. These include disdain, social learning, argumentative skill deficiency, psychopathology, or even genetics.[122]

The problem with this kind of aggressive communication is that it damages the target's self-concept—these tactics are intended to harm, and indeed they do. They weaken the other person's sense of self and undermine their self-confidence. For these reasons, they are considered destructive behaviors.[122]

Parents and Verbal Aggression

In terms of our parents' role in our own communication behaviors, research has found that adults' verbal aggressiveness was predicted by their perception of their mothers' verbal aggressiveness. That is, the more verbally aggressive people perceive their mothers to be, the more verbally aggressive they themselves are. Interestingly, even though fathers generally tend to be more verbally aggressive than mothers, the father's influence on the role of the child's predisposition toward verbal aggressiveness is not so strong as the mother's.[122]

The level of verbal aggressiveness we learn from our mothers is something we take into our future romantic relationships. Indeed, research has found that as adults' reports of their mothers' verbal aggression increased, the less emotional support and interpersonal solidarity these people had in their own romantic relationships. This suggests that having a verbally aggressive mother can cause a slew of interpersonal relationship issues later in life. Further, those of us with verbally aggressive mothers tend ourselves to be verbally aggressive in our own adult romantic relationships. Researchers suggest that having a verbally aggressive mother sets up a cycle that causes less satisfying and less productive adult relationships. Researchers have also found links between verbal aggressiveness and destructive outcomes including spousal abuse, sibling abuse, and overall interpersonal violence.[122]

Aggressive communication is no joke, even though its tactics can be disguised under a smile and joking tone of voice. It causes a great deal of harm. If you were raised in a verbally aggressive environment and particularly with a verbally aggressive mother, the cards are stacked against you in terms of your ability to have healthy and fulfilling interpersonal relationships. All is not lost, however, as Section II will show you how you can turn this around and develop healthy, satisfying relationships where no one feels the need to intentionally inflict pain with words and aggressive nonverbal communication behaviors.

Emotional Maltreatment: A Violent Environment

The research I have located classifies emotional maltreatment as including "verbal threats to the child and witnessing domestic violence".[125]

Verbal Threats

Verbal threats fall under the category of verbal aggression. As Chapter 10 will show, language matters—it can build up or destroy someone's well-being. When this someone is a developing child, the consequences of verbal threats become much more damaging than with an adult who can more easily shake off the verbal assaults. For the developing child, structures are being constructed in the environment where verbal threats are the norm, so as an adult that person is inclined to seek relationships that contain verbal threats.

Verbal violence can be defined as severe verbal aggression, cruelty of language and speech, and definite use of speech with intent to harm.[122] Indeed, these are verbal assaults. Certainly, verbal violence creates a hostile and very stressful environment for a child to develop within, and will have its own degree of damaging repercussions. We can't expect kids to come out of verbally violent homes with a healthy sense of self and a healthy outlook on life.

Witnessing Domestic Violence

Witnessing domestic violence is traumatic and incredibly stressful to a developing child. Children witnessing domestic violence suffer stress and trauma, and endure the same harm to their developing brains as children who themselves are direct victims of abuse. That is, even if the kid wasn't hit himself but instead "merely" witnessed one or both of his parents whaling on the other, his brain still suffers the same consequences as if he was in fact himself on the receiving end of the violence.

Conclusion

Mentally unwell home environments often have subtle, not easy-to-recognize characteristics. They can include any kind of neglect or abuse, such as a caregiver's emotional unavailability, emotional manipulation or verbal aggression. These unwell home environments can include any kind of stressors or trauma-inducing activity, such as the aforementioned neglect including from overprotectiveness, emotional manipulation, and/or verbal aggression, in addition to verbal or physical violence. When we can isolate and identify the individual behaviors that cause long-term harm to the developing child, we can see that these behaviors are rampant in our society, and that mentally unwell home environments are much more prevalent than we as a society may be willing to admit.

These are the roots of so many problems! These behaviors cause tremendous pain and suffering at minimum, as they cause a great deal more harm to the developing child than merely an occasional couple of tears. The behaviors that constitute a harmful home environment occur one at a time, generally subtly, and over time. They distort our perceptions of ourselves and the world in which we live, wreaking havoc on our internal structures as the next chapter will show. These are the behaviors that create the structures in which we will live our adult lives, so as adults, we seek relationships that have these behaviors because these behaviors fit with our internal structures. If you see one or especially both of your parents in the above lists, you cannot be surprised if you see your partner in these lists as well.

4. Brain Development

As we are growing up, our brains are developing. The brain develops through processes of creating, strengthening, and eliminating synapses. These synapses are the connectors between the brain's neurons, and they form pathways between the brain's regions. These synapses organize our brain and regulate everything we do, think, and feel through these pathways.

The brain is plastic, meaning it molds to experiences. The brain's synaptic plasticity is what allows a child to adapt to its environment. In an abusive environment, our brain will be shaped by that abuse, and because our brain is now shaped by that abuse, that abuse will then determine how we respond to our environment in terms of thoughts, feelings, and behaviors, at the moment and in the future.

Your Brain and Your Mother

The mental state of an infant's mother directly affects the brain development of that infant, and because she so heavily influences the child's developing brain, the child will carry these effects throughout its lifetime. In fact, her influence is so great that her interactions with the child directly impact whether its brain develops properly or not. In this way, she sets the hardwiring in this child's brain for its lifetime of managing the beauties and struggles life presents in all areas—emotional, cognitive, even motor, and more.

A mother's ability to properly attach with the infant child emotionally sets the child's conceptualization of relationships to either secure or anxiety-riddled, a setting the child will carry throughout its life unless and until that adult person expends a great deal of effort to alter that setting. Further, the child's actual personality develops as a result of its interactions with its parents, who teach the infant child about herself and who she is through those interactions. That is, part of who we become relies on our genetic material, yes, but a critical part of who we become has everything to do with how we were treated in our early lives by our parents and especially our mothers.

The brain develops and matures rapidly while still in the womb. Learning begins here. The parts of the brain connected with the emotions develop when we are tiny babies—still in the womb and in the first few years of life outside the womb. In the mother's third trimester of pregnancy, her emotional state can deeply influence her fetus's brain development, especially the brain's right hemisphere, which is particularly susceptible at this time and is the primary location of emotions.

So, how we are treated when we are babies actually shapes our brains. If your mother had a lot of anxiety when she carried you, your brain will actually develop with and incorporate her stress while you're still in the womb. She's already beginning to negatively influence (i.e. harm) your brain with her anxiety before you even take your first breath.

An emotionally well mother interacts appropriately with her baby and in so doing, helps her baby's brain develop in a healthy way. When a mother is mentally unwell, she will raise a mentally unwell child, primarily by not interacting with the child in healthy ways that would enable the child's brain to develop properly—I don't see how this result can be anything different, actually, as it's preposterous to believe that a mentally well child can result from a mentally unwell environment. The child's improper brain development sets the child up for a lifetime of anxiety and shortcomings in pretty much all areas of life.

Because early stressful experiences shape our brains, this early treatment also shapes our behavior later in life. Our caregivers are an essential part of these early experiences, and these early experiences shape the person we likely become.[126]

Neural Development
The third trimester in the womb through the first two years after birth is a major critical window for brain development. Most right brain development happens in the first two years of life. The right brain is critical in attention, emotional regulation, and the ability to be empathetic, and is involved in the regulation of morality.[127]

Right Brain Hemisphere
Neurologists have found that the right hemisphere develops its functions before the left, and more blood flows to the right hemisphere between 1 and 3 years of age.[128] In this time, the brain regions that control language, abstract thinking, emotional regulation and executive functioning develop further, and this lays the foundation for adult brain functioning.[17]

The right hemisphere develops more than the left hemisphere in the first couple of years. In the third year of life, that dominance switches to the left hemisphere.[128] These first few years are a critical period of accelerated brain maturation. Because of this, what happens in this time has profound effects on how your brain develops and the person you become. As a result of its vital importance to later life, infants and toddlers have special and critical social, mental, and emotional needs which must be met by their caregivers. If these needs are not properly met, the child will suffer for its lifetime—it's in the hard-wiring. If the right brain hemisphere fails to develop properly during this critical window, it causes a lot of problems, including mental illness and an inability to properly regulate emotions.[129]

In this critical early time, there is a lot of brain activity. The brain has huge growth spurts, a lot of synaptic plasticity, and right brain hemisphere development. Because so much is moving in our brains, our brains literally shape around the experiences we have during this time. This is why our home environment and caregiver treatment of us is so important, especially at this time.

Without proper nurturing, the right brain develops improperly. Also, our bodies show physiological indications of improper caregiver treatment, such as constipation resulting from emotional abuse.[197] So already, by the time we're two years old, we can have serious mental, emotional, and even biological issues mapped out for our lives as a result of our caregivers improperly caring for us in these critical early times.

Neural Processes

Early experiences also profoundly impact how a person integrates their emotional and social worlds. These experiences shape how people self-regulate their emotions in constructive, healthy, and socially acceptable ways. When we suffer neglect, severe stress, and abuse, our emotional systems don't develop properly or healthily.

Neurotransmitters in our brains and hormones in our bodies transmit information from one part of the brain to another, and to other parts of the body. Our experiences—how we are treated—trigger specific neurotransmitters and hormones. In turn, our brain develops in response to the specific neurotransmitters and hormones secreted. When the stress responses are amplified because we live in a stressful environment, we develop with that stress. That stress level becomes part of who we become. When stress and fear outweigh nurturance and love, our brain forms to accommodate the abundance of stress and fear in our lives.

Brain Function Under Stress
Early life abuse, particularly within the first two years of life, negatively impacts the right brain and therefore makes the person less able to cope with stress in life. This early abuse also increases the person's risk of developing Post-traumatic Stress Disorder (PTSD).[130] The right brain hemisphere, not the left, is critical in attention, emotional regulation, and the ability to be empathetic, and is involved in the regulation of morality.[127] So when the right brain development is impeded, throughout its lifetime that person is going to struggle with attention and appropriately regulating its emotions, empathy, and morality, in addition to struggling with coping and a greater likelihood of developing PTSD. The brain is plastic, so people might later compensate for the loss of positive experiences in early life, but the loss can't be completely recovered and this work can be quite difficult. Some people can never recover.

A stressful environment also causes an imbalance in the brain's functioning. When a child experiences mistreatment, that child is commonly in fear and learns to focus its brain energy and attention on survival and detection of threat. This chronically activates the brain's fear pathway.[17] This chronic activation damages the system that regulates fear, the Reticular Activating System (RAS), causing distortions in the child's natural responses to fear. Also, because the brain's fear pathway is overactivated, the other brain regions, like those we need for executive functions like thinking, decision-making, planning, and abstract cognition, will not be activated as much.

So we have childhood mistreatment causing an overactivation of the brain's fear pathway, and a resulting underdevelopment of the other brain regions, including those for thinking, attentive focus, and social interaction, rendering appropriate exercise of these behaviors more challenging than it should be. The child develops a constant expectation of danger and has real difficulties functioning in nurturing environments. The child also struggles to properly regulate reactions to social cues, causing difficulty in social interactions. This also causes problems concentrating in class, which impedes learning.

Stressful living environments and interpersonal trauma early in life affect the stress response system. Neurobiologically, early exposure to stress programs the person to show more sensitivity to stress and have a lower threshold for managing life's stressor.[131] [132] When you're exposed to stress in early childhood, this programs you to have a heightened stress response system—it takes less to stress you out than it does other people. This brings on some other conditions as well. Your brain's heightened sensitivity to stress is also associated with hypervigilance, poor emotional regulation, anxiety, and dysphoria (feelings of unwellness or unhappiness) associated with PTSD.[133] Early childhood trauma can also cause hyperarousal.[134] This kind of chronic trauma can impact the developing brain and lead to permanent structural, functional, and chemical changes in the brain.[135]

You can see how being raised in a stressful environment causes some real issues—you're more sensitive in regular life and struggle more in coping with day-to-day life events.

Brain Regions Affected

Early life stress can interfere with normal brain development. The brain's natural growth processes of creating and shaping (neurogenesis, synaptic overproduction and pruning, and myelination) can all be harmed by early childhood stress. There are additional brain problems resulting from early life stress as well: reduced corpus callosum size; retarded development of the left neocortex, hippocampus, and amygdala regions; increased irritability in limbic areas; and reduced functional activity of the cerebellar vermis (significance discussed below).[131] In other words, several of your brain's regions don't develop properly. As you might imagine, this causes a boatload of problems in life.

Further, childhood maltreatment may cause the creation of an alternative neurodevelopmental pathway that it needs for adapting itself to survive in a malevolent stress-filled world.[131] So, rather than your brain functioning normally, the stress you experienced early in life builds a different pathway through your brain in response to and for survival within that stress, causing distorted perceptions. Thus, early life trauma can enhance the possibility of psychiatric illness and behavioral dysfunction.[136,137]

Certain regions of the brain have been found to be affected by a stressful childhood. In general, these particular regions do not grow properly or even to full capacity in an environment of stress. These brain regions include:

- Prefrontal cortex
- Amygdala
- Hippocampus

- Corpus callosum
- Cerebellar vermis

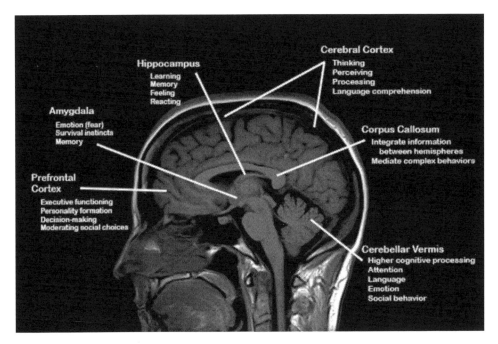

Prefrontal cortex

The prefrontal cortex is located in the front of the brain, directly behind our fore-heads. This region is critical for

- Problem-solving
- Language
- Motor function
- Judgment
- Impulsiveness
- Social behavior
- Sexual behavior

The prefrontal cortex is the final brain region to reach full capacity, achieving full development within the third decade of life (in our 20s).

In an environment of stress, the prefrontal cortex is affected in a couple of unfortunate ways. First, stress sends too much dopamine to this region,[138-140] interfering with attention and problem-solving.[141] Second, early stress alters the development of this brain region: The prefrontal cortex activates prematurely, but then has a stunted final capacity.[142]

Amygdala

The amygdala is located in the middle of the brain, as part of the limbic system, so is heavily responsible for our emotional lives and memory formation. The amygdala plays some critical roles in our ability to cope in our everyday environments.

- Accesses physiological and behavioral resources necessary to adapt to environmental challenges, especially threat[143]
- Critical in fear conditioning[144]
- Critical in controlling aggressive, oral, and sexual behavior[144]
- Helps form and recall emotional memory, learning nonverbal motor patterns, and trigger alarm responses, or fight-or-flight[145]

The amygdala is very sensitive to threatening stimuli and responds with displays of anxiety or depression. Childhood emotional neglect may increase threat-related amygdala reactions through affecting the functioning of the hypothalamic-pituitary-adrenal (HPA) axis.[146] A disrupted HPA axis function is associated with dysfunctional stress responsiveness, heightened amygdala reactivity,[147] childhood maltreatment,[148,149] and psychopathology.[150] This leads to inappropriate stress responses.

Excessive amygdala activation leads to PTSD[151-155] and major depression.[156] A stress-affected amygdala can explain impulsive violence and out-of-control behavior.[144]

Adverse experiences harm stress response regulation.[157,158] Under stress, the amygdala's development is slowed.[144] How much it reacts to stress in the childhood environment leads to individual differences in anxiety and depression.[159,160]

Severe emotional neglect has also been associated with heightened amygdala reactivity.[161,162] This heightened amygdala reactivity is associated with elevated and prolonged cortisol response to stress.[163] Extreme childhood adversity, such as that in institutional rearing, has been linked with heightened amygdala reactivity[161,162,164] and enlarged volume.[165,166]

79

Hippocampus

The hippocampus is also located in the center of the brain, as part of the limbic system. It too plays important roles in our everyday lives.

- Critical to encoding and retrieving specific information[167]
- Significant in generating dissociative states[168,169]
- Significant in anxiety and panic disorders[170-172]
- Important to behavioral inhibition, the system that stops inappropriate behavior

The hippocampus is also vulnerable to stress.[173,174] Stress early in life causes reduced overall synaptic capacity in the adult brain, which explains difficulty in memory of traumatic events and dissociation.[131,175]

As part of its normal development, some hippocampal regions have an overproduction of various cells (axonal and dentritic arborization, synapse, and receptors) after birth followed by trimming and elimination after puberty.[176-178] Early stress prevents the normal overproduction of synapses, but does not prevent their reduction after puberty. This leads to a long-term deficit in overall volume of synapses.

Some research has found smaller left hippocampus volume in adults with childhood trauma and a current diagnosis of PTSD or dissociative identity disorder.[175,179] Alterations in its development lead to the amnesic, dissociative, and disinhibitory parts of PTSD.

Corpus Callosum

The corpus callosum is the piece of the brain that joins the two hemispheres. This is how your brain talks to itself and processes information; the two sides need to work together, and the corpus callosum allows that to happen.

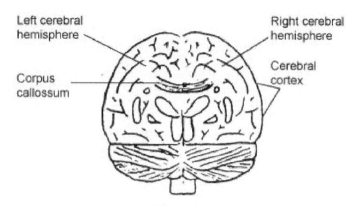

artwork copyright Karli Norell

- Left cerebral hemisphere specializes in
    o Perception and language expression
    o Logical thought
    o Analytical thought
    o Slightly more intricate development
    o Usually dominating in a variety of tasks (making most people right-hand dominant)
- Right cerebral hemisphere
    o Specializes in perception and emotional expression, particularly the unpleasant and challenging emotional variety[180-184]
    o Deficiencies can lead to poor perception and expression of challenging emotions
- Integrates motor, sensory, and cognitive performances between the cerebral cortex on one side of the brain to the same region on the other side

Early stress messes with this system, affecting the transfer of information between the two brain hemispheres[185,186] and the degree of left-right integration of the brain hemispheres.[142,187,188] Further, the two brain hemispheres don't project the same levels of serotonin and dopamine to the amygdala and prefrontal cortex, respectively. This is connected highly with levels of anxiety.[189]

Childhood mistreatment causes delays in the myelination (growth), in turn causing the two hemispheres to develop relatively independently of each other—meaning one side develops faster than the other and the two sides don't work together properly after childhood mistreatment.[190,191]

Reduced corpus callosum size means reduced communication between the two brain hemispheres. The middle portion of the corpus callosum is markedly smaller in children with a history of abuse or neglect, especially boys.[192] The corpus callosum of boys seems especially vulnerable to effects of neglect while those of girls seem more susceptible to the effects of sexual abuse.[193]

Cerebellar vermis
The cerebellar vermis is located in the middle-back of the head. It has only 10-20% of the brain's volume, but more than half of the brain's total neurons.[194] It is critical to

- Attention
- Language
- Cognition (thinking)
- Affect (emotion)[195-200]

The cerebellar vermis is very important for psychiatric health. It is very sensitive to and affected by early stress.

Problems in this brain region manifest as problems in the life areas dominated by this region, including cognitive, linguistic, socio-behavioral, and emotional disruptions.[198,199,201,202] It also plays a role in dopamine projection[203-205] and mediating stress response.[206-209] Abnormalities in this brain region lead to schizophrenia,[201,210-215] ADHD,[216-218] and depression.[219-221] Researchers have found that the vermis is important for psychiatric health, and significantly affected by early stress or neglect.

Further Impacts
Given the harm to several of our brain regions and proper functioning of our brains from an early stressful environment, it is no surprise that our lives have some distinct challenges as a result. Brain development changes also occur simultaneously with developmental stages.[125] Much research has concluded that experiences of child abuse can cause developmental delays, deficiencies, or failures of achievements in behavior, cognition, and emotional regulation.[222]

Our emotions are connected to our thinking and cognitive functioning, as well as our decision-making and higher executive functioning.[223] This is why it's important to be able to manage our emotions—so that we can be better able to decide, choose, and plan our actions.

Child abuse actually causes a type of brain damage because it impairs the proper development and functioning of several systems in our brains that are tied to our emotions. When connections in the brain are severed, brought on by childhood stress, the result is a clear deviation in normal behavior and a warped understanding of social and emotional contexts, even when intellectual functioning remains intact.[223] So, crazy and smart can and definitely do coexist.

We need our neurotransmitters to function properly if we want to be able to stabilize our well-being. The neurotransmitters in the brain that affect emotion also affect mood, responses to stimuli, learning, and memory. These neurotransmitters include serotonin, dopamine, and norepinephrine. Serotonin is important in well-being, positivity, and emotional stability. In fact, research has indicated that people who suffered mistreatment as children, including conditions of emotional abuse and neglect, cannot fully regulate serotonin as adults.[224] Less serotonin also contributes to both depression and migraine headaches, common in those who suffered early childhood maltreatment.

Infantile Helplessness
Infants cannot flee an abusive situation. When they're afraid, their facial expressions and motor movements change, and they cry. A healthy caregiver would take care of the child by comforting it, feeding, soothing it, and making it feel safe. An emotionally unhealthy caregiver neglects and ignores the child, forcing it to endure the continued stress in the situation on its own. The result in this situation is that even as an infant, the child gives up on getting its needs met and reflects a sense of learned helplessness.[64]

These kids become passive and non-responsive, yet compliant. They daydream and experience mental fugue, fantasy, derealization and depersonalization. Sometimes they feel as if they were floating or in a movie. In the defeat response, epinephrine and steroids in the body decrease. But rather than feeling hyperaroused, there's a decrease in heart rate, blood pressure, and sympathetic nervous system output. Abused babies sort of check out—their non-responsiveness might lead you to wonder if there's anyone actually inside of what appears to be a shell of a human being.

Environmental Shaping
Indeed, pretty much all of these dynamics from pre-birth through the first two years of life outside the womb place the primary caregiver, usually the mother, mainly responsible for the child's proper development. The child's brain develops

rapidly within this early time in life, and absorbs all of the elements in its most accessible environment. When Mom is the primary caregiver, that pretty much means the baby completely absorbs whatever Mom has to offer, for better or for worse. So when we have an unwell mother, we have a very messed up critical developmental stage and our brains literally don't develop properly. These problems in our brain's development bring challenges to many aspects of our lives that we will struggle against for a lifetime and actually never fully recover from, including issues with stress management, emotional regulation, intimacy, anxiety, and many more conditions.

Trauma Consequences

Trauma can come at the hands of our mothers, our fathers, or indeed, any other influence in our lives. It can happen in a few seconds, with no one else having any idea it has occurred. Trauma causes tremendous distortions in our lives in emotional, social, and neurodevelopmental aspects. Any sexual misconduct creates a trauma that lodges itself into our psyches. Sexual trauma also shapes our developing brains to hypervigilance and high anxiety as a way of life. Our brains do not develop properly when we experience trauma in early life.

Physical abuse is another form of trauma that lodges itself in the developing psyche, also creating these sorts of problems and challenges throughout life. Persistent parental/caregiver neglect also causes similar problems, as does a stressful environment that includes hostility and aggression.

Mother's Emotional Unavailability

When the mother is mentally unwell, she is pretty much going to be emotionally unavailable—she is unable to properly attend to her own emotions let alone the tremendous emotional needs of a developing infant. The child who needs to rely, evolutionarily, on its mother to teach it how to navigate these complex emotional systems instead is left to itself, alone, afraid, confused, and traumatized as a result of her emotional unavailability. This kind of trauma, brought on simply by the emotional unavailability of the mother, creates all kinds of problems for the child throughout its life.

When your mother is mentally unwell, it's no joke to you and your development, and the effects on you are nothing short of devastating in so many ways and on so many levels. The implications are highly complex, as your brain literally forms around this trauma and incorporates it as part of the world you come to know. Unraveling these distortions can take a lifetime of work, and we will still fall short—our developmental period is long past and our brain structures are fully set by this point. But there are still plenty of things we can do, as the next section will show.

Consequences of the Primary Caregiver's Emotional Unavailability

Let us leave all other forms of abuse and neglect behind for a moment, and concentrate our discussion on only the impacts of the mother's emotional availability. A mother can be emotionally unavailable for any of a number of reasons: addiction, work hours, attention elsewhere, inability to regulate her own emotions, and more. What happens to the growing child when it develops in an environment with an emotionally unavailable mother? This will mean the child's emotional needs are not met and the child is emotionally neglected. Let us dig a bit more deeply to investigate the consequences of having an emotionally unavailable primary caregiver.

The caregiver's emotional availability matters a great deal to the child because this availability facilitates intimacy between caregiver and child. This intimacy is important because it provides the foundation for neurological and other developmental growth from early life experiences.

The child's interactions with its caregivers are critical to a child's development, for good or for bad. Early life experiences with the caregiver can have direct and lasting effects on many aspects of a child's life including brain development, stress sensitivity, coping mechanisms, relationship with the self, social intelligence and overall behavior.[126,129] In other words, early child-caregiver interactions significantly affect the child's social intelligence, emotional intelligence, and general intelligence throughout development and as an adult.

The responsible caregiver's responsibility is to identify the child's internal state, match it, then help the child navigate that sentiment. This is empathic resonance. This emotional communication between caregiver and child is important because here, the caregiver teaches the child how to navigate the broad range of human emotions, laying the foundation for emotional self-management.[143]

When the caregiver is emotionally unavailable, the infants are left on their own, stressed by their confusing emotions. This stress harms the right brain hemisphere. Part of the job of the right hemisphere is stress regulation, specifically in emotional and stress responses.[225] Infants cope with the distress of zero emotional support during stressful times by self-regulating in ways associated with the right brain hemisphere.[226] Severe stress early in life, especially within the first two years, impacts the right brain negatively and because of this impact, renders the person less able to cope with stress throughout life. This also increases the individual's chance of developing PTSD.[130] The emotional unavailability of the mother during a child's infancy harms that child's ability to properly regulate stress and emotional responses throughout life.

HPA Axis
Emotionally unavailable caregivers ignore the child's emotional needs. This harms the child's hypothalamic-pituitary-adrenocortical (HPA) axis. The HPA axis regulates stress and is vital to the modulation of key hormones, including cortisol and adrenaline.

The HPA axis is deeply important to the control of vital functions, all of which help the person cope with stressors and changes in their environment. When that HPA axis is constricted, this person has problems in these life areas—managing stressors and environmental changes. Additionally, as attachment theory supports, the child may have difficulty forming healthy relationships throughout life.[17]

The HPA axis genes are important for managing a person's vulnerability to PTSD, and early life trauma impacts on the HPA axis development can render an abused person more susceptible to developing PTSD. In fact, links have been found between PTSD itself and alterations in the HPA axis.[227,228]

Social Deficiencies
Certainly these issues are not the only ones that result from being raised by an emotionally unavailable caregiver. Social deficiencies also occur. Another result, Reactive Attachment Disorder (RAD)[229] is slowed development in ways of relating to others in most social contexts. On the one hand, RAD can involve a failure to initiate social interactions or failure to respond appropriately, known as the "inhibited form". For example, consider one who does not speak at social engagements unless first spoken to, usually requires prodding to get a response, and then generally responds overly briefly, with one-word or few-word, pinched-mouthed responses. On the other hand, RAD can manifest as the "disinhibited form", where the child is overly friendly with strangers—also known as the Social Engagement Disorder.

Emotional Influences

A mentally unwell parent is certainly emotionally unavailable. As infants in these emotionally unavailable environments, we are left to our own devices to try to figure out the complex system of emotions we humans all possess. This is an impossible task to manage ourselves, and we fall devastatingly short. As infants and children, we simply lack the tools necessary to understand our emotional worlds and navigate them properly. The result is not pretty. Our coping mechanisms, ability to manage stress, ability to regulate our emotions, emotional intelligence, social intelligence, general intelligence, relationship comfort and ability, and even neurotransmitter secretions and hormonal behavior all take a hard hit when we are raised by an emotionally unavailable caregiver. This doesn't even go into the consequences of having an abusive caregiver—just an emotionally unavailable one causes all of these kinds of problems for us in our lives.

The developing child responds differently to its mother and father, and each parent has a different impact on how the child regulates its emotions later in life. Early interactions with the mother influence how we regulate fear, and early interactions with the father influence how we regulate aggression.[230] These differences could be due to differences in the ways that men and women tend to express their own trauma-related problems—research has found that women tend to turn inward with their trauma and anxiety problems, internalizing them, while men tend to turn them outward with aggression, externalizing them. So, women are observed to be more anxious or afraid, which they pass to their children through challenges in fear regulation, and men more aggressive, which they pass on through challenges in regulating aggression. This can mean that men tend to express their PTSD more externally, through interpersonal aggression, than women do.[231,232] Kids pick up on this stuff.

Attachment

One theory in psychology looks at the child's relationship with its caregiver and considers how that relationship lays the foundation for all other intimate relationships in the child's lifetime. This is Attachment Theory. It is about the mother connecting with the child at social and emotional levels primarily during infancy.

Humans have a biological need to maintain proximity to our caregiver to ensure safety. This is evolutionary and non-negotiable. This is known as the attachment system. This attachment is so important to us—it isn't only for protection; it influences neurobiological development, which affects how we regulate emotion and strategies we use to cope in adulthood.[66,233-237]

Attachment theory recognizes that humans form attachments to ensure survival.[69,234] Between an infant and its caregiver, these attachments are critical for many reasons. First, they help the infant to develop in its environment. These attachments also create and maintain internal models that provide the infant with the tools needed to predict its environment, and they maintain relationships (to improve survivability). They also create a sense of security.[238] Indeed, the child learns to survive in its physical environment as a direct result of its attachment with its caregiver.

These working models our caregivers give us contain all kinds of information. They give us information about attachment figures and the self.[234] They also provide details of interpersonal experiences and the emotional states associated with them.[239] Further, these working models give information that dictates what the person pays attention to, how they interpret the events in their lives and their environments, and what kind of information they will remember. Information on all of these processes results from the child's attachment to its caregiver during infancy. We learn all of this from our parents, usually our mothers.

These processes operate at the subconscious level rather than in conscious awareness,[234,239] and though it's possible for them to change over time, they tend to remain stable throughout the individual's life.[69] This kind of information helps individuals perceive, order, and predict their worlds, then deal with the situation at hand.

What Attachment Is
In this theory, attachment is the right brain-to-right brain social and emotional communication between the child and caregiver. This attachment deeply influences how the child can self-regulate its own emotions as it becomes older, meaning that these interactions profoundly affect the child's neurobiological development.[126]

This two-person relationship helps the infant deal with its brand-new environment and everything in it. With its mother's assistance, the infant is able to develop and grow with a sense of emotional calm and equilibrium.[240] With a solid attachment to the caregiver, the child knows he is okay, despite all of the chaos he is experiencing in this brand-new outside world.

Right Brain Hemisphere Development

We have seen from above that the right brain develops a lot during the first couple of years of life. The brain's right hemisphere primarily processes emotional information.[241] The infant's developing right cerebral cortex, the thin coating over the brain's exterior, is important as it helps the infant process individual faces, recognize maternal facial expressions intended to get a response, and respond to the mother's specific speech patterns when interacting with her child.[242] The brain's right hemisphere is central to human bonding and attachment[243] and in developing back-and-forth interactions between mother and infant.[39,242]

During the attachment period, the first two years of life, the infant is paying very close attention to the mother's facial and auditory expressions, and the infant then develops in response to what he experiences from her.

For healthy attachment and healthy infant development, the mother must relate to the infant in a way that she matches the infant's internal states. In this way she triggers production of certain elements (corticotropin releasing factor, CRF, which controls endorphin production) in part of the infant's hypothalamus that does several things: It raises plasma concentrations of noradrenaline, activates the sympathetic nervous system, increases oxygen consumption and energy metabolism, and generates a state of emotional excitement.[242] Thus, the mother's ability to interact in a healthy and emotionally appropriate way with her infant matters a great deal to the healthy right brain hemisphere development of her child.

In the first two years of life, the infant's brain is rapidly developing and by the end of its second year, it has developed several adaptive capacities. The right brain system regulates psychobiological states.[b] It is also a result of interactions between nature and nurture, or your genetics combined with your environmental experiences, in the first two years of life.[242] What the infant experiences regulates how the genes come out in the cerebral cortex, which is being developed during this time,[244] indicating a strong relationship between genetics and face-to-face interactions in shaping a human being.[242]

The social interactions between mother and child that lead to emotional development ("socioemotional interactions") directly influence the brain's limbic region growth. Emotions are primarily housed in the limbic regions, located in the center

---

[b] Psychobiological states are biological conditions resulting from psychological conditions, such as constipation due to emotional distress.

of the brain. The right cerebral cortex is especially influenced by early social experiences and also primarily involved in attachment. It is also more vulnerable to early negative environmental influences than the left.[242]

The right brain hemisphere is nonlinear, and houses a collection of early attachment experiences. It ends its first major growth phase in the second year, when the left hemisphere, which is linear, begins one. However, the right hemisphere also cycles back into growth phases at later periods of the life cycle.[245] This refocusing on the right brain growth later in life allows to continue attachment later in life. It also allows the possibility of reorganizing emotional processing throughout life. Thus, if the child's first two years with its mother were chaos, all is not lost completely, as its future will hold additional attachment opportunities.

The Importance of Attachment
Healthy attachment provides the infant with an internal emotional balance, or homeostasis. Its developing brain relies on this homeostasis as it promotes, develops, and maintains healthy synaptic connections. In other words, the context of the infant's relationship with its caregivers is responsible for how the brain self-organizes and self-develops. This demonstrates the importance of the child-caregiver relationship, and affirms the strong and sensitive emotional needs of the child—the caregivers are actually integral parts of the brain's development during this critical infant time. For caregivers, this can be both frightening and a source of hope, as the caregiver's behavior with and toward the child can either sustain a healthy child or construct the foundation for an emotionally and socially unhealthy child. Indeed, this is a huge responsibility for the caregiver, as the child's healthy future literally depends on the caregiver's ability to form a solid emotional relationship with the child.

The infant's ability to connect with its caregiver on an emotional level, through the caregiver's social behaviors, lays the foundation for the child's ability to competently manage its emotions and participate in comfortable relationships later in life. On the other hand, researchers have found that lack of attachment in infancy and early childhood can lead to Post-traumatic Stress Disorder (PTSD).

Attachment Styles
Depending on how healthy your attachment with your primary caregiver, usually when you were a baby, you will have developed one of four possible attachment styles:

- Secure. comfort with closeness and intimacy: *Come here, sit close*
- Fearful-avoidant. desire for but fear of intimacy: *I want you to be with me, but that also scares me.*
- Preoccupied. a desire for intimacy but fear of abandonment: *I would like for you to come here, but I am afraid you will just leave.*
- Dismissing-avoidant. uncomfortable with closeness and a preference for relying on the self: *It's better if you don't come too close.*

ATTACHMENT STYLE CATEGORIES
INTIMACY

Attachment Style Characteristics and Differences

Your attachment style influences how you approach relationships, yes. But it goes beyond influencing our comfort in intimate relationships. Our attachment style also affects how we mentally react to a difficult emotional stimulus.

In terms of emotional management, those with high attachment anxiety would demonstrate more negative memories when exposed to challenging emotion, while those with low attachment anxiety demonstrate fewer negative memories and negative behavioral explanations when exposed to the same emotionally challenging stimulus. Thus, because intimate relationships by their very nature bring emotionally challenging stimuli, those individuals with high attachment anxiety can't perceive a relational partner in a normal or healthy light, but rather they experience the partner in a more threatening way that makes them feel perpetu-ally off balance. So, the less secure the attachment style, the more that challenging emotions will stir negative memories and influence current behavioral explana-tions, and the more that person will perceive a relational partner as threatening rather than as normal and healthy.

The more secure styles can also help regulate playfulness, which is related to curi-osity and creativity. Anxious styles, on the other hand, do not like novelty or risk; their curiosity and creativity are stifled, even when they are in a safe environment.

Those with anxious attachment styles also experience activation in multiple brain regions that relate difficult emotions with positive ones. So, even though these people may be experiencing a positive emotional stimulus, they may have path-ways that remind them that previous positive emotional situations were eventually associated with negative ones. Therefore, this person has learned that when things are going well, they turn out poorly. As a result, they don't trust when things seem to be going well. If they're having a good time, anxiety kicks in and escalates be-cause they "know" things are about to dramatically turn, and it won't be pretty. If a relationship is going well with no discernible problems, they will be nervous in anticipation of the problems certainly about to show up—it's not right if nothing's wrong. Because anxiety is wired to emotional stimuli, even positive emotional stim-uli bring anxiety. Positive emotional influences, on the other hand, allow develop-ing infants to access a broader range of mental capabilities and actually improve creative problem-solving skills.[246]

These anxious styles can easily come with social anxiety which, in extreme cases, can be debilitating—these people are actually afraid of social interactions because for them, because of how their brains are wired, these are highly anxiety-inducing experiences. This has the effect of rendering the individual simply unable to have fun with other people. Their minds are full of anxiety, so their creativity and curi-osity are stifled. They like things just as they are, and creativity and curiosity rely on novelty and therefore risk, so are best avoided. People with anxious attachment styles are simply unable to have a good time. *Drive go-carts? Hike in the woods? Why? No thank you.*

Those with secure attachment styles, on the other hand, can properly evaluate en-vironmental signals because they regulate an openness to emotional cues in their environment, and evaluate them more accurately.[247] Those with the more secure attachment styles have a much easier time of experiencing positive emotion, playfulness, curiosity, creativity, and just plain fun. *Let's drive go-carts and go for a hike!*

The style of attachment the child develops is a direct function of the primary caregiver's relationship with that child. This primary caregiver is usually the child's mother, so the mother-child relationship during infancy literally sets the child up for a lifetime of anxiety or peace and playfulness.

If your primary caregiver was mentally unwell, then you will have an anxious attachment style, and will have to work harder at having fun and enjoying yourself and others. These pleasure sensations on their own do not come easily or naturally to you, without the anxiety accompaniment. You will have at least some degree of social anxiety because your brain regions of pleasure and stress are hard-wired together. So even though a fun activity looks like fun, whether on your own or with others, you remain apprehensive about joining in. It's easier—and safer—to isolate, staying in an environment of your own making that you can better control rather than taking the risk to have fun, as the very act of having fun brings anxiety along with it. Trying new things is hard, and anxiety levels are high when faced with the risk involved in trying something new. But if you benefited from a mentally well childhood and have a secure attachment style, it's difficult for you to understand why others can't just come along and have fun—that kind of anxiety is so far beyond your reality!

Memory
Memory development is a complex process. Memory as we know it comes together around the age of two or three.

Before that time, we have what science calls implicit memory. Implicit memory allows infants to gain perceptions of their environments and recall those perceptions unconsciously.[248] We can perceive and evaluate emotions, but are not troubled with remembering them.

Implicit memory also gives us a sense of time and of self.[40] It is largely mediated by the amygdala, home of emotions, survival instincts, and memory. It is also connected to our body's response systems that are designed to activate when encountering a threat. Implicit memory is a rapid and unconscious response system with significant evolutionary survival value.[249]

If we suffer trauma during this time of implicit memory, we will likely endure challenges to regulating our emotions, triggering our survival instincts, and re-membering things accurately.

The other main kind of memory, explicit memory, is what we generally think of when we think of memory. Explicit memory is conscious and connected with lan-guage, and begins to develop around age two.[248] It requires conscious awareness to accurately encode all information and remember subjectively.

Between ages one and two, we develop what's called semantic explicit memory which involves language acquisition. After our second year, we develop autobi-ographic memory, which involves the sense of self and events related to the self. Memory as we generally think of it develops around this age because certain parts of the brain mature at that time, namely the medial temporal lobe and orbitofrontal cortex. In explicit memory, children become able to recall details of events, understand sequence and ordering, develop spatial representations of objects, and better understand space and time.[40]

Developmental Influences
In healthy development, these systems coordinate carefully and grow to-gether—language, event recall, sequencing and ordering, sense of self and re-lated events, etc. as noted above. But under extreme stress or exposure to trauma, these systems separate. We remember things on emotional and sensory levels separate from the linguistic component.[117] This means we can't process these memories properly because we cannot bring in language to order them.

Our memories are not supposed to work this way, but severe stress causes this split. This explicit memory fragmentation influences our future emotional and behavioral responses, yet we don't really understand the fragmentation or what to do about it. Healthy kids develop their systems of detailed event recall, se-quence comprehension, spatial object representation, and space and time com-prehension integrated and together. Kids in unhealthy environments develop these various systems independently, separated also from their ability to use language to talk about their emotional and sensory experiences and memories.

The process of memory development helps an infant know how to survive, as we know what to do in the future because of what we've experienced in the past—we remember. When an infant cries and has her needs met, the neural pathways that teach her how to survive and thrive become stronger. But when the crying child does not have his needs met, his neural pathways develop under negative conditions and can lead to his later inability to nurture and love. This neglect can also lead to distortions in views of himself and others, making relationships challenging on that level as well. Such perspectives, originally laid out in implicit memory, become a part of how this person comes to view the world.

Implicit Memory and Trauma

When an infant or pre-toddler in the implicit memory stage experiences trauma, its sensory and emotional experiences are not brought into conscious awareness and properly consolidated into autobiographical memory—the memory of the self and what happened to the self—because the infant's memory system is still too immature at that stage. This limitation hinders this person's ability to consciously access memories of unresolved traumatic experiences either at the time of occurrence or later on in life. Instead of remembering the event explicitly, which cannot occur because memory was not yet in place when the trauma occurred, if the individual re-experiences some part of the trauma context, this can trigger some sort of automatic reminder of that traumatic event.[250] So, perhaps visiting the home of a rarely visited uncle later in life may trigger some sort of awareness of early abuse.

The effects of unresolved infant trauma can both lack conscious awareness and be really confusing. Abused or neglected children may not be able to retain or access explicit memories of things that happened to them. They do hold on to the implicit memories of the emotionality and physicality of early life experiences though. So, a child abused by her uncle in infancy may never know why she doesn't like that uncle, but she stays away from him.

Implicit memories of trauma can cause problems in people's lives throughout their lives, partly because it's difficult to resolve what you can't remember. In fact, it's hard to even know something is there at all. The unresolved trauma can manifest in repeated patterns of disorganized states of mind. These patterns can also imprint in neuropathways, and the individual can have problems with secure attachment states of mind and self-regulation abilities, consequently impacting an individual's ability to cope with stress.

People having suffered a trauma in infancy are also likely to have distorted internal working models of the self and others.[40] An abused child's models of himself and others would certainly be distorted, and although at some level he may be aware of this distortion, he may also be unable to identify the source of the distortion or figure out what to do about it because it is lodged in implicit memory, inaccessible with the conscious mind. These disorganized states can harm the person's ability to function properly in areas of response flexibility, emotional regulation, and communication behaviors.[40]

Early childhood trauma lodges itself in our subconscious memory, influencing our interactions (not in a positive way of course). Until infant trauma is resolved, its effects distort perceptions and behavior in wild and unpredictable ways throughout life.

Indeed, discovering an infancy trauma and healing from it can ease a huge chunk of anxiety. Just because we may not remember early childhood trauma, doesn't mean we've forgotten it either. It's still there, lodged in our psyches, haunting our thoughts, our emotions, our motivations, our perceptions, our beliefs, our interactions, our relationships. It's not easy to resolve this kind of early child-hood trauma precisely because we have no conscious memory of it, and it's re-ally hard to fix something when you don't have any idea what may be broken. What we can do is pay acute attention to contexts that serve as triggers for us however, as that is our implicit memory trying to talk to us, trying to tell us something, trying to bring an unconscious, pre-memory event into conscious-ness. Just because our triggers don't make any sense to others, and of course they never will, or even to ourselves, doesn't mean they should ever be dis-counted or ignored. If anything, we need to be very sensitive to these triggers and grateful when they arise, for they are allowing insights to our own troubled histories, giving us cues to our pains and with those cues, extremely valuable information we can use as tools to help us heal. If you suspect you suffered trauma during this implicit memory period, a hypnotist may be able to help you locate and identify it.

Trauma and Personality Development

Caregivers, in addition to being responsible for a child's brain development and attachment style which set the stage for a lifetime of ease or anxiety, are also vital to the development of the child's concept of self. Some research suggests that the self is the product of one-on-one interactions experienced.[251,252] That is, I only know who I am because you (and you, and you, and you, and you...) let me know.

We learn who we are through our interactions with others. They respond to us and we experience their responses, which help shape who we believe ourselves to be and indeed who we become. In developing a sense of self, our primary early life relationships, in which we exist not only unto ourselves but also as part of another, help. In this way, early childhood relationships deeply influence self-development.

Kids primarily learn about who they are based on the quality of their relationships with their parents. So it's easy to see that kids who are abused and neglected, who experienced some very real struggles with their parents, face some serious challenges in constructing meaningful lives and safe interpersonal relationships. They also have major self-esteem and self-concept issues.

Typical characteristics of the abused child include inability to properly manage the self, chronic dissociation, and physical problems without clear medical bases. When you combine people with these characteristics of instability with caregivers that are cruel, inconsistent, exploitative, unresponsive or even violent, it's easy to see that these caregiver influences deeply impact a child's sense of who they are. It's also easy to see that this kind of upbringing can lead to disturbances of body image; a self-view as helpless, damaged and ineffective; and difficulties with trust, intimacy, and self-assertion.[44,117,253,254]

Through their interactions with us beginning at a very early age, our parents help build and create our personalities. If we are abused or neglected, we have some distortions we're grappling with as we're growing up and developing our own sense of self. At the same time as we're trying to manage those and figure out who we are, we're dealing with key people in our environment who are downright mean and intentionally hurtful to us in so many ways, and we're struggling to protect ourselves too. Of course we come out of those years of experience with some really twisted images of who we are and the actual role of others in our lives. It's hard to ever feel safe.

We can also develop distorted perceptions of self and other as a result of early interpersonal trauma. The models of ourselves and others we develop are based on the models present in our early lives. With early exposure to trauma, these working models are distorted. These distorted models bring some real challenges to the person living within them: They provide harmful influences to a child's expectations of the future, shape that person's anticipations of others, and interfere with the ability to develop cohesive narratives of events. In a sense, we are given distorted bricks that create distorted structures from within which we attempt to live non-distorted lives.

Trauma and maltreatment mean that the internal working model of the self and others is distorted and needs to be altered later in life, which in turn deeply alters a person's sense of self and other.[40] It's just a small shift in perception though, or perhaps a small series of small shifts, but not a huge deal. If we were mistreated as kids, we have some work to do to straighten some things out so that we can live happy healthy lives. But fear not, as Section II outlines this process in detail and with multiple approaches.

Conclusion

So… let me get this straight. As I understand this information that I have pulled together and presented for you here, a stressful childhood environment causes the child's developing brain to deform, and the level of stress necessary for these neuro distortions can be as minimal as an emotionally unavailable mother. Is that what you got out of this?

The perfectly vague term "dysfunctional" has been commonly used to explain this phenomenon.

"Dysfunctional" my sassafras. How is this not freaking brain damage?

5. Post-traumatic Stress Disorder

In this book, I resist detailed discussions of any single mental condition for a variety of reasons. However, in a book about stressful environments and traumatic events as the cause of a great deal of mental unwellness, I cannot get around specifically addressing the mental condition of post-traumatic stress disorder (PTSD). Because PTSD is so damaging to our psyches, so prevalent in our society, and so easily contracted as our lives often contain traumatic events just in the usual course of living, this topic deserves a full exploration.

Defining PTSD

Post-traumatic stress disorder (PTSD) is a mental condition that often results from traumatic events. It was first recognized by the American Psychiatric Association in 1980 as a cluster of symptoms that develop after exposure to an extreme traumatic stressor where the person felt intense helplessness or horror. More recent research has identified PTSD as also resulting from repeated and severe traumatic stressors such as child abuse and neglect, and family and community violence.[34,71,255,256]

The condition was originally intended to classify adult combat veterans, but child maltreatment is also associated with PTSD symptoms.[257] Maltreatment is a trauma that leads to PTSD symptoms, especially in children, because maltreatment impacts the body's biological stress systems, in turn impacting brain and cognitive development.[258] The kinds of changes in the brain caused by poor treatment lead to PTSD.

The National Center for PTSD,[259] a division of the U.S. Department of Veterans Affairs, presents the current PTSD diagnostic criteria from the Diagnostic and Statistical Manual of Mental Disorders, fifth edition (DSM-5).[82] A diagnosis of PTSD includes the following events.[259]

Post-traumatic Stress Disorder diagnostic criteria according to the DSM-5

Criterion A (one required): Exposure to death, threatened death, actual or threatened serious injury, or actual or threatened sexual violence, in the following way(s):
- Direct exposure
- Witnessing the trauma
- Learning that a close friend or relative was exposed to a trauma
- Indirect exposure to aversive details of the trauma, usually in the course of professional duties (e.g. police officers, medics)

Criterion B (one required):
- Intrusive thoughts
- Nightmares
- Flashbacks
- Emotional distress after exposure to traumatic reminders
- Physical reactivity after exposure to traumatic reminders

Criterion C (one required):
- Trauma-related thoughts or feelings
- Trauma-related reminders

Criterion D (two required):
- Inability to recall key features of the trauma
- Overly negative thoughts and assumptions about oneself or the world
- Exaggerated blame of self or others for causing the trauma
- Negative affect
- Decreased interest in activities
- Feeling isolated
- Difficulty experiencing positive affect

Criterion E (two required):
- Irritability or aggression
- Risky or destructive behavior
- Hypervigilance
- Heightened startle reaction
- Difficulty concentrating
- Difficulty sleeping

Criterion F (required):
- Symptoms last for more than 1 month

Criterion G (required)
- Symptoms create distress or functional impairment (e.g. social, occupational)

Criterion H (required):
- Symptoms are not due to medication, substance use, or other illness

Two specifications:
- Dissociative specification. In addition to meeting criteria for diagnosis, the person also experiences high levels of either of the following in reaction to trauma-related stimuli:
  - Depersonalization. Experience of being an outside observer or detached from oneself (e.g. feeling as if "this is not happening to me" or one were in a dream).
  - Derealization: Experience of unreality, distance, or distortion (e.g. "things are not real")
- Delayed specification. Full diagnostic criteria are not met until at least six months after the trauma(s), although onset of symptoms may occur immediately.

Symptoms from each category must be present for the PTSD diagnosis.[259,260]

One PTSD study carefully outlined childhood maltreatment behaviors that can and often do lead to PTSD. These fell into six broad categories within two broader classifications: General maltreatment consisted of Failure to Supervise, Failure to Provide, Physical Abuse, Emotional Abuse, and Witnessing Interpersonal Violence. The other classification included Sexual Abuse.[261]

These researchers divided these classifications further, identifying specific behaviors that led to PTSD development:[261]

Failure to Supervise
Neglect resulting in:
- Serious accidents
- Not knowing child's whereabouts
- Being left home alone
- Unexplained school absences
- Witnessing caregiver using drugs or being drunk
- Exposure to inappropriate adult sexual activity

Failure to Provide
- Basic physical or medical care

Physical Abuse
Discipline by caregiver
resulting in:
- Bruises or serious injury sustained on one or more occasions
- Being pushed into objects
- Shaken
- Burned
- Being threatened with a deadly weapon

Witnessing Interpersonal

Violence
- Witnessing or being told about interpersonal violence
- Threats involving violence to important attachment figures
- Threatening or violent crime where significant injury or death occurred or could have occurred
- Being the victim of serious threats or violent crime not perpetrated by a caregiver
- Witnessing family members' explosive behaviors resulting in serious property damage or attempts to hurt themselves

Emotional Abuse
- Caregiver making hurtful comments at the child
- Caregiver swearing at the child
- Witnessing or hearing about other family members' physical abuse

Sexual Abuse
Isolated incidents of:
- Genital fondling
- Oral sex
- Vaginal or anal intercourse

This study found that poorer visual memory was associated with PTSD resulting from both General Maltreatment and Sexual Abuse categories.[261] Poorer visual memory may reflect dysfunction of the hippocampus and/or of other brain regions, including the right hemisphere,[262] parahippocampal area and left lingual gyrus,[263] and parietal and prefrontal cortices.[264]

Furthermore, child maltreatment puts the subject at risk for addictions, a frequent lifetime comorbid (coexisting) issue in adults with PTSD.[265] Researchers hypothesize that comorbid substance use disorders may be related to reduced hippocampal volumes and function in PTSD sufferers.[266]

PTSD Diagnosis

When symptoms occur after a person experiences a life-threatening or traumatic event or events such as those listed above, and reacts with disorganized behavior within four types of symptom clusters for at least one month, a diagnosis of PTSD can ensue.[259,260,267]

Symptoms

PTSD manifestations are categorized into four areas: re-experiencing, avoidance and numbing, negative thoughts and feelings, and arousal.[259,268]

Reexperiencing symptoms include:

- Repeated, involuntary memories
- Psychological distress at reminders
- Sleep disturbance
- Bad dreams or nightmares
- Intrusive thoughts, imagery, sounds, and smells
- Repetitive or obsessional thoughts

Avoidance and numbing, or denial, symptoms include:

- Restricted social range
- Restricted range of affect (emotion)
- Avoidance of thoughts or feelings regarding the event
- Inability to recall part of the event
- Avoidance of reminders
- Resistance to talking about what happened or how they feel about it
- Sense of foreshorted future

Negative thoughts and feelings include:

- Ongoing and distorted beliefs about oneself or others (e.g. "I am stupid." "No one can be trusted.")
- Ongoing fear, horror, anger, guilt or shame

- Significantly decreased interest in activities previously enjoyed
- Feeling detached or estranged from others

Arousal symptoms include:

- Irritability or anger outbursts
- Behaving recklessly or self-destructively
- Difficulty concentrating and effect on school or work
- Generalized sleep disturbance
- Hypervigilance (including ongoing fear of recurrence)
- Physiological arousal at reminders
- Exaggerated started response[267]

Symptoms cause significant distress or problems functioning.[259] The severity of the trauma relates to the number of PTSD symptoms experienced.[267]

Girls and women tend more likely to manifest symptoms, particularly those of avoidance/denial.[267] Men tend to express anger and hostility as a result of PTSD more than women do.[269] For women, PTSD results more in poor overall relationship adjustment and is a significant predictor of marital discord.[270]

But overall, those with PTSD are more likely to express severe aggression. Psychological aggression may be more socially acceptable than physical aggression, so it is more closely associated with PTSD than physical aggression. Regardless of gender, PTSD brings relationship difficulties and in turn, negative outcomes such as increased physical and mental health problems and disability[271] including relationship and family problems in morale, motivation, readiness, and retention.[272-275]

Stress-related and Co-morbid Conditions

Childhood PTSD can cause failures in behavioral and emotional regulation[276] along with cognitive consequences resulting in the existence of a second condition, a psychopathology.[277-279] PTSD often occurs along with other related conditions such as depression, substance use, memory problems and other physical and mental health problems;[259] in fact, several psychological issues may be associated with PTSD but not included in its direct definition. These also include: self-hatred, dissociation and depersonalization, aggressive behavior against self and others, problems with intimacy, and impairment in the capacity to experience pleasure, satisfaction, and fun. Moreover, childhood trauma exposure results in negative psychiatric and physical health conditions including PTSD,[280] depression and suicidality, anxiety disorders, addiction,[45] and major medical conditions.[16] Further, childhood trauma is also associated with developing myriad other disorders as well, including borderline personality disorder,[281,282] somatization disorder,[283] dissociative disorders,[284-288] and eating disorders.[289-291]

These behaviors and conditions often fall outside of the classification of PTSD and are not recognized as: a) belonging to the collection of trauma-related problems that appear following a traumatic event, b) resulting from the relationship between the victim and trauma inducer, c) considering the duration of the traumatic experience(s) and d) considering the availability of social support. Instead, many of these are often classified as "comorbid conditions" alongside the PTSD diagnosis.[292]

As a result of childhood abuse and neglect, kids are generally diagnosed with, in order of frequency, separation anxiety disorder, oppositional defiant disorder, phobic disorders, PTSD, and ADHD. Despite the various psychiatric labels assigned to them, these diagnoses fail to capture these kids' profound developmental disturbances or the traumatic origins of their specific issues. Instead, these kids tend to be characterized with severe problems with attachment, attention, and managing physiological arousal.

One study found that most patients with a strong likelihood of PTSD that were evaluated at a research Trauma Center in 1999 presented themselves to the clinic for other issues. These included significant poor management of emotions and impulses including aggression against self and others, depersonalization and other dissociative symptoms, chronic feelings of shame, self-blame and feelings of permanent damage, inability to engage in satisfactory relationships, and loss of previously sustaining beliefs. It was these problems, these patients believed, that made their lives unbearable, not standard PTSD recollections or complaints.[292] PTSD is often the underlying turbulence that other, more visible and tangible conditions are laid upon.

PTSD and Brain Development

All kinds of abuse and neglect are associated with PTSD, regardless of gender.[293] Nonetheless, men and women process abuse/neglect and PTSD differently. Gender, abuse/neglect, and developing PTSD are all related.[294] Across all kinds of abuse, women are more likely to develop PTSD than men. In cases of sexual abuse, women are four times more likely to develop PTSD than are men.[294]

PTSD and Brain Stunting

One important study examined 44 young people suffering from PTSD as a result of childhood maltreatment. Of those 44 participants, 34 had PTSD secondary to sexual abuse, sometimes beginning at the age of 2. Their perpetrators were their mothers (2 of 34), father or step-father (25 of 34), brother 5 years senior (4 of 34), or uncle or other close family friend or relative serving as a regular caregiver (3 of 34). Most PTSD sufferers experienced multiple types of maltreatment, with 13 of the 34 also experiencing physical abuse, and 27 of those 34 also having witnessed domestic violence. Physical abuse laid the foundation for PTSD in 4 of the 44 subjects without a history of sexual abuse or witnessing domestic violence.[125]

Multiple brain regions of these kids with PTSD were smaller than their non-abused counterparts: cerebral and prefrontal cortex volumes, cerebral and prefrontal cortical gray matter and cortical white matter, right and left amygdala and their respective gray matter, left and right temporal lobes, and the corpus callosum and its regions 4, 5, 6, and 7. Gray matter contains the majority of neuronal cell bodies in the brain and is involved in muscle control, sensory perception, memory, emotions, speech, decision-making, and self-control. Less gray matter means more struggles in these areas. Also, these kids' lateral ventricles were larger. Lateral ventricles are the brain's waterway structures containing the cerebrospinal fluid that provides cushioning for the brain, helps circulate nutrients, and removes waste—there is not a lot of neuronal activity here, so when these ventricles are bigger, that doesn't help this person in life.

Here is an adapted image from that study, showing lateral ventricles in an 11-year-old boy with chronic PTSD on the right, matched with a non-abused, healthy control subject on the left.[125]

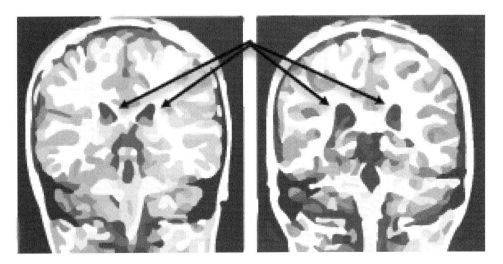

Healthy child's brain   *PTSD child's brain*

These images show the smaller brain mass/larger empty space in the brain of the abused child in the image on the right.

In this study, the PTSD sufferers showed intracranial and cerebral volumes at 7.0% and 8.0% smaller than their non-maltreated counterparts—again, that's a 7-8% smaller brain mass. They also showed larger lateral ventricles. PTSD symptoms of intrusive thoughts, avoidance, hyperarousal, or dissociation have been associated with larger ventricular volume, smaller intracranial volume, smaller corpus callosum area, and reduced measurements of the corpus callosum regions.

Some evidence even illustrated that the boys showed more adverse brain development than the girls with PTSD, suggesting that boys are more vulnerable to the effects of severe stress on their brain development than girls, even if they may manifest fewer symptoms, as noted above.

The brain's intracranial volume increases steadily until age 10, and 75% of the brain's adult weight occurs by age 2[295] with near completion of adult intracranial volume by age 5.[296] This means that what happens to us as little kids affects us for our entire lives because regions of our brains reach near-full capacity in very early childhood.

The subjects in this study showed high degrees of comorbidity particularly for mood disorders.[125]

Lateral ventricles

The ventricular volume—empty space—tended to increase with duration of abuse, meaning the brain suffered more developmental damage with longer term abuse.

Many psychiatric disorders have been associated with lateral ventricular enlargement, including child-onset schizophrenia,[297] adult-onset schizophrenia,[298] Alzheimer's disease,[299] alcoholism,[300] bipolar disorder,[301] and major depression with psychosis[302] in adults. There is also an established relationship between IQ and brain size in healthy adults.[303]

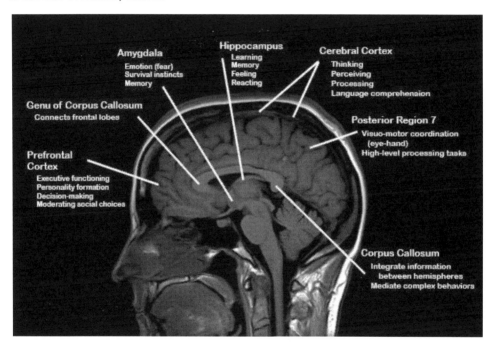

Genu and Frontal Lobes, Prefrontal Cortex

Maltreated kids with PTSD had smaller genu (region 2 of the corpus callosum), an area that helps the two sides of the frontal lobes communicate with each other. The frontal lobes are our emotional control centers and where our personality resides. They manage motor function, problem solving, spontaneity, memory, language, initiation, judgment, impulse control, and social and sexual behavior.

The frontal lobe is divided into subareas, one of which is the prefrontal cortex.[304] The prefrontal cortex is responsible for executive cognitive functions such as planned behaviors,[305] working memory,[306] motivation,[307] and discriminating between models of the world as internally or externally derived.[308] Therefore, neuron loss in this area may be responsible for the many psychosocial, cognitive, and behavior problems as well as a lot of the psychopathology present in child and adult survivors of childhood maltreatment.

The prefrontal cortex continues to develop into the third decade of life, leaving space for cortical plasticity.[125]

Hippocampus

The hippocampus is important to attention[309] and memory.[310] Because of its high density of glucocorticoid receptors,[311] the hippocampus is the most studied brain region in relation to PTSD. Research has shown a relationship between stress and exogenous cortisol, and hippocampal shrinking.[312,313] Indeed, studies of adults with PTSD have indicated memory and hippocampal dysfunction.[314,315] Some research has shown memory deficits in children with PTSD.[316,317]

Damage to the hippocampus is associated with high levels of alcohol consumption.[318]

Posterior Region 7

This research also found that as PTSD cluster symptoms increased, neurons in posterior region 7 decreased. This region dominates in a variety of tasks, particularly eye-hand coordination.

Because of what is controlled in this area, fewer neurons here can mean lower inhibition of responses. As a result, when a PTSD sufferer runs into a reminder of the trauma, the lower response inhibition can lead to the core PTSD symptoms of flashbacks, intrusive thoughts, and associated symptoms of avoidance, numbing, and hyperarousal.[125]

Corpus callosum

The corpus callosum connects corresponding regions of the two brain hemispheres. It is mainly considered as facilitating cortical communication.[319] Kids and adolescents with PTSD had smaller corpus callosums in middle and posterior regions (4, 5, 6, and 7) than their healthy counterparts. Abnormalities in a particular area of the corpus callosum can reflect abnormalities in the specific corresponding brain region.[320]

People with damaged corpus callosums show marked gaps between perception, comprehension, and response.[321] These changes can explain the symptoms of PTSD, dissociation, and the executive difficulties that come along with PTSD.

Dissociation is disruptions in the functions of consciousness, memory, identity, or environmental perception that are usually integrated, and such disruptions interfere with the smooth integration of information.[52] Thus, symptoms of dissociation may be the result of early neuron loss in areas corresponding to middle and posterior regions of the corpus callosum (5, 6, & 7).[125]

As you can see, PTSD affects the proper development of several brain regions, layering the challenges for the sufferer—PTSD may cause the poorer brain development, in turn leading to more challenges throughout life due to poor brain development.

Complex PTSD

Complex PTSD is a severe psychological condition with adverse effects in several areas. The sooner the child abuse starts in life and the worse it is, the more the sufferer is at risk for developing more complex trauma symptoms. If chronically exposed to childhood trauma, especially in the early years, the chances of developing complex PTSD increase substantially.[34,71,255,256] Repeated stressors, such as chronic childhood maltreatment including child abuse and neglect, family violence, and community violence can result in complex PTSD.[34,71,253,256]

There are stress-related conditions even more severe than complex PTSD, but for the purposes of scope, we're going to limit our discussion to the extent of just complex PTSD here.

Symptoms

Complex PTSD and other severe trauma conditions are marked by the following symptoms.

- Impairments in regulating affect (emotion, including anger) and impulses [33,71,255,256]
  - People with issues in anger management, rage, extreme jealousy, and those who stalk others and engage in self- or other-destructive behaviors impulsively would fit in this category.
- Impairments in attention or consciousness [71,255,256]
  - Those with difficulty concentrating, such as ADHD sufferers and severe daydreamers may fall here.
- Memory deficits [34]
  - People with memory issues, especially younger people, and those with blanks in their memory banks may fit in this category.
- Distortions in self-perception and relationship to the self [71,255,256]
  - Illusions of self-aggrandizement, entitlement, and self-importance, as well as severely low self-image and failure to recognize one's own worth honestly.
- Amnesic and dissociative episodes [31-34]

- o Amnesia is forgetting, and dissociation is mentally and emotionally removing oneself from a situation, which of course inhibits the ability to deal practically with that situation.
- Chronic self-destructive behaviors [31-34]
  - o Acts of self-mutilation fall here, as well as chronic substance abuse and even food abuse, either too little or too much such that it causes severe health problems such as diabetes, without a capability of ceasing the behavior.
- Distortions in relationships with others [71,255,256]
  - o These can include (mis)perceptions of others' behaviors as threats when they are not, or the reverse, failure to recognize others' behaviors as threats when they are.
- Alterations in perception of the perpetrator [71,255,256]
  - o The victim may come to view the perpetrator as good and behaving appropriately, and even develop strong emotional ties with the perpetrator.
- Somatization
  - o This includes mental issues manifesting as physical conditions, generally undiagnosable. [33,71,255,256]
- Depression [33]
  - o General loss of interest in life, loss of desire to participate in life.
- Distortions in systems of meaning [34,71,255,256]
  - o These include the meaning we attribute to our existence and our efforts. Hopelessness and despair can result from such distortions.
- Loss of sustaining beliefs [31-34]
  - o Belief systems tend to change rather than remain constant.
- Impairments in alarm reactions (fight or flight) and changes in central nervous system development.
  - o Perceptions of situations may inappropriately trigger the fight or flight response, as in sensing danger when there is none or worse, feeling safe when in danger.
- Abnormal brainstem functioning
  - o This can include anxiety, sleep abnormalities, enhanced startle response, and changes in cardiovascular functioning.

Consequences

In the presence of complex PTSD, emotional, cognitive, social, neurological, and psychological resources either fail to develop at all or they deteriorate significantly.[292] The complex PTSD that results from chronic childhood interpersonal trauma is consistently found to be highly debilitating, bringing significant mental and physical health problems. Adults can develop this condition of complex PTSD as well, particularly combat veterans.

If you're trying to have any sort of a relationship with someone with even some of these symptoms, that can feel like a constant emotional roller coaster ride—because it is. If you recognize some of these conditions for yourself and your own internal processes, you are living with a level of anxiety most people don't and do not understand.

PTSD and particularly complex PTSD are no joke and these conditions do not vanish by themselves over time. Instead, left untreated, they simply continue to wreak havoc on the person's life both through an internal nightmare and relational stress and frustration that often isolates the sufferer, contributing to increased suffering. Research is only beginning to understand this complicated condition and how to treat it.

Having one or a couple of these symptoms does not point to complex PTSD. But as in any mental health diagnosis, it is the possession of a cluster of the representative symptoms that results in a condition's diagnosis.

Conclusion

Resulting from a traumatic event in which the individual experienced intense fear, horror, or repeated neglect and/or abuse, PTSD brings a host of problems for the sufferer. Those who suffered abuse and/or neglect, and particularly sexual abuse, are more vulnerable to and more likely to develop PTSD. Its consequences include all sorts of anxieties, disturbances and disorders in the sufferer, and can also make the individual more hostile and aggressive toward others.

This chapter has presented causes, symptoms, and most common effects of PTSD. As you can see, PTSD can be blamed for just about every medical condition out there as well as a whole host of emotional and mental disturbances. This stuff is no joke. And a lot of people in our lives are walking around with it, often not even aware they have it. People who developed PTSD as children become adults with "childhood-onset PTSD". It does not go away by itself as a physical wound heals; instead, it requires dedicated focus to move past.

II.   Unwhacking Yourself: Creating Wellness

With Section I having outlined the problems and challenges we face as children and adults with stressful childhoods, Section II shows ways to ease the ever-present anxieties that result from a stressful childhood environment and cross the threshold into internal peace. Here, I offer solutions to the problems presented in the book's first section.

Having had the experience of neglect and/or abuse in our childhood homes means we have developed distortions in our thinking and perceiving. These distortions are the building blocks of our lives. It is like we are trying to live a healthy, happy life out of a home made from distorted bricks. Small wonder things are a bit wonky all the time!

Yes, growing up in an unwell environment created a host of challenges throughout our lives, and yes, we continue to struggle every day, usually in many ways, because of what we endured as kids. This is where the choice comes in: You can continue to bumble through, living your life within the distorted structures built from distorted bricks that were provided for you, or you can make a conscious choice for something different and work toward reconstruction. You can put an end to the internal chaos, turbulence, and anxiety (or at least quell it significantly) by slowly transforming your distorted structures into healthy ones. You do this brick-by-brick, little-by-little, piece-by-piece, and with every distorted brick that you replace with a healthy one, you feel a little better. Keep working on replacing distorted bricks with good ones and pretty soon, you will find that you feel a whole lot better! Your troubles will ease, your confidence will grow, and everything in your life will improve. You will also be easier to be around because you'll be nicer, kinder, gentler and more peaceful in your center, which means you will be better able to contribute to the genuine well-being of those in your life.

The anxieties we carry have a lot to do with our own internal distortions and not really knowing how to think or behave in actual healthy ways, since in stressful childhood homes we were deprived of those tools both physiologically (neurologically) and environmentally, and trying to live the healthy life we all want from within distorted, unhealthy structures. Obviously, this brings some frustration, adding to the heap of challenges we already face in our lives due to our improper neural development, as we have seen. Once you gain an understanding of what healthy thinking and behavior look like and you take conscious steps to achieve that, your life begins to get better. The healthy thinking and behavior patterns ease the anxiety, replaced with the confidence that you are doing the right thing. Brick by brick, you replace distorted thinking and behavioral patterns with healthy ones and bit by bit, you feel better. The "bricks" of health included in this section come from a variety of disciplines and traditions, some straight from the scientific research journals and others drawn from ancient wisdoms and teachings.

The most important acknowledgement along this path from anxiety and anguish to mental wellness is the very first step—recognizing that you'd like to feel better than you do. I remind you, your struggles are real, both inside your own head and in all of your relationships. Your anxieties are real, and they make perfect sense given your experiences. Your turmoil is not a product of your imagination; just because it is inside your own head does not make it fabricated or illusory. As Section I showed, the struggles you face have legitimate roots, including an internal gauge hard-wired to high anxiety and pretty much all together missing essentials for healthy emotional regulation, thought patterns and self-views, and social involvements. This isn't your fault of course. It is, however, your job to take care of.

This upcoming section offers a step-by-step approach to achieving and improving mental wellness. It covers all major dimensions of human life, and presents a range of legitimate wellness strategies for strengthening and straightening out each dimension: It is full of healthy bricks for you to draw from in replacing the distorted ones you were given. One by one, you replace unhealthy patterns with healthy ones, and bit by bit, you create a life of ease and wellness that you can enjoy for the rest of your life.

Loving Your Self

When we take care of ourselves, we say "I love you" to ourselves. If nothing else in this life, we deserve to be loved at least by our selves. No one can take care of you except you. Only you can make yourself feel better. Only you! But you know what? You absolutely deserve to feel better. And you are absolutely worth every bit of effort, large and small, that it takes to feel better. You deserve a better you, and everyone in your life would love to see a better version of you!

Multi-Dimensional Healing

Healing from the kind of mistreatment we endured as kids requires a multi-dimensional approach because we were hurt in multiple dimensions. We have been harmed in so many areas of our lives—mental/psychological, emotional, and social, with many of us suffering additional repercussions in our physical health. Basically, stress and trauma mess us up in every single area of our existence except the left-brain intellect unless the abuse is quite severe. So, in order to heal, we need to address every dimension of our existence, and we can do that via the left-brain intellect. We can consciously and cognitively transform our selves and our lives, one very small step, one single interaction, at a time. We can also rely on a foundation of spiritualism as the go-to rock to help us through, providing a strong base as we make some changes in our lives. Growth can be scary because it is entering the unknown, the novel, the unpredictable. So that's okay—go at your own pace and as you're comfortable. It's not like you don't have the time since that's all any of us has here on planet earth... Time...

Section II of this book presents viable approaches to strengthen each of these areas. Focusing on just one area at the exclusion of the others will not get you there. The damage to us is too deep and complex. You can't just go to a mental health therapist, for example, and expect her to make you better. That approach should help with one dimension, the psychological one, but even your psychologist will advocate additional methods, such as some sort of spiritual practice, attention to physical health, learning emotional management, and adjusting your relationships. Everything works together. This section presents logical, easy-to-understand and easy-to-incorporate routes to healing through the spiritual, physical, emotional, psychological, and social dimensions, and comments on intellect focus as well.

The Self Wheel

The whole individual is like a wheel of different dimensions all working together. Think of it as a wooden or metal wheel rather than a wheel with a pneumatic tire. In a wooden wheel, when one side is missing or weak, the wheel does not roll properly at all. Instead, you feel a bump in your ride every time the wheel comes around to that flat or even missing part. The whole self involves six dimensions: spiritual, physical, emotional, psychological or mental, social, and intellectual. These are represented in the self wheel. All of the dimensions need to be fully functional, at optimal performance, for the wheel to roll properly and smoothly—and for you to roll appropriately and smoothly down the road of life.

The Self Wheel

When any one of these areas is damaged or weak, it's like we're running on a wheel with a missing chunk: Our self doesn't function fully properly. In order to relieve the anguish and suffering in multiple facets of our lives, we need to strengthen each of these areas separately and fully.

You are engaging in the intellectual route at the moment by reading this book—you are grasping concepts through the logical, rational part of your intellect that you will use to help you heal. You are reading and absorbing the ideas presented here, and understanding, at a cognitive level, how they can help you improve your life. As you do this, you're sitting on the couch or on the bus, your attention here and separated from the world, decoding the symbols on this page to deduce meaning, interpreting language, following the logical progression of ideas, grasping the concepts presented. This is the intellect engaged. As adults, this intellectual route is paramount to healing. In understanding the dynamics at play in our own psyches and where we need to be to practice healthy thinking and behavior, we use our consciousness, our logical intellect. Actually incorporating the concepts accesses the other dimensions of the self wheel, but the processing comes through the intellect, which provides direction and instruction. As adults, we can learn a great deal through our intellects first, then with an intellectual understanding of the benefits and methods of certain techniques and perspectives, incorporate them into our lives in the appropriate ways.

The multi-dimensional approach, I argue, is the only way to properly overcome the multi-dimensional harm done to us during our critical developmental years. As kids, we didn't have a choice. We suffered harm on many levels and in many ways, and therefore came to know life as harmful. As adults, we do have the choice to move past that harm, with a conscious, concerted effort, by focusing on healing in each of these harmed areas. We have to strengthen each component of the wheel that is part of our self. The harm was done to us all at once—we were harmed in many ways simultaneously by a string of individual actions. We are a bit fragmented, splintered as a result, and struggle in many or most of the dimensions of our lives. The solution is to address each of these dimensions singularly. We create new neural pathways reflecting healthy thinking and behavior. In this way, we can piece back together the splintered elements of our selves, and function as a whole being with everything working together properly. In this way, the wheel rolls smoothly down the road of life.

In This Section

Section II presents a multi-dimensional approach to healing from the mistreatment we endured as kids. It starts with the spiritual dimension because, I argue, the spiritual work lays the foundation for everything else. If we do the spiritual work, everything else falls into place much more easily and our healing is a lot faster. If we don't do the spiritual work, well, the work becomes a lot harder. As a spiritual foundation, this book recommends a practice of mindfulness meditation with a focus on compassion for self and other. Mindfulness meditation is non-religious, and growing scientific research finds brain-growth results from even an 8-week mindfulness practice. And guess what? Mindfulness meditation can help grow brain cells in most of the very areas that suffered growth deficiency due to a stressful childhood environment—effectively reversing the results of and complications from that stressful childhood environment. It is also the key to living a happy life because it teaches you to enjoy every moment: It points out that this very moment is the only time in which life is lived. This chapter also contains information on other, more esoteric healing techniques for those wishing to go a bit more deeply.

The spiritual dimension is followed by the physical dimension. Mindfulness aims to be the focus for every moment, so it comes first. Our physical health needs to be the focus of every single day, so it comes second. It's easy for some of us, perhaps many of us, to neglect our physical health—self-indulgent behaviors including lying around and/or consuming whatever we want make us feel better for the moment. It's a lot harder to do things that are good for us and that we know to be good for us than just doing whatever we want with our time and putting whatever we want into our mouths. But taking care of our physical bodies is paramount to good over-all health. When we take care of ourselves, we say "I love you" to ourselves. We need this. Many of us didn't get this message as kids, that we're loveable, so we need to give this message to ourselves. Taking care of our bodies with proper diet, rest and exercise sends a clear message to ourselves that we love ourselves, and will do whatever we can to take good care of ourselves. Parents out there—you feed your kids nutritious meals, yes? You make them eat their proteins and their vitamins, and you do this because you love them, yes? We need to turn this same care and concern for proper nutrition and general physical health that we extend to our loved ones onto ourselves. You are so very worth it. This is an incredibly important chapter. Even if you already follow a regular exercise regimen and consider yourself quite healthy, please don't skip this chapter. It has a lot of other important information in it too.

From there, the emotional dimension chapter follows. Developing emotional intelligence is actually really easy if you follow a spiritual practice of mindfulness, but even if you don't, developing emotional intelligence is actually pretty straightforward compared to the other areas. I bring in research on emotional intelligence here. I also offer a brief presentation on Emotional Freedom Technique (EFT), also known as "tapping". Many find this a very simple yet very effective way to eliminate unwanted emotions that can sometimes be really hard to shake off. This is a short chapter, so I present it before diving into the more complex topics.

Psychological development comes next in Chapter 9. This is quite a large chapter. It begins with a discussion of what mental wellness looks like, followed by tips on eliminating anxieties and distortions one at a time, and then targets self-esteem strengthening. Anxieties and distortions go hand-in-hand; our anxieties largely result from our distortions. If we were raised in homes with a fair degree of distortions and anxiety, we ourselves are simply going to have a fair degree of distortions and anxiety. The apple doesn't fall far from the tree, and really, how can it? We absorb everything our parents give us whether we want to or not. It's not a big deal though—we identify these distortions one at a time, and eliminate them, replacing those distorted bricks with good ones. I don't recommend starting with the biggest trauma of your life, but rather, with the tiny things that niggle at you. You will see that once you eliminate even the tiny distortions, your anxiety will ease by that much. The chapter then moves to self-esteem building. Everyone on the planet could benefit from self-esteem building, actually. It seems like self-esteem development is hard work so we groan at the thought, but it's actually pretty easy and straightforward. I've found some excellent tools that make self-esteem development logical, practical, and not at all painful or difficult. It just involves shifting the way we look at ourselves and maybe making a few minor adjustments in our behavior. It's not difficult at all. The chapter ends with a note on ethics, as a guide for appropriate behavior.

The social intelligence piece comes next. This is a lengthy chapter because I've spent a lot of time and energy in this zone. This material comes primarily from a university course I taught several times on interpersonal communication. The chapter presents dynamics of relationships so that we can better understand people's needs within relationships, rendering us better equipped to manage those relationships effectively and successfully. This chapter covers listening, language, nonverbal cues, conflict, politeness, and more. It's a very rich chapter and if you take the material to heart, internalize this knowledge and incorporate it into your daily life with others, then your life, and theirs, will be richer for it. Once again, these concepts are not at all difficult to grasp, and I've worked with them so many times that I present them in a straightforward, no-nonsense way that makes it all seem like you already know this stuff. This whole chapter is based in communication science.

Together, these chapters recommend alterations in your thinking, perceiving, and behavior based on a deeper understanding of healthy and unhealthy practices and habits. We are just turning unhealthy habits into healthy ones. That is all! Certainly, there are a lot of tips and techniques here and this work is not meant to be achieved in a short period of time. Transforming your thinking and behavior happens one interaction at a time though, so it augments your life rather than detracting from it. The material presented here provides fodder for the internal dialogue you have constantly waging anyway—your mind never stops moving, so why not give it something healthier to work with? Embrace the tips and techniques that seem easiest first—why not? Choose as you see fit from the wide variety provided here. Choose one piece from multiple dimensions at once if you like.

This section ends with commentary on the intellect, with a focus on developing the attributes of our right brain hemispheres. Section I showed that the right brain development is skewed under a stressful environment, and further, most of us in "advanced" cultures neglect the attributes of our right brain hemisphere—intuition, feelings, holistic thinking, art, music, and more—instead prioritizing the skillset of our left brain hemisphere—logic, linear thinking, calculations and computations. Most of the chapters of Section II contain some components not backed by modern science, but this last one is the only chapter not directly supported by science other than general knowledge about which attributes the right brain hemisphere dominates. In that sense, it is also the lightest chapter in the book and a nice way to finish.

That's it. These are doors to healing from our childhood mistreatments. As always, I do not claim that they are the only routes. I do claim, however, that if you follow them, your life will improve, and quite dramatically.

Healing and Intuition

The healing route doesn't have to be all that painful and at the same time, there will be moments of some unpleasantness as you recall and work through the roots of the things that give you anxieties. In this recognition that you need healing, be smart about it. A mindfulness practice helps tremendously with this. You need to be able to feel your emotions in order to work through them. Your emotions serve very important purposes in your life—the uncomfortable ones send you signals that something is wrong and needs your attention. Maybe you're allowing harmful treatment. If you're numb to your emotions, you can't feel these emotions in their full strength, which means you aren't motivated to change your conditions and heal. Feel your pain so that you can not only understand it, but so that you can hear your intuition and be guided to something that eases that pain at its root. Don't be too afraid of it—let it speak to you and listen to it. Let it come out, and let it guide you to a better you as you better understand what is really going on inside of your own self so that you can root out the pain and discomfort and place ease and tranquility in those spots instead.

To find something that eases your pain, listen to the gentle urgings in your gut area. Which way are you gently pulled at the moment? When you find something that eases that pain (except for indulgence in food, intoxicants, shopping, gambling, media, and other numbing tools), follow it, even if it doesn't make a lot of sense at the moment. There will be a small feeling of ease within you at the thought of doing something in particular—this is what you're looking for. Maybe it's going to a movie alone, or maybe it's choosing a G-rated television show over one filled with death and violence, or choosing to not read the newspaper or watch the news today. Maybe it's ordering a salad off the menu instead of the crab cakes. Maybe it's going for a walk or picking up those weights gathering dust in your corner. The urge in your center will be shy, but it's there. Find it, and follow it. This is your path to freedom. This will build a better you. This is being true to yourself which, as Chapter 9 will show, also builds self-esteem, thus making you better two-fold.

Follow what feels right, even if it doesn't make a lot of sense at the moment or even if you think you don't want it because of some perception you hold from past experiences. I myself ended up joining a cagefighting/MMA gym by accident—I thought I was signing up to learn boxing! And I never would have joined if I'd realized I was in a cagefighting gym as that has such a certain reputation, and I didn't want that for myself no way! But in the four years of my membership, that particular sport turned out to be absolutely key to my healing. If I had known what I was getting into in the beginning, I'd have avoided it and would still be suffering from all the anxieties that vanished as a result of my making that mistake in the first place. I'm glad I listened to my inner voice, the one that urged me to check it out and join, rather than the socially constructed conscious one that said cagefighting just wasn't for me. It changed me, and it changed my life.

If a small fleeting thought brings you an instant of ease, do that thing (as long as it's appropriate, of course). These gentle urgings are your intuition guiding you along the path to wellness. This is your truth. Follow your truth. Always. If you find that the gentle urgings your intuition is guiding you toward are along a path that's not very socially acceptable, such as an organic plant-based diet or visiting a psychic or engaging in some other form of the occult or alternative therapy, still follow that path, but maybe don't publicize it to save yourself from the social grief. Be smart about it and don't get hoodwinked by savvy grifters, but do it for yourself. Live your life for yourself, not for the approval of those who do not face your internal turmoil every day. Your wellness path is your own, and only your own. You must choose to take care of yourself. You must choose self love, sometimes over social acceptance, but that is always a non-choice if you want to actually feel better. Little by little, you will find yourself strengthening.

At some point, you will want to check in with a bona fide mental health provider to ensure that you are moving in the right direction and that you are actually straightening out your distortions rather than simply reshaping them. Just like traveling to a new city, it's not easy to know you are going in the right direction when you are entering uncharted territory, so it's good to stop and ask for direction and confirmation from someone deeply familiar with the terrain you're in, then carry on along your way.

Further, as you change and grow, others in your life will likely be staying in the same place. You are the one showing changes in thinking and behavior, not them. They might be embracing your changes, or they might be resisting them—some even quite profusely. So, you may well be accused of being crazy as you make your way toward greater mental wellness. Under these conditions, when everyone you have known and loved for a long time tells you that you're crazy, it's not always easy to continue to believe the path you're on is accurate—and realistically, as you make your way through uncharted territory trying to figure it out, some of the changes might not be entirely for the better, though you've no way of really knowing that. For these reasons, it's good to check in with a mental health professional at least at some point along the way.

I hope you enjoy and more importantly, I hope this information helps you along your own path to stronger mental wellness.

II.   Unwhacking Yourself

6. A Spiritual Practice

A dedicated spiritual practice is the single-most important aspect to reduce anxiety and facilitate healing from stress and trauma. It quells the mind, lowers anxiety, and sets a serene internal landscape for other healing to occur. It's much easier to learn to better manage our emotions or our relationships if we are internally calm to begin with and know how to maintain that calm. This calm helps us respond in a timely manner, not react instantly.

Childhood mistreatment causes stress and anxiety in adult lives, leading to a wide range of other problems, as previously presented. A dedicated spiritual practice assuages that anxiety.

Spirituality Science

The science supports this position. Religiosity and existential relationships with spirituality have been shown to produce many desirable results.[322] Spiritual well-being is linked with positive mental and physical well-being and quality of life.[323] In fact, the greater the level of spiritual well-being, the lower the levels of partner abuse trauma,[324] combat-related trauma,[325] and suicide and hopelessness. This suggests that spiritual well-being protects against the hopelessness that often accompanies abuse.

Those with strong spirituality can have lighter cases of the more negative abuse symptoms, such as anxiety, lowered self-esteem, hopelessness, and depression.[326] In fact, feeling a relationship with the divine has been shown to improve the mental health of those sexually abused as children.[326,327] Several studies have shown that strong spirituality reduces the hopelessness of those abused as kids. Child abuse is traumatic, but that trauma can influence the individual toward spiritual growth.[328] Other research suggests that suffering abuse pushes the individual to seek a sense of meaning and purpose in their lives, so they turn to spirituality.[329,330]

Despite its clear benefits, a good deal of research also shows that abused people tend to hold a negative perspective of the divine, and are less likely to believe.

However, not all spirituality necessarily involves a relationship with the divine, as this chapter will soon explain.

Healing with Meditation

A strong meditation practice is grossly underestimated when it comes to its ability to heal. If you meditate using any approach except satanic something, you will heal; some methods may be more effective than others at this and neuroscience has demonstrated a mindfulness practice to be exceptionally useful, but any method is better than no method, so pick one that you're comfortable with. The more disciplined you can be about your meditation, the better you will become, faster. You will become stronger. With each passing year you will notice that you are leaps ahead of where you were last year at this time.

In most cases, it's not the meditation alone that brings healing though, I want to be clear—the meditation calms you down so you can create an internal landscape to do some productive work. Without meditation, it's harder to achieve the healing that will make you feel better because you're still operating from a base of pretty significant anxiety. That anxiety gets in the way of you moving forward. It's a little like trying to run quickly through a thick forest with lots of vegetation and no clear trail—those plants, logs, vines, and holes you can't see are definitely going to get in your way and slow you down. Incorporating a meditation practice gives you a well-cleared trail to run down—free from the pesky obstructions in your way that slow you down. But, to continue the metaphor, if you want out of the forest, once you're on the trail you have to put one foot in front of the other and keep moving forward to get out of there. You can't just sit down on the trail and expect to get out of the forest because now you're on the trail. Meditation is the trail that makes it easier for you to get out of the woods. But, you still have to do the work to get yourself out of those woods.

There are many types of meditation. In all of them, the goal is to quiet your mind from its usual chatter and movements in a million directions, and refocus on something specific. Meditation doesn't mean stopping your mind except in lesser practiced versions. There are guided meditations with visualizations that you can find online or in local meditation groups in many areas. Pay attention when doing your web searches though, and never meditate on any idea that makes you feel uncomfortable or that you find questionable. If this occurs, ask someone who knows more about it than you do, but always follow your intuition. If you walk into a room full of people with the intention of meditating with them, check your intuition to be sure you're comfortable. Purely Buddhist meditation is always going to be safe—how much trouble can you get into focusing on your breath or staring at a wall?—but still check your intuition if meditating with a group because people are not always as pure as the practice.

There are many spiritual practices out there, and several types of meditation. Over time, you will notice that your anxiety levels are lower and corresponding peace levels higher after a period of meditation practice.

The practice of mindfulness meditation changes lives because it changes the physiology of the brain, strengthening the parts where joy, peace, calm, and happiness reside. The science on that is coming up in a bit.

I have not encountered scientific work on any other spiritual practice that changes the brain to induce greater calm and serenity.

Discover Mindfulness

As many mindfulness teachers define it, mindfulness is simply "awareness". There are a variety of meditation practices that fall under the umbrella of mindfulness. These include focused attention or the Sanskrit *Samatha*, which calls for maintaining focus on a specific object. When a distraction comes, the meditator acknowledges the distraction then disengages from it by gently bringing the attention back to the meditation focus. Open monitoring meditation or the Sanskrit *Vipassana* is a non-directed acknowledgement of any sensory, emotional or cognitive event that arises in the mind without evaluation, interpretation or preference. Zen meditation is one form of Vipassana practice.

The work of Zen Buddhist Master Venerable Thich Nhat Hanh relies on mindfulness as a path to joy and happiness. He is definitely a leader in a current global movement toward increased mindfulness meditation in everyday life.

Mindfulness meditation has different trajectories—Thich Nhat Hanh is definitely not the only one advocating mindfulness. Mindfulness made its way into the West via scientist Jon Kabat-Zinn and a program he developed in the 80s called "Mindfulness-Based Stress Reduction" (MBSR)—this was how he packaged mindfulness meditation in order for the West to accept it, and it worked.

Mindfulness Science

Research has repeatedly shown that meditation itself and specifically mindfulness meditation brings incredible results to our brains and our lives. In this section I present just some of the science on mindfulness meditation and its effect on the brain.

Mindfulness Meditation and the Brain

The brain is more active during meditation than in a non-meditative state. Neuroimaging studies show increased regional cerebral blood flow during meditation.[331] Studies in electroencephalography (EEG) have shown significant increases in both alpha and theta activity during mindfulness meditation[331,332], with that activation related to proficiency of practice[331]—the more you practice, the more brain activity that occurs. Neuroimaging research has shown that mindfulness meditation activates the prefrontal cortex, where much cognition occurs, and the anterior cingulate cortex, involved in emotional regulation, and that over time a meditation practice is also associated with enhancement in the cerebral areas related to attention.[332]

Zen meditation reduces blood pressure significantly and Vipassana meditation has shown effective in reducing alcohol and substance abuse in prisoners.[332] Zen meditation can help protect from cognitive decline through inhibiting the reduction of age-related grey matter volume and attentional performance.[333]

Modern science has found incredible health-improving results from mindfulness meditation practice. This area of research is vast, and I cannot possibly cover all of it here, but I do want to present some of this science for you. In the some forty-ish studies I discuss here, I am merely scratching the surface of the science on mindfulness meditation.

Improves Wellness

First, mental conditions have been shown to improve through a mindfulness meditation practice. A review of 52 research studies showed consistent findings that cultivating a more mindful way of being brings less emotional distress, more positive states of mind, and better quality of life.[334] Mindfulness meditation produces greater positive states of mind than mere relaxation,[335] and primarily leads to reduced ruminations.[336]

Depression in fibromyalgia sufferers reduces;[337] ADHD and behavioral and neurocognitive impairments in adults and adolescents can also be improved.[338] Even substance abuse, alcohol-related problems and psychiatric symptoms were reduced in a group of mindfulness-meditating released prisoners, and they adapted better on the outside than their non-meditating peers.[339]

Further, mindfulness meditation reduces reactivity to unpleasant emotional stimuli,[340] reduces state and trait anxiety, enhances social skills and improves academic performance in mentally challenged adolescents.[341] In those with social anxiety disorder, a mindfulness intervention increased self-esteem and decreased anxiety, and increased positive and decreased negative self-endorsement.[342] Mindfulness also reduced depression, anxiety,[343] and rumination,[344] improved interpersonal sensitivity[345,346] and brought more adaptive coping strategies and self-compassion.

Attentional performance is improved,[347-349] and mindfulness meditators specifically showed better attentional performance than concentrative meditators and non-meditators, particularly when confronted with unexpected stimuli.[348,349]

Over time, meditation training has been found to influence emotional processing in response to positive and negative images, even in non-meditative states.[350]

Stressed-out cancer patients showed decreased mood disturbance and stress symptoms,[351] as well as significantly lower scores on total mood disturbance and depression, anxiety, anger, and confusion; and fewer overall symptoms of stress including less emotional irritability, depression, cognitive disorganization, and habitual stress patterns.[352]

Physiological symptoms also improve with mindfulness meditation practice. One study by Jon Kabat-Zinn found that a mindfulness meditation-based intervention delivered by audiotape during ultraviolet therapy for psoriasis sufferers reduced psoriatic lesions.[353] Immune function improves after even a short mindfulness meditation intervention, as indicated by the presence of more antibodies in the bloodstream following an influenza shot as compared with a control group.

Small Effort, Huge Payoff
Work involving Dr. Jon Kabat-Zinn showed that patients with diagnosed anxiety disorders showed clinical and statistical improvements after an 8-week mindfulness meditation intervention, and most patients continued this stress-reduction practice three years later.[354] Also, compared with listening to a recorded book, just four days of meditation training, by those with no prior meditation experience, reduced fatigue and anxiety while it increased mindfulness and improved visuo-spatial processing, working memory, and executive functioning.[355]

Even just a 5-day, 20-minute per day meditation practice integrating body-mind training (i.e. mindfulness), as compared with relaxation training, resulted in significantly better attention, stress control, and mood, with lower anxiety, depression, anger, and fatigue along with a significant decrease in stress-related cortisol and increase in immunoreactivity.[356]

Physical pain and unwellness conditions can be alleviated quickly through mindfulness meditation as well. Pain unpleasantness is reduced by 57% and pain-intensity ratings reduced by 40% after just four days of mindfulness meditation training.[357] Chronic low back pain in older adults, aged 65+, was significantly improved following an 8-week practice.[358] Chronic pain resulting from arthritis, back/neck pain, or two or more comorbid pain conditions showed significant pain reduction and functional limitation improvement after an 8-week program, while chronic headache/migraine sufferers showed minor improvement and fibromyalgia sufferers showed slight improvement in psychological distress.[359,360]

Brain Benefits
Furthermore, the brain actually changes as a result of mindfulness-based meditation, and many research studies support this. Neuroimaging studies showed eight brain regions consistently altered in meditators. These include areas key to meta-awareness (frontopolar cortex), memory consolidation and reconsolidation (hippocampus), self and emotion regulation (anterior and mid cingulate; orbitofrontal cortex), intra- and interhemispheric communication (superior longitudinal fasciculus; corpus callosum), and exteroceptive and interoceptive body awareness (sensory cortices and insula).[361]

A mindfulness meditation practice has consistently been found to influence the brain, the autonomic nervous system, stress hormones, immune system, and health behaviors, including eating, sleeping, and substance use.[334] In a study with researchers from Harvard, MIT, and Yale, MRI scans showed that meditators have thicker brain regions associated with attention and interoceptive and sensory processing, including the prefrontal cortex and right anterior insula. These prefrontal cortical thicknesses were more pronounced in older participants, suggesting that meditation might offset age-related cortical thinning; further, the thickness of these two regions correlated with meditation experience—the greater the years of practice, the thicker the regions. Most affected regions identified in this study were found in the right hemisphere, which is essential for sustaining attention.[362] In fact,

MRI tests of patients with social anxiety disorder showed increased activity in the brain network associated with attention regulation.[342]

Other MRI scans showed greater gray matter concentration in the right anterior insula, which is involved in interoceptive awareness, and greater gray matter concentration in the left interior temporal gyrus and right hippocampus as well, corroborating an assumption that mindfulness meditation training actually changes the structure of your brain in the regions activated during meditation and relevant for the task of meditation.[363] An 8-week intensive meditation program resulted in changes in gray matter concentration within the left hippocampus, and increases in the posterior cingulate cortex, the temporo-parietal junction, and the cerebellum based on MRI images; these brain regions are involved in learning and memory processes, emotional regulation, self-referential processing, and perspective taking.[364] Another study showed significant increases in left-sided anterior activation, a pattern associated with positive emotion, after an 8-week intensive intervention.[360]

Research out of UCLA found significantly larger gray matter volumes in meditators in the right orbito-frontal cortex, right thalamus, and left inferior temporal gyrus, and significantly larger volumes in the right hippocampus. Both the orbito-frontal and hippocampal regions are involved in emotional regulation and response control, so larger volumes in these areas can account for meditators' singular abilities and habits to cultivate positive emotions, retain emotional stability, and practice mindful behavior.[365]

And there's so much more. After an 8-week intervention, MRI tests examining the amygdala, implicated in emotional processing to stimuli, showed lower responsiveness to all kinds of stimuli, be they positive, negative, or neutral, when in a non-meditative state.[350] A study out of Denmark examined MRI scans and found higher gray matter density in lower brain stem regions associated with cardiorespiratory control of experienced meditators.[366] With regard to physiological manifestation of impacts, post-meditation reductions in pain were associated with activation of the orbitofrontal cortex, an area involved in reframing the contextual evaluation of sensory events, and also associated with thalamic deactivation, which may act as a gating mechanism between conveying impulses toward the central nervous system and executive-order brain areas.[357] The bottom line is that a mindfulness meditation practice has been shown to change the physiological structure of the brain even after only 8 weeks, with benefits primarily to the brain's emotional systems.

Mindfulness research is illuminating new ways that awareness, attention, acceptance, and compassion may promote optimal health in the dimensions of mind, body, relationships, and spirit.[334]

This is a lot of scientific information to sort through, so to make it easier to see just what kind of research is being done in the area of mindfulness and its impacts to life, the table below summarizes the results of a mindfulness practice mentioned above juxtaposed with an abbreviated list of conditions resulting from early childhood stress and trauma brought up from Section I.

Consequences of Early Childhood Stress and Trauma	Impacts of Mindfulness Meditation
	Alpha and theta activity, related to proficiency of practice[331]
Cognitive, Emotional, and Behavioral Results	
Emotional regulation impacted[127,222] Emotional expression deficient[180-184]	Emotional distress reduced[334]
Anxiety and hypervigilance develop[17]	Anxiety reduced[342,343,355]
Anxiety difficulty[45,49-51]	State and trait anxiety reduced[341]
Fear pathway chronically activated[17]	Anxiety and panic symptoms in those with anxiety disorders improved[354]
Minor stressors overwhelming	Habitual stress patterns reduced[352]
Strong irritability results[35,36]	Emotional irritability reduced[352]
	Adaptive coping strategies improved[332]
Depression develops[45,49-51,219-221]	Depression reduced[343,352]
	Fibromyalgia-related depression reduced[337]
Substance use (abuse) results[16,47,48]	Substance abuse and alcohol-related problems reduced[334,339] (with Vipassana meditation)[332]
Psychiatric conditions can result	Psychiatric symptoms reduced[339]
Mood affected poorly	Mood disturbance reduced[352]
Cognitive disruptions[198,199,201,202]	Cognitive disorientation reduced[352]
Cognitive disruptions[198,199,201,202]	Neurocognitive impairment improved[338]
Ruminations result[107]	Ruminations reduced[336,343]
ADHD develops[216-218]	ADHD improved[338]
Self- and other-destructive behavior	Behavioral impairment improved[338]
	Visuo-spatial processing improved[355]

Memory dysfunction[314,315] and deficits with PTSD[316,317]	Working memory improved[355]
Executive functions less developed[17]	Executive functioning improved[355]
Attention problems develop from hyperarousal and elevated prefrontal dopamine levels[141]	Attention improved [347-349,356]
Interpersonal sensitivity problems[45,49-51] Empathy impacted[127] Internal working models of others altered[40]	Interpersonal sensitivity improved[345,346]
Socio-behavioral disruptions[198,199,201,202]	Social skills enhanced[341]
Self-image disturbances[44,117,253,254]	Self-esteem improved[342]
Internal working models of self altered[40] Self-image disturbances[44,117,253,254]	Increased positive and decreased negative self-endorsement[342]
Internal working models of self altered[40] Self-image disturbances[44,117,253,254]	Self-compassion improved[332]
	Reactivity to unpleasant emotional stimuli reduced[340]
	Health behaviors influenced[334]
Eating disorders result[16,47,48]	Eating influenced[334]
Sleep disturbances result	Sleeping influenced[334]
	Influences non-meditative state emotional processing over time[350]
	More positive states of mind[334]; better than relaxation training[335]
Tendency to seek interpersonal violence; susceptible to repeated abuse	Quality of life improved[334]
	Mindfulness increased[355]

Physiological Results

Cardiovascular issues, stroke, elevated cortisol levels result[23]	Blood pressure reduced (Zen meditation)[332]
	Chronic pain reduced[357,359]
Chronic low back pain results[22]	Chronic low back pain in aging adults improved[358]
Headache and migraines result	Chronic headache/migraine sufferers improved[359]
	Reduced psoriasis[353]
Fibromyalgia results	Fibromyalgia distress reduced[359]
	Cancer-related mood and stress improved[351]
	Immune function improved[360]

	Immune system influenced[334]
	Autonomic nervous system influenced[334]
Stress response disrupted[206-209]	Stress hormones influenced[334]
.	Fatigue reduced[355]

Neurological Results

	Regional cerebral blood flow increased[331]
	Frontopolar cortex (meta-awareness) alterations[361]
Attenuated hippocampus development[131] Memory dysfunction[314,315] and deficits with PTSD[316,317]	Hippocampus (memory consolidation and reconsolidation) alterations[361]
Attenuated hippocampus development[131] Emotional regulation deficits[222]	Right hippocampus (emotional regulation, response control) significantly larger[365]
Hippocampus development attenuated[131]	Left interior temporal gyrus and right hippocampus greater gray matter concentration[363]
Hippocampus development attenuated[131] Memory dysfunction[314,315] and deficits with PTSD[316,317]	Left hippocampus (learning and memory processes) gray matter changes[364]
	Left-sided anterior greater activation (positive emotion)[360]
Right brain hemisphere (dominates perception and emotional expression, particularly unpleasant emotions) deficient[180-184]	Right orbito-frontal cortex (emotional regulation, response control) significantly larger volume[365]
Emotional regulation deficits[222]	Anterior and mid cingulate; orbitofrontal cortex (self and emotion regulation) alterations[361]
Amygdala development slowed,[144] heightened responses to emotional stimuli cause anxiety and depression.[146]	Amygdala responsiveness to emotional stimuli reduced[350]
Emotional regulation deficits[222]	Posterior cingulate cortex (emotional regulation) increases[364]
Corpus callosum size reduced[131,191]	Superior longitudinal fasciculus, corpus callosum (intra-and interhemispheric communication) alterations[361]
	Sensory cortices and insula (exteroceptive and interoceptive body awareness) alterations[361]

Prefrontal cortex development altered, with premature maturation but stunted final capacity[142]	Prefrontal cortex and right anterior insula (attention, interoceptive and sensory processing) thickening[334]
Self-referential models distorted[40]	Temporo-parietal junction (self-referential) gray matter increases[364]
Cerebellar vermis abnormal.[198,199,201,202] Leads to psychiatric disorders: schizophrenia, ADHD, depression	Cerebellum (perspective taking) increases[364]
Right brain development attenuated[129]	Right hemisphere regions (sustaining attention) greatly affected[362]
Attention impacted[127,195-200]	Brain areas related to attention grew over time[332]
	Right thalamus increase[365]
	Left inferior temporal gyrus increase
Brain stem functioning abnormal; changes in central nervous system development.[101] Results in anxiety, sleep abnormalities, enhanced startle response, altered cardiovascular functioning and modulation	Lower brain stem (cardiorespiratory control) higher gray matter density[366]
	Orbitofrontal cortex activation (reframing the contextual evaluation of sensory events) reduces pain[357]
	Thalamic deactivation (easing flow of information toward central nervous system and executive-order brain areas) reduces pain[357]
	Brain influenced[334]
	Helps protect from cognitive decline through inhibiting age-related grey matter reduction (Zen meditation)[332]

The list of problems in the left column does not comprehensively include all problems presented in Section I, but the main problems made the list and as we can see, are offset by a mindfulness meditation practice. Also keep in mind that this is only scratching the surface of the research on mindfulness meditation and its benefits, and there is tons more out there.

This table illustrates the power of mindfulness meditation at directly offsetting so many conditions that result from a stressful childhood. Science has shown again and again that a practice of mindfulness meditation can show amazing changes to

135

your life and how you feel in a very short time—it actually changes your brain by developing the areas whose imbalance causes us to feel terrible most of the time. As you can see from this side-by-side comparison, it actually offsets most of the harm done to our brains during a stressful childhood.

A Mindfulness Practice

The practice of mindfulness has modern roots in ancient Buddhist practices. The philosophy of Buddhism is thousands of years old and grounded in four ideas regarding the human experience (the Four Noble Truths):

1. There is suffering.
2. This suffering has an origin.
3. Suffering can be ceased.
4. There is a path to the cessation of suffering.

As you can see, Buddhism is literally all about recognizing suffering exists in this world (Truth 1) and finding a way out of it (Truth 4). The way out is possible (Truth 3), but we have to recognize the root of the suffering to enable this cessation (Truth 2).

To me that seems pretty logical, and difficult to argue against no matter what religious background you have.

Know that Buddhism is more of a philosophy than a dedicated religion, and it is atheistic. There is no god that Buddhists pray to and they don't even believe in a god. The Buddha was just a man who had it all figured out—that's it. They bow to him out of respect for his wisdoms—just as in many Asian cultures, they bow to one another as a respectful greeting. The position is that we all have a buddha nature, a buddha within us looking for and waiting for enlightenment. We can all be a buddha.

The Buddhists discovered several thousand years ago that compassion-based mindfulness meditation, primarily with a strict focus on the breath, relieves suffering. So, the idea of mindfulness meditation for suffering cessation may have begun with the Buddhists, but mindfulness meditation with a focus on the breath is not about Buddhism. All you're doing is breathing, which obviously you do all the time anyway, and bringing your mind's attention fully to your breath, which has nothing to do with anyone outside of your own body. So, please do not feel that if you're practicing some mindfulness meditation that you are practicing Buddhism (unless you want to). Mindfulness meditation has many prominent leaders in the West as well. All mindfulness leaders that I'm aware of offer slightly different flavors of the same fundamental message.

Another important prong of mindfulness meditation is the compassion element. Meditating mindfully will help your brain grow and help you live a much easier and more positive life for yourself, yes. The Buddhists recognize that suffering is felt within, but we as participants in this world also participate in the suffering of others for better and for worse: We can help alleviate others' suffering through compassion, or help exacerbate it through uncompassionate thoughts and behaviors. So, not only do we meditate mindfully to help ourselves but we also want to increase our compassion for others, and mindfulness meditation helps us achieve that. In fact, this act in itself helps build empathy, which those of us from stressful childhood homes are very likely lacking.

Zen Master Venerable Thich Nhat Hanh

Like all religions, Buddhism has many trajectories in practice. I always like learning from top teachers, so I have sought out the teachings of possibly the greatest mindfulness teacher of today, who follows the thousands-year Buddhist traditions of mindfulness and meditation practiced by dedicated Buddhist monks everywhere yet has updated it for modern times: Zen Master Venerable Thich Nhat Hanh. I believe Thich Nhat Hanh truly does have all of the answers to life's most vexing questions, and I rely on his poignant explanations to help me move forward. His work has made me such a better person. However, if his work doesn't speak to you, by all means, find someone whose does.

Thich Nhat Hanh is Vietnamese, and lived through two Vietnamese wars. Affectionately called Thay (pronounced "tie"), the Vietnamese word for *teacher*, his primary residence for most of his life has been in Southwest France at a monastery called Plum Village, named for its orchards of plum trees the monastics work and harvest to help support the monastery. Anyone can visit Plum Village for a retreat of a week or longer depending on the time of year. I had occasion to participate in such a week-long retreat in spring 2016. Never have I been in an environment so peaceful, joyful, fun-filled, lighthearted and happy as my time in Plum Village with the 70 or so sisters at the convent in the French countryside. Being in that environment helps you understand how to incorporate these wonderful blessings that mindfulness offers into your daily life, every moment of every day! Thich Nhat Hanh has several practice centers throughout the world where his teachings are followed and further taught, spreading his wonderful message of joy, happiness, love and compassion, the gifts of mindfulness, to all who would like to hear.

He has also written 100 books or so about how to live with joy and happiness through mindfulness. I recommend any and all of them. If you've never meditated before, he has a small set of "How To" books that are simple and straightforward and will help you start along this path to peace. He also addresses complex issues such as anger, fear, and managing difficult circumstances (*No Mud, No Lotus*) in his writings. Again, they are all excellent, so if you're interested in learning more, just pick one that seems to catch your eye. Some of Thay's books take on a distinctive Buddhist flavor, sure. But his basic meditation books and many of his writings on deeper matters are non-religious. They are philosophical ways of viewing the world that help the world, and your place in it, make a little more sense, which makes it easier to get through the day and brings great joy, pleasure, and happiness to your daily life.

What Mindfulness Is

Mindfulness is a condition of your mind wherein you are constantly aware of what arises within your mind and body, and address whatever arises within you, emotionally, at the moment in which it first arises. Consider for a moment the work of a lifeguard. A lifeguard surveys the water she is responsible for, watching for signs of trouble. She doesn't pay rapt attention to the water, giving it her 100% focus at all times—that would be exhausting! But she keeps an eye out. Most of the time everything is fine and everyone in the water is having a good time. Every once in a while she spots something that could be an early sign of someone having difficulty, so she watches this person carefully. Once she determines this person needs help, she acts in whatever way she deems appropriate. Maybe she calls out to the person to ensure he is okay, or maybe she swims out to rescue him.

How it Works

In mindfulness, you develop a second, observational level in your mind that acts as a lifeguard. This lifeguard of your mind surveys the seascape of your thoughts, emotions, and sensations, watching for whatever comes up. When something troublesome arises, disturbing your tranquility, the lifeguard of your mind recognizes it immediately and begins to act. Your lifeguard brings its full attention to that rising sensation, considering whether it is a sign of potential trouble, and decides how to act. The resulting action may involve simply calming the mind through a variety of techniques or, in more severe cases, getting you out of the situation entirely.

In a responsible mindfulness practice you also build compassion, for yourself and for others, to ensure that not only are you aware of every little thing you are doing and experiencing, but also that everything you do and experience comes from a place of kindness and compassion. In this way, you grow and become a better person. That's it.

You develop this lifeguard that surveys your internal landscape, and you train this lifeguard to immediately recognize and identify whatever arises—all of your sensations that you feel rising in your body, including emotions, all of your thoughts so that they may all be positive and life-giving, and all of your external influences so that they may bring positive results within you. In this way, with the help of your own personal lifeguard, you maintain your internal seascape of serenity, peace, and calm. Whenever something comes up that upsets that internal calm, you instantly recognize it and manage it responsibly.

Emotional Control
This responsible management depends on what arises, but because you are now fully conscious of what's rising within you, this identification gives you the power to make conscious choices about your resulting behavior. You no longer react thoughtlessly, from the gut, feeling under threat. You no longer lash out. In fact, you don't even allow the sensation to grow that much within you to the point where you want to lash out, nipping it in the bud instead. Now, when you sense something upsetting your internal landscape, you bring your attention to that sensation and deal with it immediately and calmly.

You pay attention to this sensation and bring it into your full awareness. You ask yourself what you are feeling at this moment. Identify the sensation. Is it sadness? Anger? Jealousy? Do you feel offended? Guilty? Shameful? First, remember that as a human being, you experience the entire range of emotions and all of them are meant to be experienced—don't ever beat yourself up for feeling something you think you shouldn't be feeling. Instead, objectively name the sensation.

Buddhism has identified 51 sensations within us human beings. Identify which one or ones you're experiencing at the moment. Then, in your conscious adult mind, decide what to do and how to act.

If you are in the presence of someone who is making you feel shameful, you might excuse yourself, in a socially appropriate way, and get the heck out of there, at least until you recover and feel you can manage the situation while retaining a sense of calm and ease. If someone has made you feel angry, definitely excuse yourself and go calm yourself down before continuing to address the situation—Thay teaches, very adamantly, to never speak out of anger, as this only causes problems, always.

When it is the challenging sensations that arise within you, mindfulness teaches you to recognize them just as they are rearing their head and manage them at that level, while you still have full control of yourself and before the situation escalates. In Thay's teachings, you manage these sensations simply by bringing your focus to your breath, which I'll discuss in a moment.

An important component of mindfulness involves focusing on the present moment. As we saw in Section I, childhood mistreatment results in all sorts of anxieties that bleed into our lives in all sorts of unfortunate ways. We are left with a great deal of suffering from past hurts, and fears and anxieties about our futures.

Mindfulness trains you to stay in the present moment, and shows you that the present moment is full of beauty, grace, and peace. You are safe in the present moment—completely, 100% safe. No one is attacking you (and if they are, you politely excuse yourself, forever protective of your own inner tranquility), and you are surrounded by immense beauty and lucky to be alive. That is where you direct your attention—to the beauty of life. Once you turn your focus here, to how fortunate you are to experience the beauty of this life for this moment, and to how beautiful your breath is that allows you to sustain life, whatever was bothering you dissolves, and you are instead consumed by joy, gratitude, peace and happiness.

And that, my friends, is what it's all about. That is the coping mechanism that mindfulness meditation helps you achieve. No more suicide moments, no more fear of the moment, no more social anxiety! Instead, total control of your inner landscape and an abundance of positive, peaceful, joyous thoughts.

Remember in Section I, I presented information about how severe childhood stress can make your brain develop in abnormal ways? Well, mindfulness meditation has the reverse effect. It also changes your brain, but where childhood stress makes the part of the brain housing fear and impulsive reactions grow, mindfulness meditation makes the part housing happiness and contentment grow. Indeed, it can counter the effects of childhood trauma on the brain.

Achieving Mindfulness
Developing mindfulness relies on mindfulness meditation. It's a very simple meditation, though not at all easy. I present it for you here.

Note that you don't try to still or quiet your mind when you meditate. Rather, you focus intently on the target of that session's practice. It is a shift of focus. That is all.

The Practice

In the core of mindfulness meditation, you focus on your breath. You bring your attention to the inhale and think "I am breathing in," then to the exhale and think "I am breathing out". You can shorten it in subsequent breaths to "in" and then "out". You can trace the airflow as it enters the edges of your nostrils, and feel it as it makes its way through your air passage into your lungs, then follow it on the exhale in the same way.

After you get going with this "in" and "out" for a few breaths and when your mind begins to wander, which it will about a million times, you can change the script to something like "joy" on the inhale and "peace" on the exhale, or vice versa. Mix up ideas of joy, peace, love, compassion, and kindness as you inhale and exhale. This exercise alone will help ease your anxiety and make you a more joyful and gentler person both to yourself and others.

Our minds are not designed to stand still. They are designed to move and dance around, a lot. When this happens to you, don't think "I can't meditate". Instead think, "I am normal". And every time it happens, every single time, you grab your mind, and bring it back to your focus: "in", "out", "joy", "compassion". With time and practice, you will find that you gain better control over your mind and it gets away from you in meditation less and less. This is where you are going!

The Buddhists have discovered that focusing on the breath during meditation develops mind-body awareness. It is this practice of focusing on the breath that develops the ability for your mind's acute awareness of your body and your internal sensations. This awareness of your internal sensations is what develops this objective overseer within you, this lifeguard. This is how you so easily recognize something troubling your serene internal terrain, and deal with it the instant it arises.

It may take a bit of time for this lifeguard to grow within your internal seascape, and for everyone this amount of time will be different, so if it takes you a little longer, don't dismay! Just stick with it.

Daily Focus Opportunities

It is recommended to meditate 20 minutes a day, every day. As your practice grows, stretch this time to 45 minutes, 60 minutes, 90, or as much time as you can give it. The more you can practice, the greater the benefits to your life.

In reality, not everyone can dedicate 20 minutes every day to sitting on a pillow meditating. If you can give it 10 minutes or even 5 or even 2, that's better than nothing. Just like anything else you're training at, the consistency of a short daily practice is more beneficial than sporadic lengthy meditation sessions, like 60 minutes one day a week. The point is to do whatever you can, as often as you can.

Thay's teachings include flexibility, as he is very pragmatic about life's demands. He totally gets it. Sitting meditation is probably ideal, but that's not the only way to achieve the great benefits of mindfulness. You can also turn any event into a meditative event by focusing exclusively on that event. If you are walking, focus on your steps and coordinate them with your breath: "In-2-3-4 Out-2-3-4-5-6". Bring your focus to your body and your breath. Feel your feet landing on the surface beneath them. Feel your leg and foot muscles flex as you use them to raise each leg then place your foot as you step. Feel your arms sway in rhythm.

Whatever you're doing, bring your full awareness to that activity. Preparing food, washing your hands, bathing, walking, exercising, even relieving yourself—each is an opportunity to practice mindfulness. Just bring your full focus to whatever it is you're doing, and be acutely aware of what your body is doing at that moment. Observe your body as it changes position, and feel the different muscles flex and release as you move. This is practicing mindfulness! The more of this you can incorporate into your day, the greater the benefits you will see to your life.

We all have these opportunities all day long—walking to the bathroom or between offices at work is one small example. Ascending and descending flights of stairs, or waiting in line, others. If we take advantage of these moments when our body is busy but our mind can be free by bringing our awareness to our body, we are developing a great mindfulness practice. Over time, this will become ingrained as habit, and you will see tremendous benefits to your consciousness and therefore, to your life. If it's at all possible to supplement these moments of mindful activity with some minutes of dedicated sitting meditation every day, even a short time, you will see tremendous rewards.

Mindfulness in Practice

Once we have achieved this consciousness of our bodily sensations and developed an ability to recognize sensations when they arise within us at the moment they arise, we have developed the power to consciously choose how we manage these situations. We no longer lash out in anger or behave impulsively. We are nicer, kinder, gentler, and much easier to get along with because our inner anxieties are easing. We live in a constant state of inner tranquility and we like it that way. When something comes along that upsets that tranquility, it's very easy to recognize, and immediately.

Managing Life's Difficulties with Greater Ease

The greatest challenge, and the true test of our mindfulness practice, comes when something angers us or in another way generates challenging sensations we have to struggle with. We experience jealousy, envy, fear, frustration, agitation, resentment, or something similarly not-so-fun. That's when the rubber meets the road with our mindfulness practice, so to speak. In these moments, we see how far we have come.

When these sensations arise, and they will, it is our job to recognize them at their root—as soon as that iceberg just barely begins to rear its head. We feel the arousal of energy within us. We feel the sensation rise within our bodies. Now, our job is to instantly bring our awareness to that sensation. We admit it's there, identify it by name, and decide how to act.

The first thing we're going to do is breathe and bring our full attention to our breath. "In, Out". We might take a few steps at a normal pace and coordinate those steps with our breath. "In-2-3-4 Out-2-3-4". Bringing our attention to our breath is our number one tool for resolving all of life's challenges. It sounds so simple—and indeed it really is! Which is why it works. You get your mind off of the issue and the resulting uncomfortable sensation by bringing your full awareness to your breath. Once you have calmed down and the uncomfortable sensation has pretty much left you, then you can decide on a rational and responsible course of action.

Honoring Uncomfortable Sensations

Thay teaches that it's important to not tamp down our uncomfortable sensations. If we're feeling sad, we recognize it and acknowledge it with something like, "Hello Sadness. Thanks for showing up. I didn't realize this situation made me sad but now I know that. Thank you for letting me know." Then we determine a course of action.

Some sensations are rooted deeply and complexly. It's important to recognize them and look into them to discover their roots.

Sometimes this happens over time, especially with those roots in our childhood trauma. We always treat ourselves with full compassion, whatever we're looking at and whatever we're doing. We allow ourselves to feel whatever sensation arises, just not let that sensation take over. If we're feeling sad, we allow ourselves to sit with that sadness for a moment. We even allow ourselves to cry if we need to, to help release the sadness.

What is important is to recognize that we don't have to stay in that sadness. It's important to acknowledge it and feel it, identify its roots if you can or sometimes recognize that it's too complex for us to figure out all in the present moment. Then it's important to transform these feelings into peace and compassion, not merely tamp them down with thoughts of the birds and the flowers around us. These uncomfortable sensations will be noticed and they will be heard, in one way or another, until they are transformed, so tamping down and continuing to ignore them is not always a smart move.

Thay's Teachings In a Nutshell

I recount for you here some of the basics of Thay's teachings so you can see that his ideas are approachable, logical, and very useful. For further information on the complexities of managing difficult sensations, I direct you to the teachings of Thay himself. He has written numerous books, as I mentioned, and you can check out his Youtube channel for endless talks.

You can also look for a Thich Nhat Hanh sangha in your area. A sangha is a Buddhist meditation and study group. In the Thich Nhat Hanh tradition, participants meet and meditate together then discuss how to manage life's challenges by incorporating the path Thay has laid out for us. Joining a sangha will bring you much greater benefits than you could ever achieve on your own. There are some online sanghas if there are no convenient ones in your area. Search plumline.org for more information on online sanghas.

Once again, I wouldn't worry about Thay's teachings conflicting with another religious tradition you may follow. If you don't want to agree with all of Buddhism's other concepts, such as reincarnation and karma, you don't have to. This philosophy and its dedicated practitioners are very open and accepting, driven pretty much just by the desire to relieve suffering in themselves and others. They have a lot of answers and hold a lot of keys to achieving this. Just go for the mindfulness support and direction. It will help immensely.

It's for Everyone

I have often heard people say, "I can't meditate. It doesn't work for me. My mind won't stop." Meditation is not about stopping the mind. Sure there are some traditions where the goal of the meditation is to empty the mind, to think of nothing at all. That's not what I'm talking about here.

Everyone can meditate. Every single human being. All of our minds wander. Every single one of us has a wandering mind when we try to meditate. All of us. This happens especially at first. When we notice it wandering, we gently bring it back to the meditation's focus. The more we meditate, the more we train our minds to wander less. I personally have been meditating for nearly 25 years and my mind still wanders a lot. But every time it does, I bring it back. It's getting better, and some days are better than others. Despite my mind wandering, I benefit tremendously from my meditation practice. It works!

Compassion Development: Lovingkindness Meditation

A lot of people in this world lack empathy. They care very little if at all about hurting others. Sometimes inflicting that suffering is intentional and sometimes, no amount of suffering they can inflict is enough.

This is the opposite of a well-developed conscience, the opposite of empathy.

When we grew up in environments where our loved ones repeatedly harmed us, intentionally or unintentionally, there's a good chance we didn't develop a level of empathy appropriate for civility—other people's pain does not upset us, even when we are causing that pain. In a civilized world, this is not a healthy thought pattern.

Buddhism has a simple meditation that helps develop empathy. It's called lovingkindness. This meditation is also general well-wishing of individuals, so therefore does not conflict with any existing religious beliefs. Here's how it works.

Lovingkindness Meditation

Relax, close your eyes, take a few deep breaths. Calm, center, peace, ease.

Bring to mind someone you love dearly. This could be a family member, a pet, a child, or any loved one. Hold that person in your mind. Wish them the following:

- May you be happy.
- May you be healthy.
- May you be safe.
- May you be free from pain.
- May you be loved.

Repeat the series three times all the way through, holding this person in your mind.

Next bring to mind a neutral person, maybe a stranger or someone you crossed paths with recently. Repeat the five phrases all the way through three times, holding this person firmly in your mind.

Next, bring to mind someone that you're struggling with. This could be a family member, coworker, client, former partner, anyone that lights a bit of rage within you. Repeat the five phrases all the way through three times, holding this person firmly in your mind.

Next, bring yourself to mind. Repeat the five phrases all the way through three times, holding this person firmly in your mind.

That is the meditation. It's very simple. Yet, you would be surprised at how it eases your well-being, and also improves your relationships with these people.

Feel free to change up the people that you bring to mind. If you're struggling with someone, it's better to bring them up repeatedly until you feel better, but don't force yourself. Go at your own pace.

Like most things, the more you repeat this meditation, the more effective it will be at easing your suffering as well as developing your compassion for self and others, and conscience to not cause suffering to any others. It you can do this twice a day, that will yield you great results in a short time.

Energy Work

The mindfulness path is amazing, no question. It gives many practitioners beautiful lives and if practiced, will change your life one moment at a time. Other alternatives also exist for those looking for healing at a deeper energetic level rather than or perhaps in addition to through cognition as the mindfulness approach offers.

Energy work is generally poo-pooed in North America while it is widely accepted in Europe and most other parts of the world. In those other places, people don't question the existence of energy or its manipulation for healing. There are legitimate educational institutions in many of the world's most advanced nations, yes also in Northwestern Europe, that teach energy healing. It is a legitimate practice. Only North Americans and particular United States-ians seem to have a problem with it, for whatever reason.

This is probably a good time to make that point that true ignorance is rejecting something you don't understand...

Reiki and Chakras
Reiki is slowly mainstreaming in North America and becoming more socially acceptable. It is a way that energy is manipulated for healing effect. Reiki works primarily with the energy running through your spine, making adjustments and opening blocked passageways allowing your energy to run more freely.

Another, slightly more esoteric option is to get your chakras cleared and aligned. Here, the practitioner accesses and adjusts your seven main energy centers, each located at its own place along the spine, each spinning a certain color vibration, and each responsible for a particular area of your life.

- Root chakra, base of the spine, red. Basic human survival concerns such as safety, shelter, money, food, and the right to live.
- Sacral chakra, two inches below the belly button, orange. Home, relationships, emotions, creativity, sexuality.
- Solar plexus chakra, diaphragm, yellow. Power, will, social self, fight or flight, instinct.
- Heart chakra, heart, green or sometimes pink. Love, giving and receiving, joy, inner peace, compassion.
- Throat chakra, throat, blue. Communication, speaking our truth.
- Third eye chakra, forehead between the eyes, purple. Focusing and seeing the big picture, intuition.
- Crown chakra, top of the head, white. Our connection with spirituality, wisdom, transcendence, universality.

The word "chakra" is Sanskrit for wheel; the chakra system is well known in the East and was discovered a couple of thousand years ago. Boat loads of reading materials are available on chakras if you're interested in learning more about this system of energy centers and how they relate to our daily lives. I introduce it only briefly here. When you experience a trauma, it is said to lodge itself in one of your chakras, creating stress and imbalance in the area of your life overseen or regulated by that particular chakra. A chakra clearing can help reduce or remove this lodged trauma, clearing the pathway once again and allowing the chakras—and thus your life—a healthy balance. Its results often leave the client feeling amazing afterward—rejuvenated, renewed, light, and at ease.

Deeper Energetic Healing Work

It is said that trauma fractures a person's energy, splintering off a piece of the self. For this reason, the person doesn't feel the same after that, pretty much regardless of the amount and type of mental health therapy engaged in. This splintering can feel quite odd and the sufferer may feel like no matter how hard she tries, she can never feel as "whole" as she did prior to the traumatic event—something always feels like it's missing.

There are energy workers who can help heal this division in the individual's energetic space. The service is often called a soul retrieval, and its purpose is to heal trauma. Indeed, coming out of a soul retrieval can leave you feeling like a new person—if trauma occurred at a young age, you literally do not know what it's like to not carry around the trauma, so it can feel quite odd at first to be without it. In a short amount of time however, things will smooth for you and you will become a purer version of yourself. Many find the soul retrieval incredibly worthwhile.

Choose Energy Practitioners Carefully

Whatever sort of energy work you engage in, be sure the service is legitimate before you allow any energetic manipulations. There are groups of people who prey off of those vulnerable and looking for help, giving the entire industry a bad name. These people are recognizable by a few common traits. First, they often insist that you need more help, and the help you need is not cheap. They instill fear, and then claim that you shouldn't worry, they can help you fix whatever they have identified is broken with you (for some exorbitant fee). I have also heard the line, "My services are free. I only have to charge for my time." That is a huge red flag. I was once told 5 of my 7 chakras were dead and I needed several days' worth of treatment to restore them, for around $1200. Of course, it's not possible that chakras die, but naturally, I was very concerned when I heard this! This practitioner's fear-mongering worked for a minute.

An ethical practitioner won't try to convince you to come back for more treatment but rather, will try to calm you, make you feel safe, and merely ask if you'd like to schedule anything else or if there's any other way they can help you.

Also, the scheisters often receive most of their learning from family members, not dedicated instructional institutions. This is not to say they are not gifted—in fact, their gifts make believers out of people. Just watch their ethics. In selecting a healer, in addition to checking their credentials—you want to see some bona fide training for the more advanced treatments, especially a soul retrieval—and evaluating the legitimacy of their work through the online consumer comments, one tactic is to test out a new energy practitioner with a small and simple service first, such as a tarot card reading or some other relatively inexpensive service that involves a marginal access to your energy field, and get a feel for that person.

This is definitely the time to sharpen your intuition! If you get a weird sense from any of these people, don't return to them—ever. And definitely never let them manipulate your energy space. There are too many unknowns in this sort of practice. This is not the time to use reason, but rather the time to go completely with your gut. If it doesn't feel right, leave and don't return. If they push you for more money and to make a future appointment, don't. Find someone else.

The Tarot

To help quell anxiety quickly and non-invasively, tarot card readings can provide great insight that helps immensely. This tool has been around for hundreds of years. The cards give quick answers—usually validations to what you already sense that you're feeling but hadn't been able to articulate. Hearing your own truth from a sheer stranger is a powerful way to face and accept what's in your life at the moment; with that awareness clear, you can make some educated choices.

Before you freak out about tarot cards, remember that they are merely pieces of paper with pictures on them. They are paper and ink. They are not magical or dark or possessed. They work because the particular pictures you are drawn to are interpreted as reflections of your life at the moment. It is a divination tool along the same lines as reading tea leaves or faces or whatever other divination tools people have devised and used over the millennia. Many people have found a great deal of solace in getting some sort of answers to their most vexing questions of the moment through tarot card readings. Other similar readings can also provide great peace.

Your Healing Journey, Your Choices

Whatever helps assuage the anxiety, do it. It doesn't matter what "society" says about these techniques—society isn't inside of your psyche suffering deeply; that's just you and you're all alone in your suffering—society isn't exactly stepping up to help you through it. So, choose methods that work for you, and to heck with what anyone else thinks.

These sorts of readings can help you feel better, every time. Just remember that it's wise to take them with a grain of salt rather than absorbing them as absolute truth, even though they may jibe with your experience about 90% of the time, and when viewed in that light, as fun "definite maybes" as opposed to absolute truths to base your life on, they can be incredibly useful and helpful. Tarot readings can ease your anxiety every single time you get all whacked out and also teach you some incredibly valuable intuitive skills of your own—to hear your own truth and sense your own intuition much more clearly, which is incredibly empowering.

Conclusion

There are other meditation practices as well as those presented here, such as transcendental meditation, that you may wish to explore. The point of this chapter is to urge you to select a spiritual practice and engage in it regularly, allowing it to become a way of life. Incorporate the values of the belief system you decide upon—they all converge on values of love for self and other, kindness, and compassion for self and other. I strongly recommend a mindfulness practice and have shown you plenty of evidence why I say that, but if for some reason that's not for you, choose something else.

Whatever you do, do something. You need some practice to help calm the mind which, in adults mistreated as kids, is bound to jump all over the place from one pained thought to the next, keeping you tortured and suffering. Allow a solid meditation practice with a healthy and healing focus to replace the cycles of tortured thinking spinning around in your head. Over time, this works wonders for your well-being. And while you're meditating, you may consider indulging in these additional energy healing services. You may find them incredibly powerful events that launch you forward on your healing path.

7. Physical Health

Strong physical health is really important to living a balanced life. If you don't feel well physically, nothing else works properly—you're cranky and irritable, which affects your thinking, your relationships, your emotional balance, and even your spiritual practice for the worse. If your physical health is weak, your being is out of balance. Your self wheel has a flat spot.

The three essential components to pay attention to in developing and maintaining strong physical health are diet, rest, and exercise. This is not new information. I'm no expert in any of these areas, and I don't intend to delve deeply into any of these topics here. This isn't that kind of book, and there are plenty of books and other resources out there that do focus on these areas, so I will defer to their expertise. Here, I'll just touch on the essentials and invite you to investigate further if you feel so inclined.

Diet

What you put into your body matters to every cell in your body. Your body gets its nutrients to keep functioning from the items you put into it. If you're consuming foods and beverages with low nutritional value and high poisons, you can't be surprised when you develop disease. Disease is the body not functioning optimally because one or more systems is out of whack.

Vehicle Care and Maintenance

The body is a vehicle for the spirit, and has much in common with automotive vehicles actually. A car has many different systems that keep it rolling down the road. There is the steering system, the cooling system, the suspension, the fuel-burning system, and many more. All systems work together to keep your car running and functioning properly. When one of these systems is out of whack, the car does not run properly and should not or maybe even cannot be driven. For example, if you give your vehicle low-quality fuel, you will eventually see some problems in the fuel-burning system, which can bleed into other systems as well, but you may well end up with a variety of undiagnosable—and unfixable—problems. If you give your car diesel instead of gas or vice versa, you will have some serious problems pretty much immediately—that engine was designed to run on different fuel, so it can't use what you've given it and instead, you've just killed it. Make that connection with your physical body...

The human body is also a combination of physical systems that work together to keep you going. We have the blood system (circulatory), the brain system (nervous), the bone system, the muscular system, the digestive system, the skin system (endocrine), the breathing system (pulmonary), and others. What we consume through our mouths hits the digestive system first. The job of the digestive system is to extract all of the nutrients possible from what you have put in there so it can send those nutrients to the other parts and systems for fuel. If you don't consume enough of some kinds of nutrients and too much of things your body can't use well, you will eventually see this nutrient imbalance manifest in your body as disease—some part of you is being engorged and overworked, and some other part is being ignored.

Also, if you give your body toxins, well, toxins are designed to kill so, you're simply poisoning yourself with every swallow—a little like pouring battery acid into your radiator or fuel tank, one drop at a time...

From there, the body uses whatever it can from the fuel you have given it to run all of the other systems and all of the individual parts within each of those systems. If there are not enough nutrients and/or too many poisons in the food you have given your body to run all parts of all systems properly, something will break down—this is not proper vehicle maintenance. We call these break-downs disease.

Unfortunately, unlike our cars when a part goes bad, we can't just replace a broken or damaged part in our bodies with a sparkling new one—you cannot simply replace the entire circulatory system and affected parts of the excretory system in your body because you have diabetes, for example. You cannot just order new parts be freshly manufactured for you in Detroit. Instead, if you want all of your bodily systems to run smoothly and properly, you have to give your body all of the proper fuel it needs all of the time. The body's only fuel is food and drink.

Mainstream, Painstream

It's no secret that the standard American diet is killing people. A steady diet of overly processed foods, devoid of nutritional value and often outright toxic, is making people sick with all kinds of illness from arthritis to cancer to diabetes to heart disease, and the list goes on. Throw in the excessive amounts of fat and chemicals from consuming animals and their fluids, and we've got a great environment for disease to develop and proliferate. On top of that, the chemicals added to our food are enough to make you sick in and of themselves, not to mention the unnatural, genetically modified foods (GMOs) that a great deal of governmental science assures us is perfectly safe to give our bodies.

Common mainstream information does not always have your best interests at heart. Companies want to sell their products, so food companies will of course emphasize any nutrient content in whatever it is they're selling. But don't let them persuade you that their product is good for you just because it has a vitamin or two—you eating their products is good for *them and their bank accounts*, so they'll try to be sure you swallow their stuff and come back around calling for more. It's your body, and you need to take proper care of it, for yourself. It's not enough to blindly follow recommendations for the masses. In fact, consider just how sick the masses are!

You and you alone are responsible for your own health. Huge corporations and the governments they direct aren't driving your vehicle—you are; they aren't making choices for your body's fuel—you are; they aren't putting items into your grocery cart one at a time.... yes, you are. When you get sick, you cannot blame the system or society for telling you what to eat and thus making you sick; you can only blame yourself for not fueling your body properly. It's your body, and 100% your own responsibility to keep it running smoothly.

If you want to be truly healthy, you have to take responsibility for your own health. You have to go outside of the mainstream beliefs that a lot of very powerful organizations put a lot of money into constructing in the minds of the masses. You have to be willing to see your diet differently.

If you want to be healthy, you have to actually pay a lot of attention to what you're putting into your body, and the sensibility of that choice. You can't just mindlessly buy in to what our authorities tell us is safe or good for you and expect to live happily ever after. There are boatloads of highly credible materials out there advocating diets that are different from the mainstream. Do some exploring in books and movies about the food industries and health; Netflix offers several documentaries on this topic, for example, and there is a growing amount of material on healthy lifestyles. Inform yourself.

Dietary Requirements

I've done a lot of reading about nutrition. Here are some nutrition basics.

Calories

Calories are our energy sources. We need them in order to survive. When we take in more calories than we burn off (calorie surplus), we gain weight. When we take in fewer calories than we burn off (calorie deficit), we lose weight. When we take in the same amount of calories as we burn off, we maintain our current weight. There is no secret to weight loss. This is it. It's all about the calories.

One pound of body weight is equal to 3500 calories.

How many calories our body burns depends on a several factors: sex, size, metabolism, and activity level. Men burn more than women, larger people burn more than smaller people, those with active metabolisms burn more than those with slow metabolisms, and active people burn more than sedentary people. This is not new information, I think!

If I am a moderately active female of average age weighing 150 pounds, I will probably burn about 1800 calories a day. If I am inactive, that figure falls to 1500. Calorie figures are slightly different for everyone though, depending in part on the rate at which your body metabolizes your food.

The trick to healthy weight management relies on getting all of our required nutrients while staying within our calorie goals. This is one reason why it's so important to eat healthy, nutrient-rich foods rather than foods made from white flour, white rice, and sugar—those foods will bring in the calories, but not provide much nutrition. I'm pretty sure a carbonated soft drink has close to zero nutritional value while it brings in hundreds of calories per bottle, and any kind of oil is 200 calories per tablespoon again with nearly no nutritional value which can explain why fried foods are so fattening. So, it's easy to go over your calorie goal yet remain under your nutrient requirements with these kinds of foods. This results in malnutrition, even with larger (fat) people.

Macronutrients

Macronutrients, also called macros, are the major nutrient groups our bodies need in order to function. These include protein, carbohydrates, and fat. The body needs appropriate amounts of foods from all of these groups to function properly.

All foods contain one or more of the macros.

Common protein-rich sources are legumes, nuts and seeds, and animal flesh and fluids.

Common carbohydrate sources are grains, starchy vegetables, and sugars including fruits.

Common fat sources are nuts and seeds, avocados, oils, and land animal flesh and fluids.

For healthy weight management, you calculate the number of calories from your total daily caloric intake that you wish to allocate to each of these three macros. Bodybuilders are masters at these calculations and manipulating them for their own specific bodies and goals.

Protein

When determining your macro levels, you start with the protein requirement be-cause this is a fixed amount based on your weight and exercise levels. The science varies a bit on these recommendations, but often recommends about 1/3 gram of protein (0.36) per pound of body weight for sedentary people.[367] So, if I weigh 150 pounds, my daily target protein intake is about 54 grams.

Exercising people need a little more protein. Recreationally active people need about ½ gram per pound of body weight: between 0.45-0.68 grams. Competitive athletes need a bit more, at 0.54-0.82 grams per body weight pound, while the teenage athlete needs 0.82-0.91 grams per pound of body weight. Body builders need 0.64-0.91 grams of protein per pound of body weight. The body cannot utilize more than 0.91 grams of protein per pound of body weight.[367]

The body does not store excess protein, and digesting excess protein taxes your system. Proteins are not easy for the body to break down because they are complex molecules. The body also produces ammonia when it breaks down protein. So if you're overeating your protein, you're taxing your body's organs and causing an excess of ammonia to enter your system. Since the body does not store excess pro-tein, there is no reason to consume more than your daily protein target and in fact, there are legitimate reasons to not overconsume protein. Beware the personal trainer who insists you should be eating 150 grams of protein daily! Unless you weigh 235 pounds of course.

When determining how much of each macro you should be consuming each day, begin with your protein calculation.

Protein carries 4 calories per gram. So, 68 grams of protein will yield 272 calories. If your caloric goal is 1800, you have a little more than 1500 calories left for the other two macros.

Carbohydrates and Fats
Once you've determined your target protein intake, you can play around with the other two macros, carbohydrates (carbs) and fats, to get the remainder of your desired calories.

Your body needs both. You can select a low-fat/high-carb diet, a high-fat/low-carb diet, or balance the two. You cannot opt for a low-fat/low-carb diet. You need your nutrients.

Carbohydrates carry 4 calories per gram, like protein.

Carbohydrates are essential to a healthy diet. The brain is made of glucose, which is a form of sugar. The body breaks carbohydrates into sugar. The brain uses about half of the sugar energy in the body. We need carbohydrates for glucose production, and healthy, well-fed brains, for starters.

Fats carry a whopping 9 calories per gram. This is why it's so easy to overdo on the fats—it's not that eating fat makes you fat (no, the fat you eat is *not* the fat you wear), but fat has more than twice the calories of other foods so you're just eating too many calories when you eat a lot of fat.

But fats are essential to a healthy diet. Some vitamins, like A and K, are fat-soluble—they need fat in order to absorb properly. So if you're not eating fat, you can easily be deficient in these vitamins.

Micronutrients
It's not enough to reach your macro and calorie goals every day. You also have to pay attention to your micronutrients. Micronutrients are all of the individual vitamins and minerals such as Vitamins A, B, C, D, E, Zinc, Calcium, Magnesium, and so forth.

Micronutrients is why you need to eat a lot of vegetables and vary your food intake.

All foods have their own unique nutritional profile. When you vary your foods, you're getting a range of nutrients.

A Healthy Plant-Based Diet

It's very easy to get all of your essential nutrition on a healthy plant-based diet.

Ensure every meal has a serving of protein (legumes or seitan). A serving is about ½ cup or 8 ounces, or about 250 grams.

For healthy weight management for women, eat two servings of starchy foods daily. Starchy foods are all grains and starchy vegetables. Starchy vegetables are corn, potatoes, and all squashes. A serving is about ½ cup or 4 ounces, 115 grams. Choose whole grains (brown) over processed ones. To heighten your health, choose gluten-free grains such as quinoa, amaranth, brown rice, and gluten-free whole oats.

Eat around 35 mg of fat daily, depending on your macro targets. This is easily achieved with a serving of avocado or a small handful of nuts.

Eat about 3 fruits daily. Fruits have essential nutrients, but they also have a lot of sugar.

Eat loads of vegetables daily—at least 1 cup (230 grams), per meal. Ensure you are getting vegetables from the cruciferous family (broccoli, cabbage, collards, cauliflower, Brussels sprouts) and leafy green family (spinach, chard, kale) daily. After that, eat the rainbow of colors in your vegetables. Eat raw vegetables whenever you can. Green juices and smoothies[c] are excellent, easy-on-the-tongue ways to get your veggies down.

Your plates for 2 meals will have ½ cup (115 grams) protein, ½ cup starchy food, and 1 cup (230 grams) vegetables. The third meal should have no starch.

Snacks should be vegetables and protein like hummus.

These portion targets are for women, moderately active. Men will need more food. Just up all quantities for men, perhaps double.

---

[c] The difference between juices and smoothies is the pulp content. Juices are typically made in special vegetable juice extracting machines that separate the juice from the pulp. You end up with a glass of pure juice and a separate mountain of pulp. Smoothies are made in the blender with whole fruits—you put the whole fruit or vegetable into the blender, then pour it all into a glass. If you have a smoothie but want a juice, pour the smoothie through a cheesecloth or nylon hose to separate the juice from the pulp.

That's it!

Oh and, be sure to drink your water! The body needs about 8 8-ounce glasses daily, which equates to about a half-gallon or 2 liters.

Of course, avoid all processed foods, sugar, chemicals, and alcohol. On soy products, be sure it's organic because so much soy produced in the world is genetically modified.

It's okay to splurge every once in a while, but do it smartly. Have 1 or 2 cookies, not the whole box. Have a sliver of cake, not the whole piece. Have dark chocolate instead of milk or white chocolate.

If you stick to this intake, your body will reward you with optimal healthy weight and good health!

Food Quality
Not only do the types of food matter to our overall health, but we also need to consider the nutritional quality and added chemicals of the food we choose.

Pesticides
Think first about the pesticides they put on agricultural products. Would you drink that pesticide straight from the bottle? No? Then why would you settle for eating it on your food? It's the same exact thing as drinking it straight from the bottle, just in smaller amounts at a time. But over time, those poisons build up in your body, and you might as well be drinking that poison straight up. If you pour battery acid into your gas tank one drop at a time, will there eventually be a problem?

Plenty of fiction stories over the millennia have involved slow murder by poisoning of the victim's food—first the victims get mysteriously sick, usually involving ailments the doctors can't diagnose because no one suspects they are being poisoned, then they die a "mysterious" death. Our reality is no different except we are consciously and voluntarily poisoning *ourselves*.

Cyanide or glyphosate—pick your poison. Either way, you cannot be surprised if you're sick. Kind of a given, don't you think?

Genetic Modifications (GMOs)
Think about the genetic modifications they make to our food. Think about why they make these modifications in the first place.

Most of these modifications are to make the item more resistant to pests so they can yield more product per hectare. So... they're modifying our food items and inserting pesticides directly into the seed. Awesome.

Genetic modifications also extend shelf life so produce doesn't rot as fast. So... they're putting not only insecticides but also preservatives directly into the food items through its seed. Awesome.

If you do a little digging on the internet, you'll find scientists who have helped genetically engineer this stuff that won't touch it themselves—they say it isn't food. So despite the perspective our government tries to sell you, let's just say you should pay attention, and you should most definitely be concerned.

The Value of Organics
To get around heavily pesticided, poisonous, yes—poisonous, and genetically engineered food products, buy organic. Organics are not made with GMOs and have a lot less poison than the regular products. It's not pure, of course. You can't get completely away from all of the poison in our food in this culture today. But if you eat organics, you're putting a lot less poison into your body, and that in itself will help your health. Plus, organic products have higher nutritional value—because the nutrition hasn't been genetically modified out of them—so you have to eat less of them in order to both become full and to get your nutrients from them.

The results from an all-organic diet can be surprising. For me, after the first six months of an all-organic diet, my grass and pollen allergies, which had plagued me for 20 years, completely disappeared. Now when I eat non-organic produce, I have an allergic reaction: My nose runs and I sneeze a few times. My body tells me when the food I'm eating has been heavily poisoned; my body's sensitive to the poison since it's not saturated in it. If your body is used to eating poison, you've built up a tolerance for it and you won't notice when you do. Also, I cannot eat any of the wheat in the U.S. unless it's organic—I get an upset stomach and I do not feel well. My body has had enough of the poisons they put on U.S. foods, and it will not tolerate any more. It just makes me sick.

You shouldn't think that you'll notice an immediate difference in how you feel or even in how your food tastes if you start an organic regimen. If you buy an organic apple instead of a heavily poisoned one, you won't notice any difference. But over time, if you adopt a fully organic diet, your system will carry fewer poisons and feel much cleaner, and you'll probably have to eat less because you're getting full faster as the organics have higher nutrition. You might even lose a health annoyance or two. As an added bonus, organic produce is also generally much more flavorful. Eating organics is a lifestyle choice that will make a difference over time, not in even a month or two.

Nutritional Value

For maximum nutrients, including essential fiber, eat only whole grains. The really processed foods—the white ones, like white flour, white rice, and white sugar—have had nearly all of the nutrients stripped out of them. To make white flour, they remove all of the nutrient-rich bran (fiber) and germ (nutrient-dense; will sprout a new plant) from the grain, leaving only the nutrient-poor endosperm (grinds to fluff). So when you eat a piece of white bread, you might as well be eating a piece of paper for all of the nutritional value that bread has. I am always amused that you see white flour "enriched" with nutrients—they take all the nutrients out then have to put some back in so you're not just eating the equivalent of fluffy glue.

Even science has shown that a diet rich in whole grains and other health-full foods can help increase the brain's gray matter.[368] Use whole wheat flour breads and pizza doughs, brown rice, and never ever use white sugar for anything—that stuff is plain poison.

Switching from white to brown is a simple change in your diet that will give your body and your brain tremendous benefits in many ways. If you're used to eating fluffy, airy white flour, it may take a bit of retraining of your palate, but it's an easy change to make.

Food Choices

Pay attention to what you put into your body. It is your body's fuel. Our bodies only run on what we give them. If you give a car cheap gas, it will have some problems down the line, and usually those problems are not easy to identify. It's the same with cheap, mass market food. It will mess with you. Love yourself, love your body, and give it nutritious foods.

Why Plant-Based

Finally finally, the government is publicly acknowledging that a plant-based diet is good for you. Finally, the truth has outweighed the extremely powerful animal industry influencers that sway what gets included in the USDA Recommended Daily Food Chart.

It's the Ethics

I know that animal consumption remains mainstream. The only real arguments for eating animals? "It tastes good", and pure ego, domination and all. More and more science is advocating a plant-based diet for optimal health.

More and more work is showing how consuming animals is just not good for anyone or anything. Research demonstrating how an animal-based diet is contributing to all of our globe's biggest problems is finally becoming mainstream. The problem lies with all of the land, soil, food, and water necessary to fuel these animals that are killed for human consumption. If those resources were used for agriculture instead, or left alone in their natural states rather than cleared for beef cattle, such as some of the rain forests, our world's problems would reduce dramatically. Instead, we are contributing to a lot of problems for everyone on the planet simply with our choice to eat animals.

It's not right to cause a lot of problems for a lot of people just so we can do whatever we want. To further the misanthropic argument here, it's the people in the world's poorest countries who are suffering most at the hands of the self-indulgent life choices of those in the world's richest countries. For me, that's an extra layer of insidiousness that I do not want to support.

Part of loving yourself is holding to practices you are proud of contributing to. The self-esteem discussion in Chapter 9 explains the importance of behaving in ways that you respect. When you do the right thing, you feel good about yourself, in turn raising self-respect, self-confidence, and self-esteem.

A further argument for a plant-based diet lies in compassion for all living things. All animals and most humans in the animal food industry suffer immensely. It's not right to cause suffering in others so we can do whatever we want. Love yourself, and develop compassion for all others.

The final main argument advocating a plant-based diet lies in your body's health. Setting aside all of the chemicals you're ingesting when you eat animal flesh and fluids, the ingestion of animal flesh itself causes a long list of its own problems, heart disease being one of the main ones. Again, love yourself, and refrain from putting things into your body that will bring it harm.

Plant-based Eating is Simple

A plant-based diet isn't hard—just replace animal products with plants. The typical replacement for animal flesh is legumes, which have a lot of protein and relative few carbohydrates. So, just replace the animal flesh with beans on your plate, and you will be fine. Cheese is hard for a lot of people to give up—it's literally addictive. There are some decent plant-based cheeses out there, or just go without for a while to reset your taste buds. Eat a lot of fresh vegetables and go easy on the plant-based prepared foods.

If you want to up your plant-based game, eat 70% raw foods[369] and drink a fresh (organic) vegetable juice daily. Go on a juice fast periodically to cleanse your system and improve your health dramatically in a short time.

Improve your diet, and know that you are doing right by your body. Take care of yourself. This increases confidence and contributes to a general sense of well-being for you, easing anxiety. Your physical ailments will also ease a great deal.

The Sugar Toxin

I would be remiss not to mention sugar in this discussion. It is a toxin, and it is addictive. It is in nearly every product out there. Too much sugar will cause its own set of problems. Try to stay away from it. The less you eat it, the less your body craves it.

Reduce your sugar intake slowly. Start by substituting something without sugar for sugary drinks, and use natural sugar products like cane or maple syrup as sweeteners. Watch out for the highly processed stuff like corn syrup and agave nectar.

Artificial Flavors and Colors

I also have to mention chemical additives. They will cause problems just like every other toxin. Stay away from "artificial flavors and colors" for sure. Also stay away from preservatives of all kinds, which means boxed, canned, and other processed foods. If you go organic, you'll usually be much better in this area, but beware the processed plant-based stuff. It may be plant-based, but it's still processed!

The Tragedy of Palm Oil

One more thing—you may not realize that today's prepared foods practically all contain palm oil, and most vegetable oils themselves contain a great deal of palm oil in the mix. The argument here is not that palm oil ingestion is bad for you. The huge problem is that palm oil production kills animals rampantly and destroys the natural habitats of hundreds of thousands of animal and plant species, including the orangutans, threatening their very existence. Land owners literally go on killing sprees to get rid of the animals in their way of making money through palm oil production.

So it's not cool to use palm oil or consume items containing palm oil—and by "not cool" here, I mean purchasing these items makes you complicit in the mass killing and destruction of hundreds of thousands of life forms, so yeah, blatantly socially irresponsible.

Have a conscience. Don't allow species' homes to be destroyed and their lives and indeed their very existence threatened so you can have creamy potato chips. Choose items made with some other kind of oil all together—sunflower, canola, safflower, whatever. Palm oil is in nearly all mainstream foods these days because it makes food creamier, so it's not easy to get around. Read your labels. When you see "palm" anything, that's what I'm talking about. It goes by different names on labels but it all comes from the same tree and causes the same problems.

I know, this is a big one, and it's actually quite tragic. Responsible companies do the right thing though, and they will proudly let you know they are not using palm oil, so look for that. Whether it's organic, sustainable, palm fruit, palm kernel, or whatever, it all causes the same kind of damage to our furred and feathered friends, threatening their lives every day.

Doing the right thing builds incredible confidence because you know you're being a good person and doing what you can for the right reasons. It feels good to know you're not contributing to harm. This makes you feel like a good person which in itself reduces some anxiety because you feel better about yourself.

Essential Vitamins on a Plant-Based Diet

If you go plant-based, there are a couple of things nutrient-wise to pay attention to. The main thing is vitamin B-12 as it's difficult to get B-12 on a plant-based diet. Most plant-based people supplement B-12, preferably with a sublingual tablet. Also pay attention to your zinc, folate, iron, and vitamin D intakes and levels on a plant-based diet. Smartphone and computer applications such as Cronometer for smartphones help you calculate the nutrients from your food to ensure you are getting what you need. Don't worry about the protein—consuming about 1.5 cups (340 grams) of legumes a day along with your vegetables and various whole grains will meet your protein requirement easily. If you're exercising more and need more protein, choose a quality pea, hemp, or rice protein powder (~30 g protein, 100 calories, <5 g fat, ~20 g carbs).

Eat a Healthy Diet

Food companies have capitalized on Americans' desire for fast food preparation, and have happily—and very profitably—filled that demand with a bunch of stuff that tastes good, but will make you really sick if you live on it. We need to pay a lot more attention to what we put into our bodies, and make the direct connection between what we eat and our physical and even our mental health. Everything in the body is interconnected.

If you eat the way your great-grandparents did, with home-prepared, fresh, non-poisoned, non-genetically modified foods (but absent the animal and with brown foods instead of white ones), and plenty of vegetables, you will be fine. Those foods are rich with nutrients and will contribute to your good health.

Wherever you are with your diet, improve it. Until you are eating a rich and fully varied diet of plant-based whole foods, at least 70% raw,[d] [369] gluten free,[e] sugar free, chemical free, drinking a fresh vegetable juice at least once a day, combining your foods for optimal digestion and nutrient absorption, and engaging in regular cleanses,[f] your relationship with your food intake can improve.

Loving Yourself, Developing Conscience

When we were mistreated as kids, we got the message that we were not loved. Most of us go through life feeling unlovable. Maybe we weren't wanted by our mothers, and maybe her mistreatment sent the message loud and clear that we didn't deserve to be loved. But we are here! We breathe the air and drink the water just like everyone else. We walk on the streets, pay our bills, and do the best we can to get through the day just like everyone else. We have just as much right to be here as anyone else. We are here!

Maybe we weren't treated with love or respect as kids, and maybe this taught us that we don't deserve these things. But indeed, we do deserve these things. Merely by virtue of us being here and participating in this life on earth, we deserve these things! The thing is, we cannot rely on others to give us these things, this love and respect. We have to give them to ourself. I am responsible for making sure I receive

---

[d] It lowers "bad" cholesterol. Be sure to supplement B-12.

[e] Gluten is kind of like glue in your system. It clogs things up. It also causes inflammation.

[f] Some of these suggestions have mixed support. Do your own research and draw your own conclusions here.

love, even if that comes only from me. You are responsible for making sure you receive love in this life, even if that comes only from you.

Loving someone means taking good care of them. It means ensuring their needs are met and that they are content and well. It means doing what you can to contribute to their well-being in all ways. The physical body is included here.

Loving yourself means taking good care of yourself. It means ensuring you have proper nutrition and you're not eating things that will make you sick. This means converting to an organic, whole foods, plant-based, sugar-free, chemical-free diet, and palm oil-free to do the right thing. This is as healthy as you can get. And you know what? You are worth it!

Make this transition slowly. Don't go out in your next grocery outing and replace everything you're used to with things you're *supposed to* be eating. It won't last and you'll just be frustrated and give up. Your taste buds have been set for certain things, and they will crave those things, making everything else not taste good to you. Over time, with changing your diet, this changes and your taste buds start to crave things like broccoli and whole wheat toast. Substitute things out slowly, and incorporate new things a bit at a time. What you like and want to eat changes. There are many books and blogs available to help guide you through the transition to plant-based eating if you would like to find further suggestions.

Organics for a Better You
Investing in your health through organics and proper diet says "I love you" to yourself. You are worth good food that will nourish your body well. You deserve to not be poisoned with every bite. Taking care of yourself in this way makes you feel better about yourself, which builds confidence. And as we know, where confidence exists, anxiety fades. So taking care of your physical health also makes you feel better and stronger in other ways as well, as you prioritize your self in your life.

I know organics cost more, in some cases quite a lot more. If you think you can't afford organics, think again! You need to put your health first. If that means reexamining your budget to funnel more into the grocery envelope, so be it. Prioritize your food choices because you love yourself and you prioritize your good health today and as far into the future as you will walk this earth. You want to maintain excellent health in the long run, and organics will help with this—less poison, less damage. The money you spend on your groceries will be saved in your medical expenses down the road, so it is an investment in your health and your future.

Without good health, your future will be bleak. So what could possibly be more important than investing in your self?

Can you make spending cuts in other areas to be able to spend a little more at the grocery store? Do you wear expensive clothes or drive an expensive car yet eat cheap foods that are poisoning you? Do you eat in restaurants quite a lot (almost never organic) but think you can't afford actually healthy food? What you eat has a direct effect on your medical expenses, including the over-the-counter stuff. Think about it. Use your noodle. Put the pieces together. Prioritize your self. Prioritize your excellent health. You are worth it!

Another thing you can do is look for organic products at discount grocery stores. These secondary markets often have a growing supply of organics available.

Also, ease up on your food pickiness and go for the whole food organics that are on sale rather than whatever it is you're used to. Prioritize your body's health, not your tongue's pleasure!

Cleaning Up Your Diet

I used to be a picky eater, and I savored European-style white breads with a fine selection of European cheeses. I always had four or five different kinds of imported cheese in my fridge and I ate them daily. I lived on regular white pastas, prepared sauces, breakfast cereal and milk, corn chips and salsa, a few fresh fruits and some veggies, strong dark coffee, and nice wine—just like a lot of other people. Then I started getting migraines every day. Every stinking day! Rejecting Big Pharma and refusing to take a preventative pill every day, by tuning deeply in to my intuition I realized what I was doing. I connected my physical pain with my diet, and I stopped eating all of those foods that I absolutely loved. They were, quite literally, making me sick. Of course I miss them, but my health is so much more worth it. And occasionally, I indulge a bit.

My diet is now organic, plant-based, whole foods, sugar-free, chemical-free, palm-oil free, and alcohol-free to the fullest extent possible. I now eat for my body and my conscience rather than my tongue. It's not nearly as much fun, of course, as regularly indulging in all of that processed food. And every once in a while I will splurge with a bit of European-style white bread and some plant-based cheese, and I'll have a cup of coffee once a month or so. But those old favorites have lost their appeal actually and they really don't even taste good to me anymore: The bread tastes like paste and cow cheese like a mouthful of gamey animal fat.

I'm also not as attached to my food as I used to be. I am, however, attached to my good health. So my food now needs to be nutritionally rich, and as for taste, I aim for sensational but am satisfied with edible. I'm also attached to a conscience that directs me to not indulge in anything that will bring pain and suffering to any other living being. I like being able to think about where my food comes from, every step of the way, and know that no one has suffered, not human or animal, in the process of getting this meal onto my plate. That is worth so much to me. (I recognize there are limits to this argument, but it's enough for me to know I'm genuinely doing the best I can to live with a conscience and cruelty free.)

I want to be a good person, which means inflicting no suffering on others. Animals have emotions and characters, and they are included in my no-suffering ethic. I also want to take as good of care of myself as I possibly can. Those two priorities keep my diet, and my conscience, clean.

With those priorities, eating clean is easy. I can't really eat in restaurants much because they generally cater to mainstream eaters, but I feel amazing, with a clean system and a clear conscience. And that is totally worth it. Social outing in a restaurant? I eat before I go, just to be sure I don't go hungry because the only thing on the menu I can eat is a salad, which will last about 20 minutes until I'm hungry again. Yes, I have often left restaurants hungry after having eaten—and paying top dollar for—a plate of vegetables. Not surprisingly, this also makes me cranky! So I will have a protein shake or something first.

Taking care of myself in this way, eating as absolutely cleanly as possible, boosts my confidence and my self-worth. I am more comfortable in my own skin because I know I am doing everything I can for my body's best interest. I also have a very clean conscience when it comes to where my food comes from. I cannot express how much better it makes me feel about myself knowing these things. I simply feel like a good human being, which is deeply satisfying.

Diet and Mental Unwellness

Anything that is bigger than you—for which you have a compulsion that you cannot fully control—is, to my mind, an addiction. As we saw in the first section, an addiction is a property of mental unwellness.

As we all know, food can be an addiction, just like drinking yourself into the grave or gambling your life away. Our lack of control over our food intake results from mental unwellness. When our relationship with food brings disease, either from too little, too much, or too much of certain items like sugar and processed foods, and we cannot control our food consumption despite the disease we are bringing on ourself, that is an addiction of food, perhaps also known as an eating disorder.

There are several food-related conditions most definitely. But in fact, probably nearly all of disease is food-related because your food is your body's fuel, and if you're not fueling properly, you'll create a diseased condition somewhere or other.

Whatever ailments you have and don't want to have, I invite you to take responsibility for what you put into your mouth, and make conscious choices that will elevate your good health, not cause you endless problems. If this is difficult or maybe not possible for you to gain control over the hand-grab-to-mouth-drop action, don't worry—just continue reading this book and work through its tips and techniques. You'll get a handle on it. As your mental wellness improves, so does your hand-to-mouth control.

Rest

You need your sleep. Think about a small child who has gone without her nap. She is cranky and irritable, she cries and throws tantrums, and she is absolutely non-compliant. Adults are just big kids. We may have learned to control our tantrums for the most part, but whatever lack of sleep does so obviously to a small child, it does the same to us adults, just more subtly.

There are some great books written on the importance of sleep. That's not what this book is about so I will defer to those experts instead. I will only say, getting enough sleep is part of loving yourself. It is part of treating yourself with respect, love, and dignity. It is honoring your self. It is taking care of your self.

I'm someone who needs a lot of sleep—around 9 hours a night—so when I get less than that for a few days in a row, I suffer. Everything in my life suffers, and everyone in it does too. My cognitive abilities, my social relationships, my mood—everything suffers when I'm sleep deprived. We're all like this!

I used to be a night owl and would struggle to wake up in the mornings, relying on coffee to get my brain out of the morning fog. I stayed up late because it was quiet, but it didn't get quiet until after the rest of the world had gone to sleep, around 11 or so, so I would wait a bit past that to enjoy the stillness of the night. That was fine until morning came too soon, and I stumbled around making the coffee that I needed in order to function. Looking back, that was a pretty silly way to treat my body, and the rest of me actually since everything is interconnected.

Now I go to bed around 8 or 9 pm, sometimes even earlier if I'm tired. I like getting up early and greeting the day. If I don't have a full night's sleep, I'm not going to see the early morning, no way! So if I want to see that, I need to get my tail in bed at night. So, I do.

Oh and, if insomnia gets the better of me, which it certainly does from time to time, I do mindfulness meditation in bed, focusing intently on the path of air as I breathe it in and out, and instantly catch the Z's.

Love yourself enough to give yourself the rest you need. Prioritize your well-being. Prioritize feeling good. Prioritize your sleep.

Exercise

The third prong of the physical element is exercise. None of us is getting any younger. As we age, our physical abilities reduce. The less we move, the more difficult moving is.

I want to be mobile as I age. I don't want to rely on any walking aids and I definitely don't want to be immobile. I want to be able to go where I want, when I want, on my own. This independence is important to me. I look at other people, those my age and older, who have mobility challenges. Things hurt for them. A lot of them can't run or definitely climb any more, and many of them struggle to even walk. I don't want to be like this. I want to be able to move as I want to move.

If I hope to get there, to maintain good mobility in my elder years, I have to plan that out today and every day. I have to move, now. I have to exercise to keep my muscles, bones, and joints strong and supple. I don't have to exercise a lot, but I do have to exercise—every day, or at least nearly every day.

Brain Science on Exercise

It turns out, science shows us that exercise is also good for the brain, reducing cognitive decline and reducing the likelihood of developing dementia as we age.[370-373] One study looked at the exercise habits of 1740 individuals aged 65+ and found that 34% fewer were diagnosed with dementia five years later when they exercised with a variety of physical activity, such as walking, hiking, bicycling, and swimming, at least three times a week.[374] Indeed, after reviewing many studies on the topic, these researchers conclude that exercise improves cognition.[375]

169

In another study of older adults,[376] those who walked for about an hour three days weekly showed increases in gray matter volume in the frontal and temporal cortex, and anterior white matter.

It's Not Easy for All of Us

Exercise is definitely far from my favorite thing to do. I was blessed with many gifts, but a love of exercise or affinity for athleticism was not among them. Exercise for me is drudgery. It is not easy to get my tail off the couch, away from my computer, out of my books. But I know that I have to. My desire to retain mobility as I age outweighs my desire to sit on the couch all the time. And I love myself so I force myself to move my tail every day. My usual exercise is walking because I can't flake out on that—however far I walk, I have to turn around and walk back; I don't get to stop exercising when I feel like it, which I can do if I'm exercising in the home like with yoga or an exercise video. If I'm on a walk, I have to exercise until I reach home, no matter how tired I am. This is good for me.

To maximize my time, I flex my entire leg—and indeed through my entire core if I can remember—with every step. This helps build strength and for me, it's a lot easier to do it this way than to do separate dedicated strength training. I also do squats while I'm brushing my teeth...

I do not love exercise, but I understand that it is absolutely essential for good health. If I don't exercise, I will not be able to move at all like I want to. My desire to age with mobility outweighs my desire to stay on the couch all day. And now, exercise is getting easier.

Do the Sik Stuff

There are some physical activities we've all always dreamed of doing. Maybe you've always thought it would be cool to swing from the trapeze, or twirl in the aerial silks, or surf, or scuba dive, or clog dance. These little desires are your own. But they call us. And if we can indulge these little desires, that exercise is no longer work—it becomes a source of fun! How great is it when something that you have to do because it's good for you is also a source of fun!

For me, I always thought how cool it would be to box and to wrestle, and I always thought how cool it would be to surf. But I also felt that all of these activities were off limits to me. Women didn't really do these kinds of things during my youth, and I did not want any of them badly enough to help blaze that trail through the patriarchy. So they remained in the realm of "wouldn't that be cool if I could".

Eventually, I have indulged myself in all three! I managed to make them happen. And how wonderful and so super fun they all are for me! I've had severe anxiety in approaching each of them—in my 40s—but was able to overcome that anxiety and you know what? All of them are every bit as cool as I thought they would be. I love all of these activities and when I'm in a position where I can't practice them, I miss them! They also all make me strong, in many ways. Of course this is an added bonus to the pleasure I have while engaging in them. Suddenly, my attention is turned to the fun of the activity, not the obligation to exercise. It's perfect. Next up? I bought a skateboard...

You have to take care of your physical body with a regular exercise program. You know this—I know you know this. We've all heard it a million times. Show yourself love, honor your self, by engaging in regular exercise. Find something you like so you don't have to hate it or dread it. Do it because you want to be able to move gracefully on your own through your golden years. Do it because you love yourself.

Anxiety, PTSD

A lot of us have PTSD either latently, from childhood stress, or from fear-inducing experiences as adults. If we have it from childhood, we probably don't even know we have it since we've learned to live our lives with it as part of our normal existence. Some of our adult PTSD-inducing situations we intentionally chose and others of them just happened to us as a result of circumstance. For example, I have a friend who developed PTSD as a result of a natural disaster that left her homeless and city-less—not a lot you can do about that. Another was walking across the university campus between classes one weekday morning and witnessed a naked man douse himself in gasoline and light himself on fire. A third ended up in a motor vehicle accident and tried to pull the other driver from his burning vehicle, failing. All three developed PTSD as a result of their respective traumatic experiences. Sometimes these situations just happen to us.

However you developed it, PTSD can essentially be reduced to a single word: anxiety. It's totally outrageous levels of anxiety. Anxiety is essentially fear. PTSD gives you immense anxiety and fear. Normal situations freak you out. You feel afraid all the time. In some cases, you feel like someone will suddenly jump out from behind something and attack you, victimizing you all over again. This is the fear you live with every moment of every day.

Sufferers of PTSD experience high anxiety all the time. Their circle of safety is very small, and doesn't include very many people. Gatherings of friends and family can bring great amounts of anxiety to the PTSD sufferer. This is a challenging way to live your life.

Even those of us without PTSD often have some level of anxiety if we were raised in a stressful environment. We definitely have our default anxiety gauges set higher than most.

Building Strength

In order to overcome fear, it makes sense that you increase your strength. The physical plane is one clear way to increase strength. Better physical strength and better health make you feel better about yourself, increasing self-confidence and reducing related anxieties—it's easy to feel fearful all of the time if your body is weak and you know you would be an easy victim. So get your body into better physical condition so you can feel better about yourself in the world.

The physical strength training is intentional and you can see its progress in your muscle growth and ability to lift heavy things more easily than before. It does involve more than just physical muscle development, however. Well-rounded and complete strength-building on the physical plane involves the three essentials: diet, rest, and exercise. You have to take care of your body. It is the only one you have.

The Value of Martial Arts

If you suffer from PTSD, there's an added benefit to learning and practicing martial arts—it helps you heal. I swear, it happened for me and it's happened for friends of mine who also suffered from PTSD. But even if you don't have PTSD, martial arts can help reduce anxiety and make your life easier.

I should mention one caveat here though, to be responsible. This method is not appropriate for everyone. If you've had psychotic breaks that involved violence, please, for the love of humanity, do not join a martial arts training academy, at least until you get your illness to a totally manageable level and stabilize it for many years first. You learn lethal combat skills in martial arts, and they must always always be practiced with full consciousness, conscience, and respect for the skills you have and the damage you're doing to your adversary. If you have had periods where you were mentally and/or physically out of control, this kind of training is not a good idea for you—it will be too easy for you to kill someone should you have another break, and no one needs that.

Gaining Strength

Martial arts training gives you physical strength, internal and external power, and prowess. It gives you the ability to fight. If you need to defend yourself you know you can, and you know you have a chance at not only defending yourself but even beating your attacker. You learn how to hurt people with your body. In striking arts, you learn to use the art of eight limbs—two each hands, feet, elbows and knees. In grappling arts, you learn techniques to use your whole body to dislocate most joints in the human body by pushing them past their range of motion points, and how to use your body weight to your advantage, immobilizing your attacker. You learn to observe people's moves to predict what they'll do next, how people react, and how to counter their moves, achieving dominance. It is incredibly empowering.

If living in fear is where you are, a great way to overcome that fear is to learn some combat skills.

As your skills at defending yourself and fighting improve, so does your confidence. When you are confident that you can defend yourself if necessary, you are empowered. As you feel empowered, your fear declines. The longer you stick with this training, the stronger, more powerful, and more confident you will feel in relation to others. Thus, you no longer fear a surprise attack because you know you can manage it if it occurs. This reduces your anxiety level significantly. You won't notice it right away but after a couple of years of regular training you will note that you feel a lot less anxious than before—you feel better, more confident, and more peaceful walking around in your own skin.

The Value of Grappling

In particular, because PTSD can make you so jumpy and fearful when another person touches you unexpectedly, I recommend some sort of grappling training such as Brazilian jujitsu. Grappling requires full bodily contact with another person, with near-full aggression and sometimes full force. Your bodies are intertwined as you each vie for physical dominance. Training this full-body contact helps heal from PTSD on a couple of levels.

First, you get used to people touching you so it's not a shock when someone taps you on the shoulder, even if it's from behind. Second, you learn that not all unexpected and unforeseen touches are threats. Third, you learn combat skills so even if that tap on the shoulder is a threat, you know you can manage yourself.

In these ways you become more comfortable with people touching you. As your comfort level with others rises, your discomfort level with them declines. As you become more comfortable, you become less anxious. This is the PTSD dissipating.

Indeed, psychologists have found that a good method for overcoming PTSD is to place yourself in a similar physical situation as the traumatizing event, but where you have power this time. Thus, even though grappling is great for overcoming PTSD from multiple causes, it can be especially beneficial for those victims of sexual offenses.

I joined a martial arts gym accidentally—I thought I was signing up to learn how to box. Little did I know I had joined a cage fighting gym! But it turned out to be one of the best things that ever happened to me. It was the grappling training in particular that for me, helped me move past my PTSD. Learning to dominate in full-body combat, on the ground, was incredibly empowering. Those arts are more technique-driven than strength-driven, so even as a woman with skinny little arms, I could have a chance at victory even against a man. I knew that I could defend myself and even better, really hurt someone if they tried to harm me. I learned how to dislocate joints in the arms and legs, totally immobilizing someone. I learned how to choke someone into unconsciousness in about eight different ways. And one day, I learned how to break someone's neck using my body weight and my knees. I learned that if someone messed with me, they would get a surprise, and they would get hurt. I had power. I was no longer afraid.

Moving past my PTSD was an added bonus for me in learning these martial arts. I just wanted to learn how to box initially, and eventually, after a full year, I worked up my nerve to join the submission wrestling class and learn some wrestling moves. Wow. It was so fun! And it turned out to be so very empowering and, surprisingly, healing.

Hygiene
A discussion of hygiene seems to fit best under the heading of physical care, so here it is.

If hygiene is difficult for you, it's time to exercise some self love and take better care of yourself.

Hygiene matters because it sends a message to other people about who you are and how you think about yourself. If you're not clean or well-groomed, people will have reservations about you and have a harder time wanting to get near you or trust you. They will see that you don't care about yourself, and often perceive this as you not being trustworthy. In effect, you are shooting yourself in the foot. It will be harder for you to be socially accepted, which will make relationships more difficult for you and it will be harder for you to get ahead professionally. None of us needs these kinds of obstacles in our lives.

If you are a parent, you make sure your kid is clean and well-groomed, yes? And you do this because you love your child and you want what's best for your child in every possible way. You don't want your child to be the object of ridicule or mockery, or to receive lower grades because he smells bad. Poor hygiene is not a good reason to be on the receiving end of social ill, but this is what happens. So you do everything you can to prevent this.

Hygiene Musts
Love yourself enough to clean and groom yourself. Always be well put together and presentable. Make sure you do the following, regularly:

- Trim and clean your nails of your hands and feet. They should never have a dark line under them. Toe nails and men's finger nails should never grow more than a couple of millimeters from where they depart from the skin. This is gross.
- Clean your hair. It should never be stuck to your head or appear greasy or unwashed. This is also gross.
- Tame your hair. It should never be unruly unless achieving that look takes you a lot of hair product and 30 minutes or longer in front of the mirror. This shows disarray.
- Bathe often enough to keep body odors away. Don't try to mask poor hygiene with cologne or perfume. Again, this is gross.
- Wear clothes that are clean and presentable. The clothing you wear in public should never have large spots, large stains, or large holes, or be excessively wrinkled or just plain dirty. This shows disarray and if your clothes stink, this is gross.
- If you wear glasses, keep them clean and in good condition. The lenses shouldn't be all smudged and the frames should not be in disrepair—use tape or a paper clip only as an emergency, until you can immediately have them repaired. This shows disarray.
- Keep your facial hair trimmed—both men and women! Men, trim your beard and mustache every once in a while. Don't let it grow wild for too

long. People of both genders, as we age the hairs in our eyebrows, noses, and even ears get long and weird. Keep them neat and where they belong by trimming them when they need it.

These are essential basics for good hygiene. They show the world that you have a minimal level of self-respect and self-care. Never allow yourself to leave the house unless you have all of these items checked off, even if you're going out to exercise unless you're going swimming. Love yourself enough to not be offensive to others because of your poor hygiene.

Love yourself enough to take care of your body's basic needs.

Posture

Most of us have pretty poor posture—our back rounds and shoulders slump forward, forcing a kink in our neck just to keep our head up. Not only is this not great for our spines, but it sends a message to others that we lack confidence and self-esteem.

Posture is not difficult to change. Like everything else, you just have to give it a focus.

Posture Improvement

You can improve your posture every minute of every day. The reality is that most of us are too busy throughout the day to give much thought to our posture, but we can improve it if we practice it. In times when our minds are free, such as when we are walking between locations or for exercise, we can practice better posture. The more we practice better posture in specific times, the easier it is to practice better posture all of the time.

To improve your posture, pull your body into a position that you think is appropriate. Look in the mirror. Your spine should be completely vertical and straight, from the tailbone through the neck. The head should be easily supported by the vertebrae in the neck; it should just sit atop the neck and effortlessly swivel. There shouldn't be any kinks in the neck in order to keep the head upright. The arms should swing easily from the shoulders when you walk. There should be nothing labored about your upper body as it moves. Everything should be lined up. Pull your head level so you're looking straight ahead. You will need to use your abdominal and back muscles to hold your upper body in the proper position. If you don't use these muscles, you will slouch.

Better posture is a small improvement, but it is actually a huge improvement!

Conclusion

The physical dimension is one very important part of your overall balance. When your physical dimension is weak, your being is out of balance. The physical dimension is in some ways the easiest to address: Its manifestations are clear in your physical appearance and how you physically feel, and your efforts to develop this sphere have tangible results. You can set yourself rules for making sure you eat properly, rest enough, and exercise daily. Then, you just live up to the rules you set for yourself.

I won't try to tell you that following these rules will be easy—we all know that is not the case! But if you set your mind to it, you can do it pretty easily. A regular mindfulness practice will greatly help you stay on the path. Make dietary decisions before and at the grocery store—don't buy anything that's bad for you. Get your tail in bed at a reasonable hour so you can give your body the sleep that it needs. Incorporate some exercise into your daily routine, like taking a walk during your lunch break, for example, and if that's all you're doing, at least flex from your toes through your core. Work on your posture. Slowly, with the steady practice of each of these areas of taking care of yourself, this gets easier—a lot easier. Show yourself love by taking care of your body in these ways. If you don't, no one will. This is something only you can do.

Rebuild your life structures in ways that you choose. Take full control. Do not continue to advance the structures you were given in childhood merely because you were given those structures. Assess them honestly for yourself. If your structures don't serve you in any way and certainly if they bring you any anxiety at all, change them. You are an adult. You have that choice. And you fully have that power.

8. Emotional Intelligence

Our emotions are a very integral and important part of each of us. We can never deny we have them—all of them. Our emotions make us human, and we are lucky to experience the full range of emotions, every one of us.

Difficult Emotional Regulation
As kids from stressful homes, our emotional regulation is all messed up. We're predisposed to anxiety—anxiety! Anxious emotions are right on the surface, and can explode at any time. Our work on this emotional dimension is to learn to manage our emotional expression. Eventually, with practice, we'll be able to manage our emotions themselves as well. We are replacing our unhealthy structures for emotional arousal and expression with new, healthy, well-managed structures. A practice of mindfulness helps significantly in this area.

When we have endured trauma, our ability to regulate our emotions and their expression falters. We feel a range of discomfort and often, rather than managing these uncomfortable feelings responsibly, we lash out at whoever is making us uncomfortable, often placing blame with them for making us feel this way. Nothing could be more irresponsible. Our emotions reside within us, and we are responsible for how we feel, for managing how we feel, and for managing how we express what we feel. We develop this responsibility through developing emotional intelligence.

Responsible Emotional Expression is Emotional Intelligence
In developing emotional intelligence, we must first understand how emotions work and what they are, then learn to responsibly manage those emotions. Keep in mind, we are not trying to suppress any emotions at any time; rather, we are learning to manage our emotional expression responsibly. This is emotional intelligence. Part of this management is recognizing that we very likely overreact in certain situations, and being very mindful not to do that.

In this chapter, we will talk about emotions—what they are, how to manage their arousal, and importantly, how to manage their expression responsibly. This emotional management is the essence of emotional intelligence. After that, I talk for a moment about how to get rid of lingering emotions that bring you down but you can't seem to shake.

In some ways this emotional dimension is the most important piece of our healing—we have to get away from the anxiety that plagues us and rears its ugly head in all kinds of inconvenient and inappropriate ways in our lives through our untamed emotional expressions. We absolutely have to find other ways to manage our internal selves and put a dead stop to living with anxiety. Emotional intelligence is the route to this.

The Emotions We Have

Our human experience involves a full range of emotions. Over time, scientists have come up with a classification system for our emotions,[53] which I present here.

Our emotions generally fall into four broad categories: pleasant, sad, guilty, and anxious.[53] I intentionally refrain from using the term "negative" to talk about emotions because as one who is particularly sensitive to language use and aware that the language we use constructs how we feel toward and treat something, I wouldn't want to classify anything within the normal range of experience as negative. Something that is negative is something to be avoided. We cannot nor should we ever want to avoid experiencing any of our emotions, even the difficult ones. They each serve a very important purpose in our lives and without them, we would be getting into a lot more trouble than we already do. So when viewed in this light, each of our emotions is important and useful—just that the experience of some is less pleasant than the experience of others.

Emotions are merely an arousal of energy in response to a stimulus. Something happens to us, and our energy responds in a certain way. We can feel it rise within us, for better or for worse. Perhaps we receive a phone call from an old friend, and upon hearing her voice we become very happy—our energy rises in a positive way that makes us feel good. But perhaps she is calling because she has difficult news to share, at which point we become very sad to hear of her suffering—our energy rises with something else at its core, and it unpleasantly tugs at our gut or our heart. Emotion is a rising of energy within us in response to a stimulus.

Pleasant Emotions

Our pleasant emotions include happiness, joy, love, and like.[53] Each of these brings an elation along with it, a supreme pleasure. If only we could experience these emotions and only these emotions all the time! (Well, the good news is, you can!)

When we experience these emotions, we smile, our hearts are lighter, the weight of the world is off of our shoulders, and we skip through the day.

Happiness is general contentment, when it feels like the world is going right. Joy is felt with a tickle in your heart. Joy is an important emotion to ward off heart disease! We all need to create joy in our life. If we've been traumatized, we have a particularly hard time with this one. Spending time playing and having fun can also bring joy—if we let it.

The distinction between love and like is a fine one, but indeed, it is possible to experience each separately and one without the presence of the other. Loving someone means caring about their well-being. The feeling of liking someone means that you enjoy being around them. You enjoy their company and feel comfortable in their presence. You want to hang out with them and seek out opportunities to get together. Their presence generally brings you joy and happiness. Perhaps you love certain family members or former partners or friends—you care about their well-being—but don't particularly like them and don't want to be around them.

Sad Emotions

The sad emotions include sadness, depression, and grief.[53] These emotions often bring us to tears. They generally make us want to stay inside, perhaps covered under a blanket, isolated, removed from the world.

When someone is experiencing these emotions, if they want to be left alone, we need to leave them alone with their experience. Our tendency is to want to make everyone happy—to want to "cheer people up". This is not always the best strategy. People need to have an opportunity to feel what they need to feel, in their own time and way. As their loved ones, we need to allow them this time and space.

It's important to recognize that neither depression nor grief are merely intense states of sadness. Depression is more about loss of interest in life and its events. Clinical depression is a serious medical condition that often requires medication. It can lead to suicidal tendencies. Grief is something experienced when you've lost someone or even something important to you. Psychologists have identified five stages of grief. These include denial, anger, bargaining, depression, and acceptance. Not everyone experiences all five of these stages and they are not always experienced in this order. Psychologists also caution people to allow each of these stages to take the time they need, and remind us that everyone experiences grief in their own way.

Guilt Emotions

There are only two emotions in this category: guilt and its partner, shame.[53] In experiencing both of these, you just feel bad. It's not the same kind of bad you feel with the sad emotions or the kind of rage that arises with the anxious emotions. It's your conscience doing its job. Both guilt and shame are very important because they help us be good people in the world. Psychology tells us that guilt arises out of empathy for others—we have done something to hurt someone, and we feel bad about that. Guilt is an empathetic awareness that we have caused injury. Our precipitating action can be real or imaginary.

On the other hand, shame is how we feel about ourselves. It can come from an action that we did to hurt someone though it doesn't have to, but either way it's all about how I feel about me. It's not about empathy for others. It's about feeling like a jerk, like a bad person. It's about how we appear to ourselves and how we feel we may appear to others—like a bad person. If we are embarrassed for something we did intentionally because looking back, we know it wasn't the right thing to do, and we sort of beat ourselves up for it, this is shame. It's possible to live in a perpetual state of shame, especially if we've been traumatized as kids. We were made to feel like we're bad people and we believe this about ourselves. We need to get out of this and leave this feeling behind.

Emotional manipulators are masters at drawing out our guilt and shame. The more sensitive we are, the more likely we are to experience both of these emotions, and our manipulators know that about us and use it completely to their advantage. These are very powerful emotions for manipulators to tap into because they strike directly at how we feel about ourselves and our behaviors. Both of these emotions make us feel bad, like we messed up. Of course manipulators will want to tap that— then simply lead us by the nose because our sense of personal strength has been flattened at least somewhat, leaving us more vulnerable.

Anxious Emotions

The anxious emotions are the least comfortable to experience—both for ourselves and for all within our radius at the moment. These include anger, fear, jealousy, and envy.[53] Though uncomfortable, each has a very important role in our personal preservation.

Anger is what arises when we feel we have been threatened or mistreated in some way. Our self-preservation instinct kicks in and we want to lash out to protect ourselves, or perhaps our loved ones who we feel have been somehow victimized.

Anger is very important to ensuring we protect ourselves. It's an incredibly useful and important emotion—we just have to be very careful to express it responsibly, because it is so powerful that its expression can get out of hand easily. A wise practice is to never speak when feeling anger.

Fear is another incredibly useful emotion. It tells us when there's a possible threat in our environment, and helps us stay alive. We have a fight-or-flight instinct, which tells us when to either stay and continue to stand up for ourselves, or get the heck out of the situation because it is truly dangerous for us. Often times when we feel fear we mix it with anger—you frightened me, making me feel threatened, and that angered me.

Jealousy is what arises when we feel that an important relationship is being threatened. We have jealousy in all kinds of our relationships, not only our most intimate relational partnerships. We can be jealous that our child or even our cat seems to prefer someone else at times, and jealous when our siblings or friends seem to have relationships with each other that we are not part of. Jealousy is very uncomfortable and is also felt in the core of our being, like anger. It is also often combined with anger and fear—by talking to that pretty lady you made me feel that you don't care about me enough, and that frightens me, so I am angry with you for making me feel this way. Rather than confront the jealousy within us, many of us, particularly those less mentally healthy among us, simply insist that the threat, being the third person, be removed from the scenario, usually permanently. We do this by insisting that the object of our affection not have any contact with the person perceived to threaten our relationship with them. That is, we forbid our daughter from speaking with her aunt because their relationship is "just too close". Sometimes that third party truly is a threat to your relationship though, and jealousy lets you know this. Jealousy can keep families together—though I am not advocating its rampant expression by any means.

Envy has a similar feeling to jealousy in the body and in English, the two are usually confused. Envy is about wanting something someone else has, while jealousy has to do with an important relationship being threatened. Jealousy is about people, while envy is about things and states. Envy is experienced because someone... is thinner, is taller, got better grades, makes more money, has a better job, has a nicer house, has kids, has nicer kids, has no kids... the list is endless. Envy is represented by the saying "the grass is always greener on the other side of the fence." We seem to want what others have. When we feel envy, we also feel it in our core, in our gut as a pang of unpleasantness. It triggers feelings of hatred, mild or severe, for the person who has that thing that we want. Its sensation in the body is very similar to jealousy and also, very similar to anger. Again, envy often turns into anger—you have more than me and that makes me feel bad and I'm angry with you for making me feel bad. Envy can be a powerful stimulus to get you to move forward in life though, so it's also a very useful emotion. If you feel bad every time you see your sister who's just lost 50 pounds, that bad feeling—that envy—can motivate you to get on a health kick yourself.

Our emotions help us in so many ways and are such a very rich part of our human experience. They give us reasons to live, they let us understand our pain and loss, they help us be good people in the world, and they let us know when we are under threat. We couldn't live without every one of our emotions.

Expressing Our Emotions

We don't need to worry about expressing the pleasant emotions—at least not much. It is possible to overdo happiness and be overly exuberant with joy in certain contexts, making others uncomfortable, yes. So in that sense, even the pleasant emotions could use an eye for management. The sad emotions—we need to let them be felt, and at the same time, we need to watch ourselves to be sure they don't get carried away. You might want to try to hold off your tears until after the meeting. If we drop from sadness into depression, we may need to get some clinical help. So in that sense, we need to keep an eye on those as well. As for guilt and shame, as traumatized people, we need to be careful about not beating ourselves up too badly for something we did or maybe even didn't do yet someone is blaming us for anyway.

We need to be careful not to let these emotions make us vulnerable to manipulation so in that sense, we need to be aware of them. Easily the category of emotions that most requires our attention for emotional management is the anxious ones. Those can get us into so much trouble!

Predisposed for anxiety and all of the emotions anxiety arouses, traumatized people tend to overreact in this category, perceiving threats when there are none, and also impulsively reacting to extremes in the face of these anxious emotions—there are reasons that anger management courses have sprung up in recent decades, and that the court system has incorporated them as part of sentencing for violent offenses. Traumatized people tend to have real problems managing their anger, and since fear, jealousy, and envy can easily convert to anger, that's the entire category of anxious emotions that traumatized people have trouble with. But fear not, as this book can help with that.

Emotional Intelligence

Emotional intelligence is a concept that sprang up in the scientific literature in the 1990s.[377,378] Much has been written on this topic so if it interests you further, by all means, take a deeper dive than the one offered here. Plenty of resources are available that discuss this idea in depth.

Its crux involves responsibly managing your emotional expressions. The idea is that it's not okay to express your emotions, particularly the anxious ones, whenever you feel like it and to whatever degree makes you comfortable in whatever context you're in. As responsible people living in a civilized society, we have certain responsibilities to take care of ourselves and not upset others with our irresponsible emotional expression.

Note that emotional intelligence is *not* about not feeling certain undesirable emotions, tamping them down, or pretending they don't exist. Emotional intelligence is about responsible expression of all of our emotions as we feel them.

Developing Emotional Intelligence

Emotional intelligence, as reported in the research, is actually a very simple process[377,378]:

1) Recognize the arousal of energy within you and identify it as pleasant or unpleasant (i.e. don't try to name it, just describe it to yourself);
2) Identify and name that emotion;
3) Think about how to responsibly express that emotion in the context you're in; and
4) After its expression, look back on its expression and evaluate your behavior for its social appropriateness, given time, place, and context.

These steps are further elaborated for you here:

Step 1: Recognize the energy arousal.
You have an arousal of energy in response to some stimulus in your environment. Identify whether that's productive and positive, or not so comfortable. (I won't call them negative for word choice reasons, as this label of *negative* suggests these emotions are something we should avoid, which isn't the case at all.) So you have an arousal of energy. It is comfortable? Or is it uncomfortable?

Step 2: Name the emotion.
What's going on, what do you feel? Is it frustration? Envy? Jealousy? Anger? What do you feel? Put a name on it.

Step 3: Decide on appropriate emotional expression.
After you understand which emotion you're feeling, you have to find an appropriate way to express that emotion in the context you're in. Appropriate is the operative word here. If you need to leave the situation for a while so you can calm down and gather your thoughts, then that's what you need to do.

In order to be emotionally intelligent, it's important that your expressions of your emotions are appropriate. So, you need to learn to manage your emotional expression. Not your emotions! I'm not saying don't get angry. I am saying find a way to transform your anger and after calming down, express yourself in a socially appropriate way for that situation. If you can't do that right now, then it's your responsibility to leave the situation until such a time that you can come back and you can be appropriate with your expression.

Step 4: Reflect and evaluate.
After the fact, part of developing emotional intelligence is looking back and evaluating the appropriateness of your emotional expression for the context you were in.

Practice these four steps. Become deliberate and responsible in your expressions of emotion. Once you can remain calm and manage your emotional expressions well, you have made great strides toward achieving emotional intelligence. Nice work!

Eliminating Uncomfortable Emotions: Tapping
Sometimes we are plagued by an uncomfortable emotion we just can't shake. It may be an emotion from the sad category, the anxious category, guilt or shame, or a wicked combination of emotions from all of those categories. Try as we might to reason ourselves out of the discomfort this emotion brings, it remains—sometimes for a really long time, like many days or even weeks or longer.

Believe it or not, there is a tool out there to help eliminate these uncomfortable emotions—actually eliminate them! And it's not at all painful or difficult. It's called Emotional Freedom Technique (EFT) or "tapping", and it works.

Meridians

Tapping is built on the same essential principle as acupuncture or acupressure. In those treatment modalities, certain pressure points along energy meridians are stimulated in order to release a blockage in the body's energy flow and thus, relieve physical pain. As it turns out, these principles can be used to relieve emotional pain and discomfort as well. You can do it to yourself or have a friend tap for you. These are the meridians you want to access:

- Top of the head. Directly at the apex of your skull.
- Eyebrow. Where it begins near your nose. Choose one side.
- Side of the eye. On that eye socket bone outside of your eye.
- Under the eye. On the eye socket bone directly below your eye, in the center of it.
- Under the nose. In that little dimple there between your nose and your lip.
- Chin. Just as your chin begins beneath your lip.
- Collar bone. On the collar bone, just inside of the knot at the throat end.
- "Sore spot." Move to the middle of your collar bone, then down, equidistant between your collarbone and your armpit.
- Under the arm. Directly on your side, where a bra strap is/would be.

Tapping Points

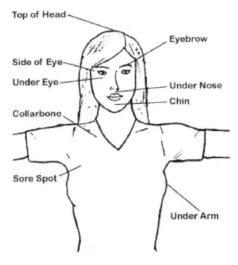

Top of Head

Eyebrow

Side of Eye

Under Eye

Under Nose

Chin

Collarbone

Sore Spot

Under Arm

artwork copyright Karli Norell

Here's how it works:

1. Take a calm breath, and identify the emotion most troubling you at the moment. Is it anger? Fear? Jealousy? Sadness? What is the emotion? Name it.

2. On a scale of 1-10, assess the intensity of the emotion you're feeling. Is it a 7? 9? Even a 10?

3. Keep the emotion in mind. Close your eyes, relax, and quiet your mind. Keep your focus on the emotion. Tap each of the nine meridians with medium-hard pressure between 5-10 times in each spot. Do this for two rounds.

4. On a scale of 1-10, assess the intensity of the emotion you're feeling. It should be dramatically reduced. If not, repeat the tapping exercise.

5. Assess your emotional condition. Sometimes our difficult emotions are layered. I once had seven troubling emotions layered after a breakup. Seven! And I worked through them one at a time with this technique, reducing them all by 70% or more. Wow did I feel better afterward!

Tapping is an effective way of reducing the intensity of the difficult emotions we all face from time to time and have a hard time shaking. I invite you to investigate further if you like. There are many resources available on the internet, and some techniques get more specific in order to manage other aspects of your life. These are the basics, and I've found this technique ridiculously useful and simple. I showed it to a friend before an important job interview for an extremely competitive position—she got the job. Increasingly, college and professional sports teams are reportedly using it to reduce anxiety before games. Try it! You'll be surprised!

Conclusion

In a nutshell, the above steps are one recommended way to develop emotional intelligence and achieve emotional peace. Another possibility is to take up a practice of mindfulness, which trains your mind to observe emotions as they arise and deal with them before they grow and become more difficult to appropriately express. Mindfulness teaches you these steps though, in nearly the exact same way. Either way, your goal is to learn to manage the expression of your emotions so that that expression is appropriate for the situation.

Developing emotional intelligence is an important piece of developing social intelligence. You cannot be considered socially intelligent if you cannot responsibly and socially appropriately manage your emotional expressions.

Developing emotional intelligence is also important to your sense of inner peace. As you learn to manage your emotions, you will find your internal seascape much calmer—you have more control over it! You can also learn to manage your emotions from your adult, cognitive, conscientious brain. You can learn to make healthy choices in how you express your emotions rather than lashing out or flipping out or flying off the handle, none of which increases anyone's desire to be around you, ever. This control over your emotional expressions helps you build confidence in your ability to be a whole and appropriate human being—if you have a history of going off or flipping out and you learn to overcome those tendencies, you can take great pride in your growth. And you should!

We didn't get the lessons on how to handle our emotions when we were kids, and for most of us, our entire lives have been spent with our emotions leading the way, for better and for worse. This section gives you tools for managing your emotional expressions and even to eliminating difficult emotions, which is critically important to developing your emotional dimension.

9. The Psychological Dimension

This chapter is kind of a biggie. A lot of damage was done to us in terms of our thinking, and this brings problems to other areas of our lives—all other areas of our lives, actually. Our thoughts direct our emotions, and if you don't believe me, think about something terrible and see how you feel, then think of something truly wonderful and see how you feel. Our thoughts cause our physical health or unhealth, and often a sense of low self-worth leads us to seek soothing, though self-destructive, behaviors. Our thinking definitely influences our social relationships, and unhealthy thinking will lead to unhealthy relationships. Our thinking and perceptions about certain activities leads us to engage in them or not, often preventing us from developing in those ways. Our thoughts keep us where we are or catalyze us to move forward. In these ways, then, our thinking is the centerpoint of this self-improvement work—we cannot heal if we don't change our thinking patterns. It's okay though—we just have to build new structures out of healthy thoughts. This chapter helps with that construction.

In This Chapter
This chapter has several components. First, I talk a little about what actual mental health looks like. This is a pretty simple, easy, and straightforward discussion so this part is short. Then, I talk a little about straightening out any cognitive distortions you might be using as coping strategies. This is also short piece. After that, I talk you through the process of rooting out thinking patterns that are bringing you anxiety and replacing them with healthy structures. From there, I present some views from psychology on what it takes to heal. In the last major section, I talk about how to build your self-esteem. This last piece is huge. In the first place, everyone on the planet could use some of this. In the second place, especially those of us with challenging upbringings really need this. We are left with crumpled self-esteem that manifests in ugly ways in our lives, preventing us from moving forward very far. I'll talk more about that when we get there. The chapter closes with a word on ethics and a presentation of ethical guidelines for your reference as you rebuild your self.

Characteristics of Mental Health

Thresholds for mentally healthy ways of thinking and being do exist. Without attempting to fully define mental health, I will offer three representative characteristics discerned from the literature: absence of core anxiety, lack of distortions, and well-developed conscience.

That is to say, research talks about anxiety of any sort as something in need of healing, so, absence of anxiety would represent a component of mental health. Research also talks about distortions of reality as representative of mental unwellness—in fact, an oversimplification of mental unwellness could be the greater the distortions, the greater the degree of mental unwellness. Therefore, absence of distortions of reality would represent a facet of mental wellness. Third, the scientific literature talks about lack of conscience or a poorly developed conscience as present in all mental unwellness, so, a well-developed conscience would help comprise mental health.

Absence of Core Anxiety

Mentally well people do not operate from a central core of anxiety and don't have anxiety-related issues. That is not to say they never have anxiety, but they do not walk around in a skin of anxiety all the time, fighting against it in efforts to enjoy life. They have little or no social anxiety, no PTSD, no addictions such as a weekly alcohol habit—no real anxiety at all.

This doesn't mean extroversion or excellent social skills. It just means a calm center. It means an easy ability to manage your weight and an easy ability to have only one drink, socially if you like, and a healthy relationship with exercise as well as everything else in your life. Cravings of any sort do not get the better of you. You have that self-control, easily.

Lack of Distortions

Lack of distortions of reality means a realistic sense of self and others. Accurate perceptions of one's own and others' self, behaviors, attributes, shortcomings, characteristics, and place in the world help characterize one that is mentally well. This includes recognizing and accounting for human error. This also means easy forgiveness in the recognition that people make mistakes as part of being human.

An example is recognizing that people get to be proud of their strengths and accomplishments and we are proud of them for their accomplishments too, without perceiving their successes as about us in any way. Another example is recognizing we all play a role in relational difficulties rather than anything being entirely the other person's fault. Another, sometimes we ourselves make mistakes and need to recognize and take responsibility for them. Also, you're aware there are multiple possible explanations for someone's actions or words, so don't immediately get angry for what you see or hear. Keep reading this chapter, particularly the ethics portion at the end, to understand more about our distortions.

Well-Developed Conscience

A well-developed conscience means you don't hurt other people or cause their suffering. You think about them and their needs, their well-being. This prevents people from behaving with cruelty and when toes are accidentally stepped on, amends are immediately sought. That doesn't mean healthy people never hurt others. It means they usually recognize and feel bad when they do and take responsibility for their wrongdoing. They can usually offer a genuine apology because they legitimately understand they were out of line and are genuinely seeking amends for their inappropriateness.

These three essential components—absence of core anxiety, realistic view on life, and a well-developed conscience—comprise the foundation of mental wellness.

What Mental Wellness is Not

None of this is to say that mentally healthy people are perfect—far from it. This is also not to say that mentally well people have no more need for growth—also untrue. Mentally healthy people also make mistakes. They are just aware enough to recognize error as a natural and normal part of human life and behave appropriately when they slip up.

Note that social intelligence and emotional intelligence are not in this list of mental wellness characteristics. These are intelligences that we need to develop if we come from a stressful childhood environment because they are lessons in civility and personal responsibility in a social world and we are likely deficient in them, but they are not components of mental wellness in and of themselves. In fact, mentally well people have a degree of social and emotional intelligence naturally, but many are also somewhat deficient in these areas.

The reverse also holds true—many deeply disturbed, deeply unwell individuals demonstrate high proficiency in social and emotional intelligences, at least at first. These can be the most dangerous kind of person because we tend to lower our guards in the face of very polite people with strong social graces, perceiving them in a glowing light. Therefore, it is a mistake to equate politeness and social appropriateness with mental wellness—these are goals we should all strive for, yes, but they are not in and of themselves indicators of mental health.

Dealing with Your Distortions

In managing our lives, we've developed coping strategies to get through the day and the many challenges that fly our way. These are presented in Section I. I present them again here for ease of reference. Please refer to Chapter 2 for explanations and discussion.

- Group 1: Healthy strategies; positive reflection.
  - o Putting into perspective
  - o Planning
  - o Positive reappraisal
  - o Acceptance
- Group 2: Healthy coping; reconciling the trauma
  - o Assimilation (it's your own fault—unhealthy)
  - o Accommodation (change your way of thinking about the world—healthy)
  - o Overaccommodation (believe the whole world is dangerous—unhealthy)
- Group 3: Damaging strategies
  - o Blame
    - Self-blame
    - Other-blame
    - Denial
    - Minimization
    - Perpetrator attachment
  - o Runaway thinking
    - Rumination
    - Catastrophizing
    - [Hypervigilance]
    - [Dissociation]
    - [Amnesia]
  - o Logical Fallacies
    - Appeal to ignorance

- Slippery slope
- False dichotomy
- ... (please see Chapter 2 for additional logical fallacies)

Most of these options are not healthy. Whatever you're doing in Group 3, knock it off. Go up into Group 1 and take a look at those options. Overcome whatever is happening in Group 3's choices by using options from Group 1. Be honest with yourself—you can't heal if you aren't. You must get your mind out of the habits of Group 3. You absolutely must. These are not healthy for you and are keeping you from progressing. They also keep you feeling bad.

From Group 2's options, you want to incorporate what happened into your view of how the world works sometimes without changing your view of how the whole world works.

You're In Control
The good news is, you can control your mind! You can control your thoughts. When you replace destructive thinking patterns with constructive patterns, you are healing. Over time, those destructive thought patterns have less control over you and your well-being, and you feel better.

Choosing Healthy Options
When you have a destructive thought pattern, any of those from Group 3, it is your job to recognize that you're having that pattern and knock it off. Intentionally change what you're thinking about and do it right now. You can change your thinking and focus on:

- Your breath. Feel your breath entering and leaving your body. Trace the flow of air. Feel its coolness as it enters your nostrils. This is where a practice of mindfulness really, really helps.
- The beauty of your current environment. Look around you! Look at nature at play everywhere. See the trees, think about what lives in them and how much we need them. See the clouds, be thankful that they carry water for us to live. A practice of mindfulness helps with this as well.
- A mantra such as "I am safe" or "I am loved" or telling yourself "You're okay. It's okay. That was a long time ago. You're safe now."
- Something beautiful in your life.

- The positive outcomes in your life as a result of that event. Transform that event from a source of suffering to one of giving you immense beauty because of where it took you. This last option is great for helping ease your anxiety at a root level. If you're not there yet it's okay—just try to get there eventually.

Positive Reappraisal
The first set of options outlined above is critical for helping transform your suffering into gratitude. This positive reappraisal is an important part of positively reflecting on a difficulty in order to move past it.

Consider this: You would not be where you are if it were not for that event or that suffering. You would not have found the path you have found. You would not have done the things you have done. You would not have the people in your life that you do. Examining your painful events as a catalyst to move you into a different space is a great way to gain perspective on them, accept them, and even be grateful for them.

Self-Talk, Self-Development
I put hypervigilance, dissociation, and amnesia in brackets above because I don't believe you can simply will your way out of those. Those are real cognitive distortions at a deeper, less voluntary or conscious level. I think those will dissipate as you heal, but I don't think you can just make them stop because you want them to. You can reason your way out of them when they happen to you by reassuring yourself that you're safe (hypervigilance) and by reminding yourself that you are part of this world and you are a whole person (dissociation). You don't have to even believe these things as you're telling them to yourself at that moment, but tell yourself anyway. It will help make you feel better and should help pull out of those desperate states of being. In any of these experiences, the first recommendation is to bring your focus to your breath, and breathe slowly and deeply for a few.

Research suggests that a major key to beginning a treatment plan for PTSD includes hobbies, skills, and activities that calm you down and provide a sense of satisfaction and competence. Most people need to feel interpersonal safety to create some sense of inner calm to distinguish between actual current situations, and the roots of current distress having occurred in the past. Fears must be quelled for people to think clearly and become conscious of their current needs. Therefore, we need to develop a body with predictable and controllable reactions to daily stressors, as developing this sense of bodily mastery and competence contradicts and offsets an identity of physical helplessness.

Exposing yourself to situations that create a limited degree of controllable anxiety and include tremendous social support can be most beneficial. These teach you to associate certain anxiety-provoking physical sensations with feelings of mastery, competence, and triumph, either alongside or in place of the traumatic memories.[292]

Reconstructing Your Internal Models

When I was a kid, I fell on the road gravel and gouged my knee. My mother took me to the emergency room. This is what happened:

1. My **wound was visible to everyone**, since blood ran steadily down my leg. I cried from the pain.

To treat it:

2. The doctor **examined the evidence** (blood running down my leg).
3. She **determined the source of the wound** (my left knee).
4. She **examined the wound carefully to determine exactly what was wrong**.
5. She **cleaned the wound**. She scrubbed it with a brush and despite the topical anesthetic, it hurt like crazy. I cried from the pain.
6. She determined **some of the gravel remnants were in too deep and could not be reasonably removed**, so she left them.
7. She stitched it up, **reconstructing** the flesh and skin, making it healthy again.
8. My wound throbbed for a bit. I still cried, but decreasingly with time.

All of this process took place absent emotion. Sure, I cried from the physical pain, and maybe I was a little afraid and had a little anxiety because I was hurt, but I did not get carried away by any emotion.

Our Mental and Emotional Bodies

Our mental and emotional anxieties work the same way. We follow the same set of steps. Watch:

1. Your anxiety **wound is visible to everyone** via your behavior. Everyone in your world can see that you have some hang-up about a certain matter, and I guarantee, no one likes being around it. It is something they must

tolerate and accept if they want to be around you, but no one likes it—they have to tip-toe around it. Sometimes you cry from the pain, even if you aren't aware of its exact source. I will illustrate with an example of wanting to learn to surf. Part of my problem was that I was afraid of the ocean. This fear of the ocean was visible to everyone that wanted to get into the ocean with me, and it was quite annoying to them.

To heal it:

2. **Examine the evidence**. Here, the evidence is your thought patterns and life choices. Look at how you're thinking and the choices you're making. Identify a certain behavior that you find unhealthy and/or anxiety-inducing.
   a. Refer back to Chapter 3 to help you identify the unhealthy patterns in the treatment you receive and accept from others.
   b. Or, identify a particular anxiety. Sometimes these anxieties are constructed completely by ourselves, with no help from anyone else. Other times, these anxieties are constructed in response to a way we were treated, as a coping mechanism. For me with my ocean fear, I noticed that every time I would get into the ocean past a certain thigh-depth, my anxiety level would rise significantly. I could snorkel in the ocean because I could see beneath me, but I couldn't go in very deep water or swim out far from shore. My anxiety at getting into the ocean water was my evidence. I examined that anxiety, and observed when it appeared and what made it worse.
3. **Determine the source of the wound**. Ask yourself, "Why do I do that?" or "Why do I choose that?" or "Why do I allow that?" or "Why do I think that?"
   a. Your wound's source is probably in the way someone treated you. What was that treatment? For me and my fear of the ocean, my father had been in an ocean boating accident when I was a small child; one man died and my dad came close. From this trauma, he feared the ocean from then on out, and I learned this fear from him.
   b. It could also be in your own perceptions of a situation.
4. **Examine the wound to determine exactly what is wrong.** Look deeply at the root of your anxiety. Try to keep your emotions out of it so you can see it clearly and accurately. If you get a little emotional that's fine, but then try to look at it again later absent emotion so you can actually see it.

    a.   What happened to you? How were you treated? This is probably in the way a parent treated you. How was that? What were the specifics of that treatment? What happened, exactly? Recreate as much as you possibly can. For me with my ocean fear example, I recreated what exactly I had been taught: "You don't want to get in too deep or it'll take you away and that'll be the end of you." In 50 F water of the Pacific Ocean, that is not an unreasonable thing to teach a child. But I had also picked up on his tremendous anxiety at the ocean so even in 83 F water, I still carried the fear. It was part of my conditioning.

    b.   Or, what perceptions did you construct for yourself?

5. **Clean the wound**. Consciously decide to take that thought pattern out of your thinking. Say it out loud to yourself. Make it real to yourself. Make it conscious. Recognize the unwellness the wound causes in the form of your mental distortions.

    a.   Consciously and firmly decide you will not tolerate those certain behaviors from others anymore.

    b.   Consciously and firmly decide you will change your way of thinking. In my ocean example, I consciously told myself that it was my father's fear, and I understood his fear based on his traumatic experience (he may even have had some degree of PTSD from that event, now that I think about it, which would further explain the level of anxiety that accompanied his relationship with the ocean). I taught myself more about the ocean's currents and understood at a cognitive level that yes, you can get caught in a rip current and it will pull you out, but you just swim lateral to the ocean to get out of that, or wait until it pulls you out and then cycles you back in. Either way, in water that's 50 degrees Fahrenheit that process can be deadly, but in 83-degree water, you can stay out in the ocean forever without worrying about death by hypothermia. I was in warm water, so my fears were unfounded at a logical level.

6. **Recognize that some traces will not vanish completely**. This isn't magic. You will continue to struggle against the old thought patterns for some time, but eventually, they will all but disappear. Keep working against them. This kind of healing release often happens in layers so maybe on the next go around, you can extricate a deeper layer. Also, the structures you have built are solid, so it's hard to tear them down and replace them. Keep

at it. Personally, I increase my confidence in the ocean every time I get in, but I carried a nagging anxiety in me that "I will get pulled out and that will be the end of me," for years despite facing and confronting it. Then I had to extricate at a deeper layer—I realized my anxiety was also from the ocean's raw power, and that it could kill me if it wanted to by picking me up in a wave and slamming me into the sand, perhaps holding me down there so long I drowned or slamming me so hard my neck or back broke. These things really happen in surfing. So, I had to face that level of the anxiety, which I did by again learning more about the ocean, being careful about depth (definitely don't surf in shallow water), exercising my breathing while out of the water, and letting it toss me around and letting those waves break on my head so I could have that experience and see that I didn't die. After a few years of actively struggling against it, that anxiety has finally vanished.

7. **Reconstruct** your thinking with your desired thoughts. Do not allow yourself to fall back into old (unhealthy) patterns. Consciously decide what you want then talk yourself through it. Mindfulness helps a lot, once again, in facing these anxieties and overcoming them, one breath at a time. Spend some time in this reconstruction if you need to. Write it down. Talk it over with a friend. Your old patterns happened unconsciously; to change them requires conscious, concerted effort. My wounded knee happened in a split second, but to treat it required hours and hours of conscious, concerted effort, including a trip to the emergency room and a team of medical professionals assessing and managing it: Harm occurs in an instant but properly treating it takes a lot of time and effort. As a result of the effort involved to move past it, it's easy to fall back into your old thought patterns—they are so normal for you and those neural pathways are well-established! You must fight against them consistently and consciously. Some of mine I've been working on for years...

    a. In how others treat you, determine how you want to be treated. Write down the traits and characteristics. Then, accept only this sort of treatment. Watch carefully for the behaviors you used to be comfortable with, the ones that harm you. Stay alert. Keep your antennae out. Be gentle with others through the transition, but don't settle for being treated in ways that harm you.

        These new terms of how you will accept being treated will mean that certainly most or possibly all of your relationships will have to change. Your relational partners will resist this change, insisting on continuing to treat you as they always have—this is very comfortable for them! And they do not intend to give up their ways just because you've changed your mind. They will fight to keep you where you were, not allowing you to change the terms of your relationship.

You must be very insistent. You must remember that you are the most important person in your life. You must remember that if you don't take care of yourself, no one will. You must love yourself enough to insist that others treat you well. This will likely mean that some or even many or most of your relationships will have to end. You might have to get a new job. This could easily put a huge crunch on your marriage if this is your situation.

Always put your own well-being first, before the well-being of anyone else—come what may! I don't mean to be selfish here, but rather, take care of yourself first—like the flight attendant instructs us to put on our own oxygen mask before helping others with theirs. Because if you're not right with yourself in this world, it doesn't matter what else is right.

b. In your own thought patterns, use logic to create a reasonable and realistic new structure. For me, I had to tell myself, out loud and repeatedly, "You can do this. If you get pulled out you know what to do. The water is warm and you can stay in it all day. If you need to be rescued, there is more than enough time because hypothermia is not a concern here."

8. Your emotional wound or distorted thought pattern has been freshly cleaned, and your unhealthy thinking pattern reconstructed. This period will be a little wobbly as you transition into your new thought pattern—just as walking was a bit wobbly after having my knee worked on. Stick with it. Be insistent with yourself. It's okay to cry a little to process through this transition. It's important to recognize exactly what happened to you in its entirety. The more details you can recall, the more you can extricate those unhealthy roots; you simply consciously decide to think differently, and then do it.

That's the Magic

And that, my friends, is how it is done. One by one, brick by brick, anxieties are quelled and essentially vanish. It's not such a big deal really. Do this with one anxiety, feel a little better. Do this with a lot of anxieties, feel a lot better.

This conscious reconstruction is a vital part of your removing your anxieties. You absolutely must look honestly and carefully at the roots of your anxieties and you absolutely must make a conscious decision to think differently. You can do this absent emotion, and in fact the less emotion you bring to this process, the more effective you will be. Don't feel bad. Don't feel guilty. Don't feel stupid. Also, try not to be too angry, or too sad, and definitely don't be afraid because you're not in that difficult physical place anymore. You are rebuilding your internal models. You are taking your life into your own hands. You are not letting anyone else control your life or your choices by the damage they did to you as a kid. In this process, you are trading out anxiety-inducing bricks for bricks of tranquility, acceptance, and personal power. Yay you!

The Power is in Your Hands

Don't allow how others treated you as a kid govern your whole life. Don't give your abusers that kind of power. Maybe they would be pleased with themselves at the extent of the damage, destruction, and control they brought to your psyche and your life, or maybe they would feel bad, but that's not relevant or important at all. What is important is that you take your life back! You take control of your own life. From here on out, you consciously decide to think differently, to live differently— in a way that you want to live. You decide what is right for you. Now you really are in the driver's seat of your own life!

Face your fears absolutely. Start with the smaller stuff and work your way into the larger issues. Even the smaller stuff brings anxiety to your daily life so as you shed those smaller anxieties, you are stronger and better equipped to take on the larger items. You're also more practiced. It feels so good to eliminate anxieties! They are what's holding you back!

Identify as many of these items as you possibly can in your life, one at a time. Every single one of them brings you some degree of anxiety and contributes to your core of anxiety. Take your time. Don't try to take on too many at once. You have nothing but time! Give each piece the time it needs and process it carefully and thoroughly. The more of these items you can work through and thus eliminate, the calmer your core and the healthier you become. With every single transformation, you will feel a little bit better. This adds up! With a lot of these transformations, you will feel a whole lot better!

This is the path to mental wellness! Welcome!

Or, the Infection Spreads

As a kid, if I had not gone to the doctor with my bleeding knee and had it cleaned and treated, the wound would have gotten infected. The infection would have grown. The wound would have gotten bigger. The damage would have eventually taken over my leg, interfering with every single step I took for the rest of my life and if still untreated, I would have died from it. It would not have gone away all by itself.

Our mental health is similar. There's no blood to indicate the source of the wound, but the wound is most definitely there and evident to others via our behavior, whether we want to admit that to ourselves or not. If we leave it untreated, it will fester with infection and that infection will eke into all areas of our lives, interfering with our well-being in every moment of every day with the general anxiety and specific distorted thinking and behavior the wound brings us. This stuff does not go away by itself. If left untreated, indeed, it can consume our lives, and it can even kill us—either directly, through suicide, or indirectly, through disease and self-mis-treatment.

It's not a big deal to treat our internal wounds. Looking at that stuff is about as much fun as having your fresh wound scrubbed with a stiff brush, okay. But the cleansing is necessary, just like with a gouge in the knee. If you don't treat it, you will continue to suffer from those wounds every day in large and small ways, and worse, you will continue to make your loved ones suffer right along with you. That is so not worth it. On the other hand, taking a few uncomfortable moments to examine your internal wounds and scrub them clean will benefit the rest of your life in ways large and small. Your experiences will be so much more pleasurable and joyful once you extricate that infection from your psyche. Your peace with yourself and your life will take on whole new dimensions. And that, my friends, is definitely worth it.

It's On You Now

What happened to you as a kid was not your fault and it was not okay. You did not ask for that treatment and you did not deserve it. But it happened. You had no choice. The choices you make now *are* on you because today, you have other options. As a kid, you didn't.

Straighten out your thinking about what happened to you a long time ago. Then, take a look at the adult choices you're making as a result. See the connections. Let your present challenges and struggles lend insight to what you endured as a kid— you're exposing yourself to the same kinds of poor treatment now but today, with your adult brain, you can see that poor treatment if you're willing to take a look. Admit the cognitive distortions you have about your past and about your present situations. Today's unhealthy choices do not make you a loser so do not beat yourself up *at all*. Just be honest and take a look at what you're doing. To heal the present, you have to gain a healthy perspective on the past.

Maneuvering Through

Try to view these events and behaviors as factual occurrences, nothing more. Be willing to see your truth with a fair and objective perspective. Try to take your emotions out of the equation so you can gain a more objective viewpoint on the events that transpired and process them rationally. Eventually, as you work through, try to remember as much as you can so you can get the fullest picture you can and understand it as deeply as you can so you can gain the best and deepest understanding of yourself possible.

Look at it all as if it happened to someone else, not you. Look at the facts, as an outsider would. See what you did, see what your abuser(s) did. See how you were manipulated. See how you didn't ask for any of it. See that it was not your fault and you did not deserve it. Consider the issues you have today as a direct result of their behavior back then. Your ultimate goal is to find peace with those events. Stop feeling angry. Stop feeling hurt. Stop feeling fear. Stop feeling anything at all for those events. They just happened. You need to admit them honestly and understand their role in your life. That is all.

Be careful not to shift into other-blame. Instead, try to see the events through the eyes of your abuser(s). I'm not saying with compassion, yet, but merely for perspective-gaining. Chances are, they themselves were so sick that they had no idea of the kind of pain they were inflicting or damage they were doing to your young psyche and soul. I'm not saying excuse or even forgive their behavior at this point— just look at it objectively. Gain this perspective. It will help you move forward in a healthy way.

At the same time as you don't shift into other-blame, it's important to gain an objective perspective on the events of your life so that you can understand them for yourself and process them, eventually putting them to rest. Part of this is assigning responsibility where it rightfully belongs. If you have hang-ups as an adult that you can trace directly to your childhood, this becomes surely the fault of your parents—it wasn't yours! This might sound like other-blame, but the difference is that in assigning responsibility, you are just looking to make sense of what happened to you. But you retain a full recognition that the matter rests entirely in your hands to resolve. You don't get to blame other people for your problems—even if that blame is actually warranted. You have to take full responsibility for your own problem resolution, and blaming someone else, like your parents, relinquishes the responsibility you must take on for yourself in this process. That's why you don't blame them. Instead, you assign responsibility as a way of understanding the whole scenario about what you endured, and identifying the roots of your problems. If you cannot identify the root, you cannot fully extricate the issue.

You're building new mental structures when you intentionally pull your mind out of one sort of destructive thinking pattern and put it into a constructive thinking pattern. You need this. The structures that were made for you as a child are harming you, every day and in many ways. This intentional refocusing helps you build new, healthy structures that will allow for and sustain your well-being. This is where you are going.

Let It Come Out
It's important that you not tamp anything down. Stuff will come up for you because that's your subconscious telling you to look at it. It needs attention because it needs your acceptance. With your acceptance you can move past it, but not before. Avoid the temptation to just always think about other things—a diversion tactic—when something begins to gnaw at you.

Let it come out. If you need to take a couple of days off of work to let it come, do so. Take care of yourself. Don't let it come out in ways that overwhelm you, but let it come out in manageable ways. If you need to feel sad for a few days, let yourself do that. If you need to cry for a while, that's okay. Crying is a tremendous release and we often need it for healing to occur—just don't keep crying over the same events, because that is a waste of your good energy and you're not getting anywhere.

Maybe you need to isolate for a bit, or even take a few days out in nature, in your happy place. Do whatever you feel you need to do to help this ugliness inside of you come out. Be willing to look at it. Be willing to see it. Be willing to admit it. Be willing to admit what happened to you and how it made you feel. Be willing to admit all of the pains and struggles you've had in your life because of this event or situation. Look at the whole picture. Look at it as completely as you possibly can.

Again, stay out of self-blame and other-blame, and stay in healthy reflection. Don't go down any catastrophic mental roads—keep your thoughts on the event and try to keep your emotions low. Let the trauma surface, slowly, so you can heal from it.

If it does not surface, it will haunt you and every aspect of your life until it does. Take care of yourself.

Once you can talk about the event without any emotion arising in you, you're past it—but not before. As long as you feel a tug or pain or fear or anger inside of you, you're not done with it yet and it still has a hold on you. Keep looking at it, processing it, reflecting on it until you feel nothing for it, until you can talk about it openly and just as easily as you can talk about what you did last weekend, or like it could have been someone else's experience. You want to have complete internal quiet when you talk about it—no emotional arousal at all. People look at you in horror when you tell them, say they're sorry you had to endure something so awful, and you shrug your shoulders. *Whatever*. It's just part of your story, just like a lot of other parts of your story that made you who you are, like how many siblings you have and where you went to school. That's where you're headed.

I'm sorry—you simply cannot heal completely from your childhood mistreatment if you don't acknowledge it and accept it. You don't have to do it all at once, nor should you. Take your time. Some issues, such as sexual abuse, can take years to fully work through. But that's okay—just go one piece at a time. It's not like you're going anywhere or have anything more important to do...

Giving it Time
This reflective processing will take some time—it won't happen in the next five minutes or the next five months. Give yourself time and love yourself enough to process those events honestly and compassionately for yourself and maybe even for your perpetrator if appropriate. Take your time. There is no rush.

Process one piece at a time, as you are comfortable. As you notice an anxiety surface in yourself, especially a small one, think about it for a bit and try to find its root so you can quell it. If you feel overwhelmed, stop. If thinking about this stuff gives you so much anxiety you start to physically shake, definitely stop. Give it some time. Think about other things. Look at the smaller stuff.

Start with the 1-pound weights—a lot of them—instead of the 1000-pound weights and slowly build strength to take on the bigger stuff. If you come at the bigger events again later and still feel overwhelmed or confused, find a professional to bounce it off of and help you sort through it. There are millions of mental health professionals just waiting for us to call and ask for help.

There is no shame in getting help—it's like taking piano lessons or Portuguese classes—you recognize that you want a little guidance to make sure you're spending your efforts wisely and heading in the right direction rather than trying to figure it all out all by yourself. When we didn't have proper models for healthy thinking and behavior, we can't really figure out what that looks like all on our own and sometimes we just need a little help to see the picture more clearly. It takes a lot of courage to ask for help and rather than showing weakness, you show tremendous strength in having the courage to admit when you need help and asking for it. Don't be afraid, and definitely don't be ashamed. Be proud that you are taking care of yourself and straightening things out. Getting help is an act of self-love.

Over time, this processing gets much easier. You also get stronger. The more you heal, the easier this processing gets.

Digging it Out
The information presented in Section I should give you a lot of insight to your struggles. As we saw, even if our mother was just emotionally unavailable—even just that!—we have some bona fide stuff to straighten out. If abuse was part of the picture on top of that emotional neglect, there's quite a lot to untangle.

Possibly, armed with the information in Chapter 3 about neglectful and abusive behaviors, you can even see your abuser(s)'s individual behaviors as part of some larger attempt to control and manipulate you. Maybe you can even see your own behaviors in the lists provided there which means, you have some real work to do. But that's okay. What else are you going to do? Might as well improve yourself so you can have a better life and influence those around you to have a better life as well.

Keep Your Eye on the Prize

The work you have to do is time-consuming, but it does not have to be that difficult or painful really. Remember that you love yourself and you want so much to be healthy on all planes. You want to feel better about yourself, your life, your loves, and everything else. Remind yourself that the troubled experiences of your child-hood do not get to own the rest of your life and control your whole life and every-thing in it. Inner peace and self-love are definitely worth the sometimes arduous path to reaching those destinations.

You will conquer that stuff. You want to get through the day in peace and serenity, wearing a genuine smile all the time. You want the internal turbulence and the mental and emotional suffering to stop! You can get there. Take your time. Gently persevere.

Psychology Science for Healing

Moving past traumatic events or lifestyles and genuinely healing from them is no small task. This never happens all by itself. Your psyche doesn't heal itself magically like a rash or a broken bone. You have to give your internal healing some pointed attention. This subsection presents some of what science has found helps people move through PTSD to find peace.

Common psychological approaches to treating PTSD include cognitive behavioral therapy and phase-oriented treatment. These approaches have had a good deal of success with PTSD sufferers who developed the condition as a result of a wide va-riety of traumas. Some treatment modalities include addressing the underlying fear structures which the PTSD is situated on, or identifying and working through your base fears such as lack of feeling safe.

The currently common psychological treatments for victims of childhood abuse in-clude:

- Cognitive-Behavioral Therapy (CBT)
  - Useful for treating those with depressive rumination; also includes sub-forms of CBT including: Behavioral Activation, Rumination-fo-cused CBT, and Mindfulness-based CBT
- Cognitive Therapy
  - Effective for trauma-related guilt and faulty thinking, common in abused individuals

- Relaxation Training
- Skills Training
- Self-protection Training
- Parent Training (to be non-abusive parents)

The goals of all of these various treatment modalities for abused people include:

- Helping the individual better relate to others and form healthy attachments
- Helping the individual develop better coping strategies for traumatic events and environmental stressors
- Allowing the individual to develop necessary skills for expressing their feelings and opening up about their emotional experiences
- Helping the individual develop and maintain necessary skills for managing painful experiences and minimizing negative emotional defense mechanisms, including withdrawal and dissociation
- Allowing the individual to speak about their traumatic experiences without shame or guilt, and release the anxiety related to the abuse
- Helping the individual identify and remove cognitive distortions and faulty thinking
- Helping the individual reduce intensity and frequency of negative emotional symptoms arising from the abusive history

The treatments vary in their approaches to achieving these goals.

In other words, seeing a psychologist can help in this area. But I will leave further exploration of these psychological approaches to the professionals in this field.

PTSD Recovery
Another important technique to recover from PTSD includes vocalizing your daily experiences, emotions, and observations. Putting this into words helps create emotional distance from the trauma and allows observation from a variety of analytical viewpoints. When you don't communicate these stressors, that leads to emotional isolation, which is a sense of being forsaken and no longer part of the human race. But feeling understood and amplifying that you know and understand about your experiences by communicating them with others (usually a therapist, but not necessarily) is joyful, peace-bringing, and above all, healing.[292]

Some research says that in order to reduce fear, and therefore treat the PTSD, you have to do two things. First, you have to attend to the trauma-related information in a way that activates your own traumatic memories. This means that you have to put yourself in situations that are similar to or otherwise remind you of the traumatic experiences you had. Second, the context of that intentional environment needs to directly contradict key components of the trauma—you have to feel safe. Your ability to decrease the fear or anxiety associated with PTSD depends on evoking, in a controlled and coordinated manner, three things: the trauma-related cues in the environment, meaning that the new environment has to resemble the trauma-inducing environment in some ways; the sensory and motor responses, meaning you have to feel and act in similar ways as the trauma-inducing event caused you to feel and act; and the meaning of the traumatic memory, meaning you have to be able to better understand the trauma-inducing event and its impact on you. In this way, you have to be re-exposed to an experience with components similar enough to the trauma to activate it while at the same time, dissimilar enough to change it.[292] Perhaps for the reasons articulated here, martial arts training is very effective for resolving PTSD, especially that with an interpersonal violence base.

The Healing is Yours
I am not a psychologist, and I don't know a lot about these methods or what psychologists can do for you to help you heal from traumas in your past. I do know that psychology science is rich in the area of PTSD treatment, so if you would like to work with a mental health practitioner to help you resolve these issues, they should have a plethora of tried-and-true resources available to them.

I would also suggest that you never place the full responsibility for your healing in the hands of an educated stranger. Your healing is your own journey, and you and you alone are responsible for it. Indeed, visit a mental health practitioner if the little voice within you is telling you to do so—just don't expect that alone to be the magic that makes the pain go away. You have to do work in the other areas of your life as well, and that is all on you.

Building Your Self-esteem
The methods presented in this entire section, except for the very last part, come from the work of psychologist Nathanial Branden.[379] I find it exceptionally insightful and poignant as self-esteem development, so I share it with you here.

Self-esteem is comprised of two parts: self-confidence, and self-respect. This chapter subsection helps build all three of these areas.

What Self-esteem is
Self-esteem is about your relationship with yourself. It is how you feel about yourself and how you perceive yourself. It is your self-identity.

When we were raised in difficult homes, we were taught that we are not ever good enough. We fall short in countless ways, and are full of flaws. Well, this may be true in that we are all human beings, but being mistreated as kids, we get this message more strongly than most, and our lives are affected in detrimental ways because of the impacts of this message.

Our self-esteem affects everything we do in our lives. It influences how we interact with others. It exacerbates our basic human needs for control, inclusion, and affection—the needs to have control over our lives, to be included in the lives of others, and to receive reassurance that we are loved and accepted. The lower our self-esteem, the higher these needs. We all know people with very low self-esteem—they are the so-called control freaks among us, the "needy" ones, who always have to be in everyone else's business and need constant ego stroking. We also know that these people are not easy to be around. This is one way that low self-esteem influences our relationships with others.

Our self-esteem also influences the kinds of jobs we accept and the kinds of companies we work for, and the kinds of treatment we are comfortable subjecting ourselves to. The lower our self-esteem, the less respect we are comfortable with receiving at work. Also, the more comfortable we are with not advancing. In fact, we might even place our own blocks in our way, perceiving only positions up to a certain level available to us; the higher, more esteemed, more lucrative positions are simply out of our reach.

Our self-esteem also determines the kinds of personal relationships we choose and the treatment we are comfortable receiving. The lower our self-esteem, the less respect we are comfortable receiving.

Self-esteem is self-reflective in the company we seek. That is, we tend to seek the company of others that treat us in ways that reinforce our current self-esteem level. This is because our self-esteem level is our own self-identity. So, we choose to be around people who see us like we see ourselves. When this self-view is at low levels, we choose to be around those who perceive us at those same low levels.

This makes us comfortable—even if these environments themselves actually make us relatively uncomfortable due to the treatment we receive within them. This phenomenon also makes it really difficult to move past our current levels of self-esteem; it's hard and sometimes scary to grow beyond our known environments and relationships.

As your self-esteem grows and improves, you as an individual also grow and improve. Suddenly you see new doors open to you that you previously perceived as unavailable options. You seek the company of people who treat you better, with more respect. You have more respect for yourself, and this shows in how you conduct yourself in your affairs. This in itself opens more doors for you.

There are no drawbacks to improving your self-esteem, only benefits. You only have to make a few internal adjustments to help you grow in this way.

The Approach

This section presents some of Dr. Branden's ideas on how to improve your self-esteem. He has developed sets of exercises to accompany these ways of thinking, and out of respect for him and his intellectual property, I do not include them here. Instead, I refer you to his book *How to Raise Your Self-Esteem: The Proven Action-Oriented Approach to Greater Self-Respect and Self-Confidence*. You will find everything you need there. The book includes sentence-completion exercises where you complete a series of question beginnings with the first tail that comes to mind, and you do this with the same question beginnings several times on different days over a period of time. Examples of his question beginnings include "I treat myself like my father treated my 5-year old self when I …" or "If I were to listen to the things that child needs to tell me, I…" Dr. Branden lays out a complete set of exercises for developing each area and I can honestly say, the more of his exercises you do in the way he recommends, the better you feel.

I strongly urge you to do the exercises and to do them completely. The more of these exercises you do, the more your self-esteem will grow. The higher your self-esteem, the more benefits you will see to your life. Your anxiety will reduce, relationships improve, and professional opportunities increase. Feeling better about yourself is quite possibly one of the very best feelings on earth! And one of the richest gifts you can give to yourself. Construct a new structure for your self-perception, and let it be a rich, full, powerful and positive one. Love yourself enough to develop a better version of you.

Self-acceptance

As people, we are all complex beings. There are many sides to us, and this is part of what makes each of us unique. We each have our own memories, thoughts, emotions, actions, physical characteristics, and subpersonalities.

Each person is our own unique combination of these many parts of ourselves. If we want to build self-confidence and self-esteem, we have to accept each and every part of ourselves—all of our physical characteristics, all of our subpersonalities, all of our behaviors and actions, and all of our emotions and thoughts.

Accepting and liking are two different things. Just because you accept something doesn't mean you like it or that you even have to like it. It just means that you accept it. Acceptance is neutral. It's without judgment. To build your confidence and self-esteem, this is what you have to do with all parts of yourself.

For example, maybe you don't really like the way you behave in certain situations. Maybe you don't manage your anger well, and you don't like that part of yourself very much. So you distance yourself from that part of yourself. You just don't ever think about it because thinking about it makes it real, and you don't want it to be real. You don't want that to be the way you actually are. You pretend it's not there. But it is the way you are. And if you want to build your confidence and self-esteem, you have to accept that that is the way you are. If you don't like that part of yourself very much, okay. Maybe you can change it. But at this point we're not talking about liking all parts of yourself or changing them: just accepting them.

So, the first thing you have to do to build your confidence and self-esteem is accept all parts of yourself. Accept all of your truths—your physical characteristics, actions and behaviors, thoughts, emotions, memories, and all of your personalities.

Own your virtues and assets, unapologetically

Some of us are really good at some things. We just are. We were given certain gifts. This might be beauty or attractiveness, a good ability to make a lot of money easily, a particular talent in art or sports, or maybe high intellect. Whatever it is, some of us just have more than others in our lives.

Sometimes these gifts of ours make other people feel uncomfortable, so they might try to make us feel bad for this. They might put us down or attack us. So to make it easier on ourselves, we just stop ourselves from exercising that talent or ability somehow. We ignore it within ourselves. We pretend it's not there. When we deny this strong part of ourselves it makes other people more comfortable with us, which means they attack us less, so that makes life easier and more peaceful for us.

When we're good at something, it's pretty easy to self-sabotage. Because when you're on top, you have a lot of haters. So to avoid walking around with a target on your back, it's just a lot easier to stop being so good at that thing. The problem is that when you do that, you betray your self. You undermine your self-confidence. To build self-acceptance, you need to accept all parts of yourself. You cannot accept all parts of yourself if you're pretending some part of yourself isn't there, even if it's a good part.

Part of self-acceptance means accepting all of these parts of yourself too—even your best qualities. Accepting these parts of yourself means not apologizing for them or pretending they don't exist. You've got to integrate them into your life and enjoy them fully.

So, a very important part of self-acceptance is accepting all of your gifts and virtues unapologetically.

Integrate fractured aspects of yourself

In addition to accepting your strengths and particular gifts, you also have to accept the parts of yourself that you've pretended don't exist because you don't like them.

We've all done things we're not proud of—all of us. This is part of being human. We've all done things that we know were not right. We know we hurt people. We know we broke the rules. We know we embarrassed ourselves and maybe even others too. As a result, what we tend to do sometimes is to pretend that thing never happened. We don't think about it and when others bring it up we deftly change the subject. We don't want to think about it, we don't want to talk about it, and we definitely don't want to hear about it. Sound familiar?

For some of us, there was a period or maybe even a couple of periods in our lives that we're not proud of and we wish never happened. Maybe we were a terribly snotty teenager, or addicted to something like drugs or gambling or sex with strangers, or maybe we were an abused child or in an abusive adult relationship, or maybe we spent time in jail. Whatever situation we were in, we don't like to think about it. So in our minds, we divorce ourselves from that period. We fracture it off. We intentionally ignore it.

no one's looking, letting other people pick up the slack that you leave. Or maybe people find your behavior uncomfortable sometimes because they say you're irrational. If this is you, if you are the person breaking these moral codes, you will not have strong self-respect, self-confidence, or self-esteem.

So the next thing you have to do to improve your relationship with yourself is to be someone who you respect. Be a person of your word. Treat others like you want to be treated. Don't flip out on people or make random rules for other people to follow just because those rules are more convenient for you. Treat others fairly.

Be the kind of person that you respect. Behave in ways that you respect. If you wouldn't tolerate a certain behavior in others, definitely don't let yourself behave that way. Conduct yourself with integrity, honesty, and rationality at all times. When you do, you will gain self-respect, which will increase your self-confidence and your self-esteem.

Live consciously—accept uncomfortable truths
Each of us has a choice: Do we want to live fully awake and conscious, or do we want to live in a cloud? Living in a cloud means that you simply don't see certain truths that are uncomfortable for you or inconvenient if you admit them, which is definitely a lot easier and a lot more comfortable—ignorance is bliss, right?

For example, appropriate to this book, let's say your mom or dad has a mental illness. And in that mental illness, this parent is really irrational sometimes and mistreats people, because mental illness does that to you. You have two little kids and you want to go away for the weekend without bringing the kids. If you are awake and not living in a cloud, you know you can't leave your kids with your unstable parent. The kids might get hurt. So with that option off the table, you have to find other childcare. And maybe you can't find other childcare or it's very expensive, which means you can't go away for the weekend without the kids. You can't do what you want. This is very inconvenient for you. But on the other hand, if you're living in a cloud, you don't have to see your parent's mental illness. You don't see the damage it does. You don't see the mental illness so you don't see that you're putting your kids in harm's way when they're with your ill parent. So, you feel just fine leaving your kids in that person's care. You get your weekend away. This is very convenient for you. Whenever someone says "hey aren't you afraid your unstable parent will hurt your kids?" you respond with "what unstable parent? My parents are fine. They take good care of my kids."

217

This is what I mean by living in a cloud or living fully awake. Are you willing to look at the reality of your life and the people in it? Or do you choose to sugar-coat everything, and pretend that everyone and everything in your life is just fine?

Some kids actually wake up in their childhood. They're taught not to lie, but then they're confused because they see the adults in their lives lie all the time. Kids who live in a cloud don't notice the adults in their lives lying.

If you want to improve your confidence and self-esteem, you have to take an honest look at the reality of your life. Does someone close to you have a mental illness or addiction of some sort? Do they have trouble managing their anger? Are they verbally or physically violent? Are they excessively manipulative?

There are a lot of people in this world who live their whole lives in a cloud. They refuse to see their own reality. Then they're actually surprised when something goes bad because they didn't see it coming. They didn't see it coming because they weren't paying any attention. They were sugar-coating things, pretending everything was fine, because that was a lot easier and more comfortable than the actual truth. These people seem to have bad things happening to them. Is it really bad luck? Maybe. Or maybe they're just not paying any attention to where they're going in life. They're just bobbling along, assuming everything will be just fine. They they're surprised when something bad happens to them.

But if you're awake in your life, if you're living your life consciously, you admit the shortcomings of those people in your life. Maybe you continue your relationship with them anyway, but you don't pretend these faults aren't there. If your wife has an anger problem, you don't pretend she doesn't. You admit it and accept it, and then maybe try to do something about it, but what's most important here is admitting it and accepting it.

If you're awake in your life, you're thinking and speaking for yourself. You're not just repeating what you heard on the news or what your neighbor said. You're assessing situations for yourself and developing your own opinions toward them. You're speaking your own truths. Sure, we get our information from others, but then if we're awake in our lives, we're processing this information on our own—in our own minds, for ourselves. We're not just repeating what we were taught because we like the source and rejecting things said by people we don't like, whether it be from our parents or teachers or political or religious leaders. We're thinking about things and drawing our own conclusions. This is a very important part of living your life consciously.

If you're awake in your life but everyone else in your family is living in a cloud, you're seeing realities that they refuse to. This means you're not seeing eye-to-eye. The realities that you see threaten their illusion. This might make them very uncomfortable—with you! Because you're pointing out realities that they have very successfully hidden from for a long time. They don't want to see these realities. These realities are very uncomfortable and very inconvenient to the version of reality they have constructed for themselves. So what I'm getting at here, is that it's very possible that your family will alienate you if you're awake and they're living in a cloud. This is actually more common than you might think. You see, if you're going to represent uncomfortable truths, then cutting you out of their lives is a lot easier for them than accepting you with the uncomfortable truths you represent.

Of course, this is a sad outcome. But it's also no reason to sacrifice yourself. If you have to choose between succumbing to their illusion or holding fast in your truth, you should always choose your truth. Self-respect demands this. And you can't build strong self-confidence if you're lying to yourself.

Pay attention to your life. Look under the surface just a little. What are the areas to watch out for? Also, think about the things people have taught you and the information you've received. Actually think about it, on your own. Use your brain. And develop your own insights and perspectives. Don't just follow the crowd because it's convenient and everyone else does. *Think.*

We are responsible for our existence, our choices, our feelings and emotions, our behaviors
It's important to recognize that we and we alone are responsible for ourselves. We are responsible for our feelings and emotions. We are responsible for our thoughts. We are responsible for our choices. We are responsible for our behaviors. We are responsible for the situations we find ourselves in. We and only we are responsible for ourselves. As adults, no one else is responsible for us.

In building our confidence and self-esteem, we admit our humanness. That is, we admit that we make mistakes, just like everyone else does. And when we make those mistakes, we don't try to escape blame or responsibility. We admit we messed up. We own up to our part in them. We take responsibility for our part. We also take responsibility for trying to make it right.

We are completely responsible for ourselves. So when something goes wrong in our life, we don't try to blame other people or the situation or say it was just bad luck. We lost the game because we played poorly together, not because our star player was sick or the field was too wet or the referee was biased. We lost the game because we didn't play well enough to win. No other reason. We take responsibility for this loss and try harder next time. We don't blame someone or something else for our failures and shortcomings.

When a relationship turns bad, we look at it carefully and try to see what we missed. What were the red flags that we chose to ignore? When we feel bad for some reason we don't blame others for making us feel that way. Instead, we look into ourselves to better understand what makes us feel this way, and try to heal it. When we mess up and make a mistake or misjudge someone or something, we admit that. We don't try to make other people responsible for our errors or mis-judgments. We again ask ourselves what we missed and reassess the situation. We take full responsibility for our feelings and emotions, our experiences, our thoughts, our relationships, and our situations. We and we alone are responsible for what happens to us. If we develop a so-called lifestyle disease, such as heart disease, diabetes, Chron's, etc., we don't just blame the culture we live in and ex-pect our doctors to magically make us well. We look honestly at our own eating and lifestyle habits. We take responsibility for ourselves.

You are completely responsible for your existence and everything in it. You are completely responsible for all of your choices and for everything in your life. Of course, that's not to say that sometimes things don't just happen to us, because that happens too sometimes. But the steps leading up to that event and how you respond to it are 100% your responsibility. No one else is responsible for how you feel, or what you think, or what you experience, or your physical health. You and you alone bear full responsibility for your own life.

You have to make your choices responsibly. You have to look before you leap. Or, the Italian version of that is to look at your plate before you eat. I personally prefer the Italian version because I can't imagine eating a plate of food without looking to see what I'm putting into my mouth! All of your decisions in your life need to follow the same conscious protocols. You have to look at your options and consciously decide that you want to experience something. You have to pay attention to where you're going, because you and only you are responsible for your own life's journey.

Once you understand and embrace this idea of full responsibility for yourself, you are much closer to realizing strong self-confidence and self-respect.

Live authentically
Living authentically is an important point for improving your relationship with yourself as it is about honoring your own wishes and needs.

When we're living authentically, we are honoring our own truths. We don't pretend to like something when we don't. We don't pretend to agree when we strongly disagree. We don't go along with the crowd when that means we compromise our own values and beliefs.

I don't mean we run around spouting our truths all the time, come what may. I'm not saying we run around arguing with people whenever they say something we disagree with. What I am saying is that we are true to ourselves. We can still be polite—and indeed we should be polite, as that's a very important part of us believing in ourselves and believing we are good people. We just don't betray ourselves. We don't lie about what we think or feel. We don't pretend to be someone we're not. When we do this, we betray ourselves and undermine our confidence and self-esteem.

You might be getting the impression by now that having strong self-esteem and strong self-confidence may not make you the most popular person in the room. People don't always like people who see the world differently than they do. But as previously noted, when you have to choose between being true to yourself and going along with the crowd, strong self-esteem and confidence demand that you choose your own truth every time. You have to be true to yourself. You have to stand for your own principles. I'm not saying you have to stand alone in your principles because again, you should be polite. Just don't pretend to support something that you don't.

This is what it means to live authentically.

Appropriately assess our own behavior
This point involves knowing yourself. It's about knowing your own values and priorities, and seeing that line between your own values and priorities and other people's.

When we are living our life with confidence and strong self-esteem, we are clear in our own beliefs. We know what we think and believe and we know why we think it and believe it. We can see the line between our own perspectives and the perspectives of others, which we feel obliged to follow.

Let me illustrate this with an example. Let's say you were raised with a strongly conservative perspective toward behavior. You were taught that sex comes after marriage, abortion is wrong, drugs are wrong, homosexuality is wrong, and interracial marriage is wrong. So you go through your whole life promoting these ideals. You never question them. You have been taught them since you were a little kid, everyone in your life promotes these ideas, and so you believe this is the right way to live life—not only your own life, but you believe everyone should live their lives according to these standards, and you judge people by these standards. When you see same-sex couples or interracial couples, you frown and sort of glare at them, letting them know you disapprove of their "immoral" behavior. When you see women's health clinics you frown, because you know they take care of women who have sex before marriage and who get abortions. You believe these clinics to be immoral and supportive of immoral behavior. You've never really given any thought to your positions. You just promote these ideals because this is what you've been taught is right.

Then one day you observe a mixed-race family in the park. And at first you frown and glare at them like you usually do. But you keep watching and pretty soon you see how happy they are together. They're laughing and playing and having a great time. They're sharing love and affection and joy. You look around and notice a same-sex couple with small children, again seeming very happy. They're also laughing together and sharing love and joy. So you start to think, how can this be so wrong if they look so happy? Or how can they be so happy if what they're doing is so wrong? So you start thinking a little about what's more important—allowing other people to make their own life choices and be happy, or trying to force others to do what you think is right for their lives. And you begin to assess what you believe for yourself, and separate your own beliefs from what you've been taught.

This is the moment I'm talking about—when you question what you have been taught and what you blindly believe, and when you begin to see a difference between what you actually believe and what you were taught is right.

Building confidence and self-esteem means you're aware of this disconnect. You're aware that the standards you use to judge others are your own standards, not the standards of other people that you've been taught to enforce. You figure out which judgments are actually yours, and which ones you learned and feel obligated to follow. This deeper knowing of yourself is an important part of building strong confidence and self-esteem.

Know your truth

We make judgments about human behavior. We judge ourselves, and we judge others. When we make these judgments, it's important to make them with compassion and honesty.

Let's look at an example. Maybe you see a married man you know out with a woman not his wife at your favorite restaurant. They are very flirty and touchy and it looks like they're well on their way to sex. You have jumped to the conclusion that he's cheating on his wife. Your judgment about cheating men kicks in and you judge him harshly. You get all offended and maybe send him a disapproving look or somehow let him know that you see him and what he is doing, and you do not approve. You're also offended that he's doing this right there in public, in your favorite restaurant, for the whole world to see.

So it looks like he's violating one of your strong moral codes and so you feel appropriate in letting him know he's out of line. Here's the thing: The truth is, you have no idea what's going on in his life—none. Maybe he and his wife recently separated. Maybe they decided to open up their marriage and see other people. Maybe the wife doesn't want sex so she gave him permission to explore. Maybe the woman's a long-lost cousin who just happens to be very affectionate and flirtatious. Who knows? You're offended that he's there in your favorite restaurant, okay. Well, it does have the best food in town, and it is the nicest place to meet someone, and it is really easy to find and very conveniently located. So there could be lots of explanations for his behavior, and lots of reasons he picked this restaurant.

When we are judging our own behavior or the behavior of others, we need to keep in mind that things are rarely what they appear. There could be a hundred explanations for what you saw, and the actual truth might not even have crossed your mind in those hundred possibilities. The actual truth could be any of the explanations I offered a minute ago or something you didn't even think of. It's important to remember this when we are judging the behavior of others.

When we are judging our own behaviors, we need to keep the same sort of open, accepting mind. We might know the truth of our own behaviors in ways that we don't know the truth of others' behaviors, sure. But in knowing that truth of our own it can be very easy to be really hard on ourselves when we violate our own principles. But when we do, we have to show ourselves the same compassion and open-mindedness that we show in judging others' behaviors. We have to remember that our behavior occurred within a certain context, and that situation offered only a limited set of options at the time. We did what we thought was best at the time, given what we had available to us at that time. And we are gentle in self-judgment.

It's important to be honest in our judgments of behavior, whether our own or someone else's. If we see something we don't like, it's important to recognize that that behavior might violate our own code of ethics. But it's equally important to recognize that things are very often not what they appear. And actions and behaviors need to be judged with compassion and open-mindedness.

Live benevolently
Part of building your own self-respect is to build other-respect. In other words, you respect the rights of other people to do what they want with their own lives. You don't impose your own moral codes on other people and expect them to live by your values. Instead, you respect that they have their own moral codes and that they have the right to live by their own values.

This can be hard to do. It's not always easy to watch other people behave in ways that you believe to be morally wrong. As an example, I eat a plant-based diet. And I eat plant-based for moral, social responsibility reasons, because an animal diet contributes to all kinds of global problems—deforestation and resource depletion, world hunger, global warming, and trash buildup, and the animal food industry brings a lot of exploitation and suffering to all of the animals and the humans involved. To me, eating animals is just wrong, and for a lot of reasons. And I believe this very strongly. But just about everyone I know eats an animal-based diet. I certainly cannot go around to every meat and egg eater I see and tell them that their dietary behavior is immoral and wrong, and that by eating that steak and lobster they're contributing to a lot of the world's biggest problems. I don't get to do that. I order my food and keep my thoughts to myself. I have to respect their choices to eat animals, just as I expect them to respect my choices to eat only plants and not pressure me to eat animals.

Living benevolently means we let others be. We understand that everyone has the right to make his and her own choices for their own lives, and we respect their right to make those choices for themselves. My values don't work for everyone. Their values don't work for me. And that's okay. What is important is that we all respect each other's rights to live our lives as we please.

When we stop trying to make others conform to our own values, that tension in our minds disappears. We are much more at peace when we let others be. We aren't putting our precious energy into senseless battles.

I'm not saying we don't try to right the wrongs of the world. When we see abuses or violations of law and human decency, we can step in. But on a daily basis, we leave others to live their own lives in peace.

Respecting other's rights to make their own decisions strengthens your own self-confidence and self-esteem. You are comfortable in your beliefs for yourself, and comfortable allowing others to just be.

Uphold rational self-interest as a guiding principle

When we're working on our self-respect and confidence, it's important to recognize that we each have the same rights and privileges in this world as everyone else. We are equally important. We are not entitled to more than the next person, and we do not deserve less.

It is important to take care of ourselves and to meet our own needs. Self-respect demands this. Our daily interactions are to be guided by rational self-interest. That is, the "rational" part of this is that we don't believe ourselves to be more entitled than the next person. We are on equal ground with everyone else. To believe that we are more important or more anything than they are is not rational.

At the same time, the "self-interest" portion of this means that we take care of our own interests. We don't self-sacrifice or self-surrender. We don't put others' needs before our own, and we get our own needs taken care of. We don't consistently sacrifice ourselves and our needs for the benefit of others, and we don't surrender ourselves when we should hold our ground. We take care of ourselves; we get our own needs met.

We operate along a guideline of maintaining rational self-interest in meeting our own needs, not of sacrificing ourselves or our needs or of surrendering to others. Other people don't always get to come first in our lives. At the same time, we don't always get to go first when others are involved. We don't bully others or run them over. We don't push others out of our way because we feel more entitled to something than they are. Instead, we find that line of decency for ourselves and others, and place ourselves rationally within the grand scheme of things. Our interactions are guided by rational self-interest.

Respect yourself as you respect others
It is an important point to remember to offer the same respect to yourself as you would offer to others. And we also need to offer ourselves the same level of compassion as we offer to others. We need to be lenient and forgiving of ourselves as we are lenient and forgiving of others.

We can be our own worst offenders. For a lot of us, it's easy to put others first and to act as though our own needs don't matter as much. We're hungry, but we can wait. We need the bathroom, but we can wait. You want to go home from work because you have a headache, but you can work through the pain. Yes, we can all withstand some degree of this waiting and tolerance and I'm not saying we never should. What I am saying is that we need to apply the same principles of compassion to ourselves as we offer to others. If we would not let a friend go hungry in this situation, we should not let ourselves. If we would not make someone else wait for the bathroom in this circumstance, we shouldn't make ourselves wait. If we would send someone else home from work because of a headache, we should go home ourselves. If we would not expect others to suffer, we should not subject ourselves to that same suffering. Instead, we need to have compassion for ourselves—for our needs, for our own suffering—and try to alleviate that suffering for ourselves as much as we try to alleviate that suffering for other people.

An important piece of this is to not allow ourselves to be mistreated. We don't just sit and tolerate mistreatment. We make it stop or walk away or whatever we need to do, but we don't subject ourselves to being mistreated. Just as we don't mistreat others, and we definitely don't expect them to sit and take it when they are mistreated, we don't allow that mistreatment of ourselves.

Self-respect demands that we offer the same level of respect for ourselves as we offer to others. We have the same compassion for our own needs and our own suffering as we extend to others. And we don't allow ourselves to be mistreated, just as we don't want others to allow themselves to be mistreated.

Success breeds confidence
This point diverges from Dr. Branden's work, but augments it I think.

Sports coaches know that in order to build a player's confidence in a certain sport, that player needs to have some success with that particular sport. A runner will have more confidence in his ability to win the race if he has won the race before. If he has already succeeded, he will have more confidence that he can succeed again. A soccer player will have greater confidence in her ability to head the ball into the goal if she's done it before and succeeded.

This is perhaps one reason why winners keep winning. They have the experience of success, which builds confidence. And that confidence helps them succeed again. As their success builds, their confidence builds. This is a beautiful spiral of success and confidence that builds upward. The more success someone has at something, the more confident that person is at that thing. And, the more confidence someone has at something, the greater the likelihood of success with that thing.

We have different levels of success in different areas of our lives, and so we have different confidence levels for those various areas. For example, you might be an excellent writer, and have had a lot of success in writing excellent copy that people like. So you have a lot of confidence in your writing ability. At the same time, maybe you're a terrible event planner. You've tried it before and it was a disaster—you accidentally hired two caterers and no musicians. You do not have success in event planning as your previous failures have killed your confidence in this area. That's okay—you can either work on strengthening those skills or simply avoid them. But the point is that your lack of success has developed a lack of confidence in this area, while at the same time, your success as a writer has built strong confidence in that area.

If you want to improve your confidence in a certain area, give yourself opportunities to succeed in baby steps. Succeed with small parts of the task. If you want to be a better event planner, maybe take a supporting role, not the lead role, and take on only the tasks of music and food. Then do these tasks well. When you succeed, you'll build your confidence. As you build confidence in smaller parts of the larger task, you can slowly build up your confidence in the larger task. Just do it one step at a time. Break down the area into its subparts and focus on succeeding in those small parts. And slowly, you will have success in all of the smaller parts and can build your success in the larger task.

An important part of building confidence is to have success. You need to succeed with something in order to build your confidence in that thing. It's okay that you're strong in some areas of your life and weak in others. This is completely normal. And when you want to succeed in a larger task, give yourself opportunities to succeed with smaller parts of that task. This way you can build your confidence in the larger task by building your confidence in the smaller tasks. You'll get there!

Summary: Building your Self-esteem
This section has presented several ways that you can build your self-esteem primarily with minor adjustments to your ways of thinking. As mentioned previously, Dr. Branden's exercises really help build your self-esteem so I encourage you to locate his book and do those exercises. The more of those exercises you do, the higher your self-esteem will grow. Do them because you love yourself and you are worth it. Do them because you love those in your life and you want to be easier to be around. Do them because you want to have more professional opportunities. Do them to quell the anxiety within you. Do them so you can be a better person.

Building your self-esteem is building a better you. Building a better you is the best way to show yourself love. At the same time, it shows love to all in your life. Building your self-esteem is totally worth it, in every conceivable way.

Ethics
Objective guides for behavior help do just that—guide behavior. When we behave in accordance with an established set of ethical guidelines we agree with, we feel proud that we are behaving ethically. Feeling proud of ourselves is important to developing strong self-esteem. When we know we are behaving ethically appropriately, we are comfortable and confident in our behavior. This confidence replaces anxiety.

Below is a list of 10 ethical principles to guide behavior from a 1988 issue of the journal *Ethics: Easier Said Than Done*.[380] It seems to me quite reasonable, so I offer it to you.

Ten Ethical Principles to Guide Behavior

The study of history, philosophy, and religion reveals a strong consensus about certain universal and timeless values that are central to leading an ethical life.

1. *Honesty.* Be truthful, sincere, forthright, straightforward, frank, and candid; do not cheat, lie, steal, deceive, or act deviously.

2. *Integrity.* Be principled, honorable, upright, and courageous and act on convictions; do not be two-faced or unscrupulous or adopt an ends-justifies-the-means philosophy that ignores principle.

3. *Promise-keeping.* Be worthy of trust, keep promises, fulfill commitments, and abide by the spirit as well as the letter of an agreement; do not interpret agreements in a technical or legalistic manner to rationalize noncompliance or to create excuses for breaking commitments.

4. *Fidelity.* Be faithful and loyal to family, friends, employers, and country; do not use or disclose information earned in confidence; in a professional context, safeguard the ability to make independent professional judgments by scrupulously avoiding undue influences and conflicts of interest.

5. *Fairness.* Be fair and open-minded, be willing to admit error and, when appropriate, change positions and beliefs; demonstrate a commitment to justice, the equal treatment of individuals, and tolerance for diversity; do not overreach or take undue advantage of another's mistakes or adversities.

6. *Caring for others.* Be caring, kind, and compassionate; share, be giving, and serve others; help those in need and avoid harming others.

7. *Respect for others.* Demonstrate respect for human dignity, privacy, and the right to self-determination for all people; be courteous, prompt, and decent; provide others with the information they need to make informed decisions about their own lives; do not patronize, embarrass, or demean.

8. *Responsible citizenship.* Obey just laws [if a law is unjust, openly protest it]; exercise all democratic rights and privileges responsibly by participation [voting and expressing informed views], social consciousness, and public service; when in a position of leadership or authority, openly respect and honor democratic processes of decision making, avoid secrecy or concealment of information, and ensure others have the information needed to make intelligent choices and exercise their rights.

9. *Pursuit of excellence.* Pursue excellence in all matters; in meeting personal and professional responsibilities, be diligent, reliable, industrious, and committed; perform all tasks to the best of your ability, develop and maintain a high degree of competence, and be well informed and well prepared; do not be content with mediocrity, but do not seek to win "at any cost."

10. *Accountability.* Be accountable; accept responsibility for decisions, for the foreseeable consequences of actions and inactions, and for setting an example for others. Parents, teachers, employers, many professionals, and public officials have a special obligation to lead by example and to safeguard and advance the integrity and reputation of their families, companies, professions, and the government; avoid even the appearance of impropriety and take whatever actions are necessary to correct or prevent inappropriate conduct by others.

Source: Michael Josephson, "Teaching Ethical Decision Making and Principled Reasoning," *Ethics: Easier Said Than Done*, Winter 1988, pp. 28–29. www.josephsoninstitute.org.

When you follow most of the guidelines on this list and strive to follow the ones you fall short of, your confidence improves—you know you are doing the right thing. You know you are a good person. You know your behavior is appropriate, even if it's sometimes unpopular.

Knowing you're behaving appropriately brings a lot of confidence, replacing previous anxiety. So you can follow these ethical guidelines because it's the right thing to do and you want to be a good person, or because you want to feel better about yourself and amplify your own self-confidence and self-respect, growing your self-esteem. Either way, if you follow guidelines for ethical behavior such as those presented above, you will feel better about yourself and you will be a better person and more decent member of society. It's a win-win!

Conclusion

This chapter has presented a few perspectives and approaches to healing and strengthening from a psychological perspective. First, I presented what the picture of mental health looks like. In order for you to get to a destination, it helps to know what that destination is. Then, I presented a method for pulling out anxieties by their roots, one at a time.

From there, I offered a brief discussion on some findings from psychology to help you move past your traumatic events. If seeking the help of a mental health practitioner calls to you, then by all means, take that route. I only urge you to first recognize that there are multiple routes to healing available to you and that the mental health therapy route isn't the only one, and second to not place responsibility for your healing in the hands of an educated stranger. Your healing is your own work, and you have to do what feels and seems right for you. The time will come when talking some things through will be useful—verbalizing things is a vital part of healing. Plus, it's good to get an objective perspective on whether certain behaviors classify as healthy or unhealthy. When we're trying to (re)define that for ourselves, it can be especially useful to bounce things off of someone who knows more about this stuff than your circle of confidants probably ever will, unless you run with mental health workers.

This chapter then offers a lengthy discussion of how to build your self-esteem, which included several individual components. Each of these components is outlined and designed to help you improve your relationship with yourself. We could all use these reminders from time to time to help us live the life of dignity and integrity that makes us each feel like a valuable human being.

Finally, the chapter closes with some guidelines for ethical behavior to instill confidence that when following these guidelines, you are indeed doing the right thing.

Healing the psyche requires a multi-dimensional approach, and even within each dimension multiple approaches are available to you. Choose the ones that make the most sense to you and keep your mind open. If one doesn't call to you today, revisit it in a year or five and see if it calls to you then. Life is long, the healing journey is long, and each step we take along the way helps us live a richer, healthier, happier life, whichever step that may be at the moment.

10.   Social Relationships

As we saw in Section I, our ability to participate in meaningful, fulfilling interpersonal relationships takes a serious hit when we come from stressful childhoods. We have developed models of relationships as stress-inducing, painful, possibly mean, manipulative, explosive and violent, and certainly unhealthy. Of course we have problems developing and maintaining healthy relationships with these sorts of detrimental relational models. Part of our problem is the kinds of people we choose to enter relationships with and their level of mental unwellness, and part of our problem is us—we don't know how to behave appropriately to achieve and maintain quality relationships.

Fear not, however; there is hope! It is entirely possible to develop and maintain healthy relationships as adults from difficult childhoods. You just have to transform your relational models into healthy ones, enabling you to enter healthier relationships in the first place, and then learn healthy relationship behavior. You have to replace your previous structures about what relationships are supposed to look like with healthy structures. That is what this chapter is about.

First of all, it's important to recognize that we're talking about all kinds of relationships here, not just the most intimate ones. Our relationships with co-workers, supervisors or underlings, friends, and family members all share the same essential dynamics. So, when we learn appropriate interpersonal communication skills and take these skills into all of our relationships, all of our relationships improve.

This chapter comes directly from a university course on interpersonal communication I taught many times. Every time I taught it, I learned something new; I saw something in a new light or understood something at a deeper level. And every time, I became better at interacting with people. Even my relationships with my students improved! This chapter covers the essential aspects of your thinking and your communications that you'll need to pay attention to in developing your social intelligence. Employ these steps wholeheartedly, and watch your life transform. Continue practicing these dynamics and incorporating them deeply into your communications, and you will reap benefits for the rest of your life in unforetold ways.

Move Slowly Here

Please know that this chapter offers an extremely brief synopsis of each of these ideas. Each idea in itself is its own book at minimum and academic discipline at most. The language section represents the entire field of linguistics, for example. Having taught this course many times, I have condensed this chapter's material to its essence, and present it to you succinctly and quickly.

What that means is please be warned not to gloss through this stuff. Move through it slowly and carefully, giving each concept the time and contemplation it deserves in order to be absorbed. Work through these ideas slowly, perhaps even incorporating one concept at a time into your life before moving on to the next one. In the university classroom, each of these concepts warrants a full 40-page textbook chapter and a full 2-hour seminar, and these topics could not even be covered adequately within that limited time.

Please take your time with this material. It is incredibly rich and deep—much richer and deeper than the space allotted to each suggests. If you find a particular topic especially intriguing, I invite you to do some digging and find additional resources on that topic; rest assured, they are out there. I also invite you to revisit these concepts regularly and often as you work to incorporate them into your way of communicating. Every time you reread this stuff, you will very likely absorb this material at a deeper level.

The more you can get from this chapter, the richer and more fulfilling your relationships will be. Especially those of us with bent models of relationships need all the help we can get!

Communication Competence

This chapter begins with a brief presentation of communication competence. This is the ideal, and where we are headed in developing our interpersonal communication skills: We want to be competent communicators.

The first piece of communication competence includes trying to ensure that all of our communications are **appropriate** and **effective** for the given audience and context. When communications are not appropriate, they will not be effective. To illustrate this idea, consider for example how your communication changes when you are in a bar with your friends, or when you are in a religious worship center. The communication appropriate to one place is not appropriate to the other, and will come across as out of place in either context. Additionally, consideration of audience will help make your communication more effective.[381] The remainder of this chapter outlines ways to be more sensitive to the needs of your audience.

With that foundation, communication competence consists of five elements: self-awareness, adaptability, empathy, cognitive complexity, and ethics.[381]

Self-awareness means being aware of your own communication behaviors. Part of this is **self-monitoring,** which means that you observe your own communication behaviors and ensure they are appropriate to the situation. As a crude example, if you are someone who tends to use foul language, you would self-monitor while you're in a place of religious worship and refrain from such language usage in this environment.

Adaptability is the ability to adapt your communication to the environment you're in. That is, you wouldn't communicate in the same way to your closest friends as you would to your coworkers. Rather, while you're at work, you would adapt your communication behaviors to the norms and standards of the communication environment at work, and when you're with your friends you adapt to that social environment accordingly.

Empathy means that you communicate with another person while putting yourself in that person's shoes, so to speak. For example, if your friend has just announced he is getting a divorce, you would consider that friend's frame of mind and refrain from bringing up how great your own significant relationship is at the moment, aware that such statements will likely only serve to make your friend feel worse about his or her own challenging current relational situation.

Cognitive complexity is the idea that another's communication behavior can have multiple sources. In part, this means that when someone is sharp with you, it could be from something you've done, yes, and perhaps that person is reacting to you. However, it could also be a result of that person's physical wellbeing at the moment—perhaps s/he has a headache or didn't get enough sleep the night before—or something in that person's life that is weighing on him or her at the moment. This is also a recognition that your perception of someone else's communication behavior may or may not be aligned with their intention when creating the message. Cognitive complexity keeps these dynamics in mind at all times.

Ethics means to communicate in ways that are morally correct. That is, when someone is particularly vulnerable, we don't take advantage of that person's weakened state to get him or her to agree to something that s/he otherwise would not likely have done. We also don't take advantage in any other way, such as using this opportunity to say something difficult that has been building up within you.

Those who are proficient in each of these five areas of communication are considered competent communicators.[382]

Mastering each of these levels generally requires some minor shifts in how you approach and behave within your interpersonal interactions, but this consciousness is good for your development. Communicating with others is a much greater responsibility than most people give it credit for: Since we sort of have the other person's well-being in our hands, it should have some forethought behind it.

In sum: **Always communicate in ways that are appropriate and effective for the given situation. Strive to include high levels of self-awareness, adaptability, empathy, cognitive complexity, and ethics in all of your communications.**

Listening

Listening well requires a lot of attention—more than most people are willing to offer. But being a good listener is very important to your communication competence and your social success.

Becoming a better listener is actually pretty simple. A "better listener" means engaging in *attentive* listening, or *active* listening or maybe *mindful* listening. It means listening with your full attention.

As we all know, that's hard work! So we develop ways to relax our minds, even though another person is talking to us. These ways we "check out" of a conversation maybe even began in childhood, and they become habitual. Now, these poor listening habits, or practices, are standing in the way of your social intelligence because they're preventing you from fully attending to the people talking to you—you're not paying attention. If you don't pay attention, you aren't fully present, which is a little insulting at best. These poor listening practices are easy enough to get past, if you know what you're up against. Here's a list of the most common poor listening practices most of us use from time to time.[381,383]

The first of these poor listening practices is **pseudolistening**. In pseudolistening, as the name suggests, you pretend you're listening while your mind is on a beach in Brazil, or on a horse in Wyoming, or just about any place except in the conversation taking place at the present moment. We all do this—it's a survival principle! If we pay 100% attention to what people are saying 100% of the time, we won't make it through our day without completely exhausting ourselves. Paying attention is hard work. So I'm not suggesting you never pseudolisten—in fact, there are some very good times and places for this, such as in meetings where a particular topic isn't relevant to you or with a friend who talks incessantly, feels the need to vent endlessly, or repeats herself continuously. At the same time, when someone is speaking directly to you or important information is being aired are not the times for pseudolistening.

Another poor listening practice is **selective attention**, or possibly **selective inattention**. Here, you only pay attention to what concerns you and "don't hear" the rest. For example, your doctor tells you that you need to drink one glass of red wine a day and jog three miles three times a week, and you hear only the part about the red wine. You "missed" the part about all that jogging.

Closely related to selective (in)attention is **fill-in-the-gaps** listening. Here, you pick up on bits and pieces, and invent the rest yourself to make the story complete. For example, your wife says she spent $500 yesterday: She bought clothes for you and shoes for her, and these were necessary expenditures because you have an important event coming up. When you retell the story to your buddies, you say that your wife spent $500 on shoes and clothes because she's going to a baby shower.

One poor listening practice that's particularly undesirable to be on the receiving end of is **defensive listening.** Here, neutral comments are perceived as personal attacks. Because they're perceived as attacks, the hearer will likely attack "in return." An example is that you compliment your friend's new dress and say it looks nice on her. She responds with "are you saying I look fat? Not everyone can have your figure you know."

The poor listening practice where you do all the talking and almost none of the listening is known as **stagehogging**. In actuality, in a normal conversation you should probably be speaking your portion of the time based on how many people you're talking with. If it's just you and one other person, that's a 50-50 conversation. If you're in a group of 4, your speaking time reduces to 25%, etc. Not all conversations work like this, of course. Just be sure not to dominate the conversation and listen when it's others' turns to talk. In another manifestation of stagehogging, the speaker sometimes also feels the need to "one-up" the other person. You know—you caught a fish four feet long so I caught a fish five feet long.

In a **rebuttal tendency**, the speaker listens with the purpose of finding something to disagree with. This is a debate posture. Also, you formulate your response in your head while the other person is speaking. If you're thinking of what you're going to say next, you can't be actively listening to your conversational partner. I think that this happens a lot with professionals in busy environments. I say this because of the responses I often get to my questions, which are not direct responses to my questions but some other point they're trying to make to show me my concern is actually my own fault.

Closed mindedness is the poor listening practice where you don't hear anything you disagree with. This is common at gatherings where there are extreme differences of opinion, especially with regard to morality-based discussions. If your mind is closed to your conversational partner, you can't actually hear them, and as a result, you can't know them well. You don't have to agree with everything the other person says to be able to listen to that person's opinion. People's perspectives are really interesting if you'll give them a chance to be heard. I personally find it fascinating, the degree of perspectives "out there" on any given topic. I love to ask questions to probe the thinking especially of those I most disagree with. It's polite to hear them out, and it's good to know your opposition's arguments.

Finally, **competitive interrupting** is the poor listening practice where you interrupt the other person for the purpose of hijacking the conversation. This says to the other person that what they're saying is not important, and what you want to say is much more important. By extension, you are much more important than they are. Competitive interrupting is not to be confused with interrupting to ask for clarification, for example.

When we engage in any of these poor listening practices, we send a clear message to the other person that we don't value what s/he is saying. Naturally, this is perceived as not valuing the other person.

We all engage in one or more of these poor listening practices from time to time. The key here is to identify which ones you tend to use the most so that you can transmute that behavior into a mindful listening or attentive listening experience. One way to identify which ones you use the most is to intentionally practice each of them in turn (warn the speaker so s/he isn't offended), and see which ones you're most comfortable using. Identify it, laugh at it, and knock it off.

As a final note on this topic, when I would ask my English language university students where listening takes place, I was expecting to get "in the ears." But my students from China all put their hands on their hearts…

In sum: **Reduce poor listening practices; increase attentive listening.**

Language

The next area for consideration is language. There are some really important things you need to understand about the dynamics of language that will make you a better communicator.

Language Ambiguity and Imprecision

The first thing you need to understand about language is that it's ambiguous and inexact. We try to say exactly what we mean, and inevitably, someone's not going to understand us in the way we intended. And they're going to get frustrated, thinking "why don't you be clearer?" "speak more clearly!" "just say what you mean!"— and we're trying! We are saying what we mean! And we're going to get frustrated that they don't understand us, because we're "being crystal clear." They just don't understand us in the way that we want to be understood. That's nobody's fault. That's one of the features of language.

There are a lot of reasons for this that language theorists have talked about and examined, though we don't have space for that discussion here. Really what's important to know here is that language is inexact and it's ambiguous. And we do our best to be clear, but you're never going to be clear to everyone all the time; it's just not going to happen.

Understand that misunderstandings are common, ambiguities are common, and that's just the way language works. It's no one's fault and definitely don't take it personally or get defensive if you don't understand someone or if someone doesn't understand you. Just be patient and try to go about rephrasing your point or theirs, or apologize for not understanding clearly and ask for more clarification, or better, apologize for not expressing yourself in a way the listener can clearly understand and slow down, and come at it in another way.

Language Power

The second thing you need to understand about language is that it's very powerful. Language has the power to make someone's day or put somebody in tears. You can build someone up and break someone down just as easily with your linguistic choices. People tend to take the words you use very seriously. So, be aware of that.

Use language consciously, and use it to speak positively to the people that you're talking to. Don't think that language is irrelevant and it doesn't matter. It's your responsibility as a competent communicator—all of our responsibility as competent communicators—to be as nice as we can be, and recognize the incredible power that language has and use that power responsibly.

One little piece I'd like to throw in here on the power of language is about the use of *but*. "I love you, but you smell bad." What do you hear in that sentence? Most people just hear the part that comes after the *but*—you smell bad. There are linguistic reasons for this, involving the rhetorical purpose of *but* as a contrastive device: Its job is to show that what comes next contradicts what came before it. Typically, when we have to deliver some criticism, we tend to say "you do really well in this area, but…" and whatever comes after the *but* completely negates what we said before. People don't hear the first part any more; they're just focusing on what you said after the *but*. So, let's get the *but* out of there, along with all of its synonyms—*however, although, though*, etc.—when you're interacting with people. Just stop using these words that contradict. Find another way to say these things. You might say, "You do really well in this area. Some areas I'd like to see you improve are…" Or, insert an *and*. "You do really well in this area, and some places I'd like to see you improve are…" Or, use *at the same time*: "You do really well in this area. At the same time, there some areas I'd like to see you improve in." That completely changes the tone.

In sum: **Language is ambiguous and inexact, so don't get offended when you don't understand or aren't understood clearly. It's powerful, so use it consciously and responsibly. Try to avoid** *but*.

Politeness

When we want to improve our social intelligence or our communication competence, we need to be polite. Basically, politeness means communicating in ways that instill good feelings in others, and it's actually pretty simple. We interact with courtesy and respect for their experience in receiving our communications.

The Concept of Face

A brief discussion of face theory here will be useful. You're probably familiar with this one. Essentially, when you *lose face* you do something that breaks the social code and you get embarrassed, and when you *save face* you prevent or recover from losing face, or help someone else prevent or recover from losing face. The theory also includes *threatening face*, which is important to talk about to better understand politeness.

Face, according to face theory, is a person's public self-image. Each of us has the same face needs, but in varying degrees. All of us construct a public self-image intended to demonstrate we are competent, independent, and socially adept. In this theory, when we receive communication that we perceive as making us look bad in any of these ways, our face is *threatened*—we are in danger of losing face. We are uncomfortable, and often don't know how to respond. That prompts us to try to save face, or others can help us save face, and restore our public self-image.[384] As polite communicators, we want to avoid putting people in this situation as much as possible. So, we need to not threaten their face.[385-389]

Face Threats

When we want to *not* threaten someone's face, we interact with them as though we respect the fact that they're competent, we respect the fact that they're socially adept and capable of getting along well with people, and we respect the fact that they're autonomous and fully capable and able to make their own decisions.[390] To not threaten someone's face is to keep in mind these three fundamental human face needs in all of our interactions, verbal and behavioral/nonverbal, and to interact in ways that minimize violating or threatening these needs to the fullest extent possible. This means that we are thoughtful and careful with our words and non-verbal cues, and may mean using more indirectness in polite requests.[391]

Disagreements can be considered face threats, as well as telling someone what to do and certainly delivering criticism.[384] So whenever we find ourselves in this position, we might front that information with an assurance that we know that the other person is competent, independent, and socially adept in an effort not to threaten that person's face.[392,393] We might say something like,[394] "I'm sure you've already thought about this. I was just wondering about..." or "You have a lot more experience in this area than I do so excuse me if I'm being cheeky here, I was just wondering if we might consider..." Another useful tactic is to learn to present information in the form of a question rather than a declarative statement, as people tend to find questions less threatening than declaratives. Also, when you disagree with someone, it is, interestingly and perhaps counterintuitively, useful to front that disagreement with the very direct statement, "I'm going to disagree with you on that." That's still a face threat, but somehow it's a warning so when the disagreement-slash-face threat comes, its blow doesn't hit so hard; they're braced for it.

241

Face Protection

In all of our interactions, we are mindful of protecting and preserving the other person's needs to be deemed competent, to be considered knowledgeable about getting along with people, and to be deemed autonomous or independent and fully able to make their own decisions. If we can protect those different face needs in the people we're talking to when we're interacting with them, we will come across as more polite. It's just that simple.

The Esteemed Emily Post

As a scholar, I am hesitant to cite a lay source for anything, particularly in my own discipline. However, I have to say that I found the most recent printing of Emily Post's book on etiquette[395] to be very helpful and I have to strongly recommend you pick up a copy. She very articulately, clearly, and thoroughly spells out polite, courteous, and appropriate social behavior in most conceivable social situations. She helps build new structures for social behavior that are solid and appropriate. For me, it quelled a lot of anxiety I used to have about how I was supposed to behave in certain situations.

Anything that eases anxiety on any level, I'm interested. With Emily Post's help, I have replaced that structure of anxiety in social situations with confidence in my own behavior as socially appropriate. I also found that nearly no one I have ever known actually practices courtesy at this level and in these ways, and wow how appropriate is the behavior she recommends! That meant we could all use a few tips from the esteemed Emily Post on how to behave appropriately in this world we share with others. I cannot recommend it highly enough. I learned a ton, it answered all of my many questions about what's socially appropriate behavior, and I only wish I had discovered it sooner in my life because it would have eased a lot of my anxiety a lot sooner. Seriously, you should pick up a copy.

In sum: **Communicate in ways that always protect the other person's needs to be deemed competent, autonomous, and socially adept**. **Be courteous.**

Co-Cultural Differences

When we think of cultural differences, we generally think about differences between people of different nations or different countries. Cultural difference is definitely that, and it's also more and deeper than that. We need to keep in mind that everyone comes from a different place—I don't mean on the globe, but inside.

We are all a product of how society treats us based on the skin we're in and where we happen to be. I'm treated a certain way because I'm a woman and not a man; because I'm 5'7" and not 6'2" or 4'11"; because of my skin color, my body size, my accent, my academic background, and my passport. Additionally, I choose certain group memberships, such as religious, athletic, and hobby affiliations, and develop a sense of belonging to those groups through a process of fitting in, or acculturating. Thus, being a part of a certain group means sharing certain characteristics—those that mark group membership. It could be certain slang, dress code, politeness level, and degree of external social interaction shared by members of a certain gym, for example, or by members of a certain sport such as boxing as opposed to surfing. All of these demographic features and various experiences lead us to have different life experiences.

Researchers call these various group memberships co-cultures. Some of my bank of experiences are different from the experiences of people with different demographic features, but they're very similar to the experiences of people with shared or similar demographic features. For example, as a woman, people generally tend to treat me as they treat most women, however that may be, until or unless they find out that for some reason they shouldn't. So, my experience as a woman is shared with other women because we are generally treated quite similarly, at least at first.

Experiences Construct Perspectives
We need to keep in mind that whatever background we come from, whatever demographic categories we're part of, and whatever interest groups we belong to, and we all come from many, many different demographic categories and social interest groups, each of these has a bearing on how we see the world. They influence how we interpret information, how we process information, the kinds of decisions we reach and the kinds of suggestions we make.

I am still amazed when people find out I did my undergraduate work at UC Berkeley and they say, "Ah. That fits. Now I understand." Apparently that academic experience shaped my thinking in ways similar to the ways it shapes the thinking of its other students, and that certain thinking style is identifiable and recognizable, even a couple of decades later, by those familiar with it. All of these different features are different experiences that we have in life, and they lend to different views of the world.[396]

What is important to remember is that we all have a very different, unique combination of our background or our demographics. There's religious affiliation, political affiliation, hobbies and activities, and sports participation and/or fandom. There's economic background and current economic status, educational background including degree types, institutions, and areas of study, and past and current professional areas and levels. And there's a whole lot more. Each of our experiences lends to different ways of viewing and interpreting the world. So not only are our DNA and our fingerprints unique to us as individuals, but our bank of experiences is as well, which means that our range of perspectives is also unique to each individual. That's just important to remember. No one sees the world exactly as you do. All perspectives are equally valid.

So when you're working with a group of people, even if they're all your same skin color, gender, and religion, there are going to be some differences in the ways these people think and view the world because of where they came from; because of the part of the country that they came from and the side of town they grew up in; because of whether and where they went to college and whether and where they went to graduate school; because of whatever kind of work history they might have and their own economic history. A very diverse group of people will increase the group's diversity of perspectives exponentially. Everyone brings their own unique set of features and characteristics with them, derived from their experiences in the environments they've been exposed to and the way the world treats them.

It's important to remember this when we're interacting with people because people are different than we are, and they see the world differently than we do. They have different perspectives than we do. And these differences need to be honored and valued—not ignored and repressed or insulted, of course. It's important to remember that we all see the world differently, and the reason for this is the various backgrounds and combinations of features that our backgrounds have.

And incidentally, the most diverse groups tend to reach the best decisions because of the vast diversity of perspectives brought to the table; it takes them longer to work through things, but their decisions are richer and more innovative than the decisions of people with more similar demographic characteristics.

In sum: **Have patience in interacting with others, as they've had different life experiences and see the world differently. Their perspectives are equally valid and valuable, even if (and sometimes especially if) they're different than our own.**

Conflict

A very important part of life with other people, conflict is not a bad thing, regardless of what you might think or what you might have been taught. In fact, conflict is natural, normal, and as I mentioned, really important. It helps us to clear the air so that we can better understand people and where they're coming from, and it helps us to know other people at a deeper level. So conflict in and of itself is not at all a bad thing. In fact it's really useful.

Gottman's Four Horsemen of the Apocalypse

The trouble with conflict comes in what happens to a lot of people when conflict arises. Behaviors during conflict can be problematic. Psychologist John Gottman, out of the University of Washington, talks about what he calls the Four Horsemen of the Apocalypse. These are four different behaviors during conflict, and when someone engages in one of more of these behaviors, there's a good chance that relationship will show some problems down the line.[397]

These so-called apocalyptic behaviors are: Criticism—we don't criticize the person we're having a conflict with; we stick to the issue. Contempt—veiled anger and hatred. We don't think like that during conflict; we stick to the issue. Defensiveness—whatever you intended to be a neutral statement, I take as an attack and respond "in kind", with an attack. That gets us nowhere in terms of the conflict; it's attack ping-pong—or more likely, squash. And the last one is stonewalling, which is just shutting down—you want to have a conversation and I just do not engage. I might just ignore you and keep reading my newspaper or my book, or leave the room or even stomp out of the room. The conflict can never be resolved if I don't stick around to resolve it.

Each of these four horsemen gets in the way of resolving the conflict. And we all know what happens with unresolved conflict...? Somehow it tends to fester and grow like an energetic tumor in the relationship. These are not productive behaviors during conflict, so we want to try to avoid those as much as we possibly can so that we can get the conflict resolved and move on.[397]

Resolution Options

When we're in conflict, we need a resolution, an outcome. There are different categories of resolution. One of them is compromise. That's probably the one most of us are most familiar with when we think of working out a conflict. Compromise isn't about me getting my way or you getting your way, but rather we both give up a little bit so we can both get a little of what we want. In that situation, for both parties it's a little bit win and a little bit lose. That's one way to do it.

There's also complete avoidance of the conflict, which shows a low regard for yourself and the other person because you won't address the issue so it can't be resolved. There's accommodation where you just give in, which shows a high concern for other and low concern for your own needs. And there's competing, which seems to believe in an either/or outcome, and shows I care about my needs more than yours.

A better way in many situations is what researchers call *collaboration*, and that is a win-win. That means you get everything you want and I get everything I want. We consider both of our needs and develop this third possibility that neither of us had considered before. When we want to reach a decision that's collaborative or reflects collaborative efforts, it usually takes a little bit more time because there's consideration and creativity involved. This is not usually a solution that we'd thought about when we walked into the conflict; it's a new idea that arises out of the communication in the conflict as both people express what they want. We want to seek a win-win—the best of all possible worlds.

In sum: **Watch yourself when you're in the middle of conflict: Avoid criticism, contempt, defensiveness, and stonewalling; and go for the win-win in seeking a resolution.**

Nonverbal Communication

Another area you want to keep in mind when you're working on improving your social intelligence is your nonverbal communication. Researchers suggest that as much as 93% of our total communication comes from nonverbal sources. There are facial expressions, gestures, vocal characteristics, space expressions, touch, and many others.[398]

Physical Distance

One area of nonverbal communication is your space bubble. Researchers call this *proxemics* and it has to do with distance—how close someone can be to you so that you feel comfortable. This comfortable distance will depend on your intimacy level with the other person—and send messages to others about your intimacy level with this person. It's important to understand that everyone has a space bubble. That means when someone you're not close with steps inside your space bubble, they're too close, and you feel uncomfortable.[399,400]

The space bubble is culturally determined so people from different parts of the world might have a smaller or a larger space bubble and need more physical distance between you and them in order to feel comfortable. If you want to make someone comfortable when you're speaking with them, be careful not to invade their space bubble. When working with international students, I encountered people from cultures all over the world and many had different space bubble needs. Sometimes a student would get too close to me so I would back away... so they would step closer... so I would back away... it was quite amusing to watch as they chased me around the front of the classroom with me continuing to back up and them continuing to close the distance. It was just a reflection of the differences in our space bubble needs.

Physical Contact
Closely related to proxemics is touch, what researchers call *haptics*. If you want someone to be comfortable with you, be careful how you touch them and where you touch them. Touch is a very intimate thing, and it demonstrates an intimacy in the relationship that the other person may or may not feel comfortable with. For example, the baseball coach can pat his players on the derriere to indicate "good job," but the classroom teacher goes to jail for this. So, be aware of how you use touch and where you use it when you're talking to another person, and be sure it's appropriate for the situation and your level of intimacy with the other person.

The Face and Eyes
The face is incredible. It has thousands of expressions, so it's important to recognize that your face is really very telling, and particularly your eyes. When we hold a gaze for a longer period, that gives an indication of some sort of attraction. So, it's important when you're talking with someone that you make sure you don't hold your eye contact with them for too long if you don't want to send the wrong impression of what you intend to be a very collegial relationship.

It's also important to keep in mind that when you're interacting with people from other cultures, this rule about eye contact varies. In the United States, holding eye contact is considered a sign of respect and demonstration of integrity, but that's not the case in all cultures. In fact sometimes and in some cultures it's viewed as disrespect because it's interpreted as a challenge.

You should know the people you're interacting with and their national cultural customs when it comes to eye contact so you don't inadvertently offend them, either with the use of eye contact or with its absence.

Gestures

Gestures, certainly, are a big part of nonverbal communication. Make sure they're not aggressive—no eye-rolling or finger-flipping allowed in socially intelligent interactions. Be careful about putting your feet on the table or turning your back on others as this is often interpreted as rudeness.

The Voice

Another important area is your voice. The voice has many different features—speed, volume, articulation, pitch, inflection (variations in pitch), tone and more. These vocal facets need to be considered when you're trying to communicate competently with someone or improve your social intelligence. You'll want to be sure to speak at an appropriate volume and speed, articulate clearly, and use some vocal inflection to avoid sounding monotonous. Also, be sure your tone isn't aggressive or otherwise threatening or condescending.

Emotional Expression

It's important to note that emotion is most generally expressed in nonverbal communication cues. If someone is crying and you ask them what's wrong, and they say "nothing," well, you can't really believe the words because clearly something is very wrong, as emotions are spilling out nonverbally. That emotions are primarily conveyed nonverbally is something to keep in mind as both one who communicates and as one who receives communications from others.

Mixed Messages

Be aware of your nonverbal communication, and be sure you're using nonverbal communication cues that match your verbal cues. In the example I just gave, someone is crying and you ask them what's wrong and they tearfully say, "nothing"—that doesn't match! They're sending a mixed message. And that's really frustrating as a listener. What do you do with that? As a communicator, don't put your listeners in that position. Be sure to match your verbal cues with your nonverbal cues. Otherwise you're going to send unintended cues and cause confusion.

In sum: **Use nonverbal cues intentionally. Be aware of what you're doing with your nonverbal cues. Match your nonverbal cues with your verbal cues so you don't send mixed messages.**

Show Value

Part of being socially intelligent or a competent communicator means that you communicate in ways that show value for the people you're communicating with.

It's important to communicate with people in ways that show you value them, as a human being and as someone in your life.

Showing Value to Others: Confirming Messages
There are three really easy ways we show value. The first is recognition, the second is acknowledgement, and the third is endorsement.[381]

In recognition, we say hello. We notice someone's presence. When someone says hello to us, we don't ignore them; we answer back. We return telephone calls and text messages. We don't blow people off. In this way, by responding when someone talks to me, I show that person that I value him or her.

The next one is acknowledgement. This is a step deeper than recognition, and goes further to acknowledge that you are a human being with your own insights, your own intellect and your own perspectives, and I might ask for your opinion on something. When was the last time your boss asked for your opinion? And further, what did that mean to you when he or she did? It's kind of a big deal because it doesn't happen all the time, and it doesn't happen enough. So, acknowledging someone else's presence and their contributions and their being in your life is more than just saying "hi", it's saying "hey we're in this life together. What do you think about this thing here?" That's very important to social intelligence.

The third way to show someone we value him or her is endorsement. That means praise or flattery. "You've done a really good job on this." "I recognize you worked really hard and it shows." It's really that simple.

These are called confirming messages in the communication research. When you practice these kinds of messages—recognition, acknowledgement and endorsement—you send a message to the other person that you value him or her. Within the context of relationships, you are demonstrating that you are attending to your relationship and you want that person in your life. This is a very powerful message.[381]

Showing Absence of Value: Disconfirming Messages
The opposite of confirming messages of course is disconfirming messages. Someone says "hello" to you and you ignore them. You get a text message asking "hey, wanna get together next weekend?" And you simply don't respond. That's one way that you can be disconfirming. These things that seem like minor inactions send huge messages about how you feel about that person and your relationship with them. Disconfirming messages don't reflect social intelligence.

Another disconfirming message is to offer a tangential response which isn't really a response but rather a hijacking of the floor. An example is someone asks you "hey you wanna go to the ball game next weekend?" And you respond with "Anyone wanna go fishing tomorrow? It's supposed to be a great day and I hear the fish are biting like crazy!" You totally changed the subject. You totally took the conversation away from the original topic of the ball game next weekend. That's another behavior that people often do but it's not productive to your relationships because it demonstrates lack of value for having the other person in your life.

Insults, hostility, aggressiveness, which we'll talk about in a minute, ignoring, pretending to respond—all are disconfirming. All of these behaviors say "I don't value you." They might say, "I don't value you in my life and maybe I don't value you as a human being." They might even say, "I don't value you on this planet so just get out of my face because I don't want you around." Indeed, these seemingly small and insignificant responses can send extremely powerful messages.[381]

To reiterate one particular point because it seems to be an increasingly bad habit practiced by more and more people as we get more comfortable in this technology age, so-called *blowing people off* or *ghosting them* is not a socially intelligent behavior. It's a very disconfirming message.

When you want to increase your social intelligence and you want to improve your relationships, it's very important that you send a message to the people in your life that you value them.

In sum: **Show value. Always send confirming messages. Avoid sending disconfirming messages.**

Self-Concept

Our self-concept is how we see ourselves. It is our identity. It is what comes next in the sentence beginning with "I am ..." Which words would you use to describe yourself? Answers might include external characteristics such as nationality or profession, or internal characteristics such as "stubborn" or "smart." We also need to believe we possess certain characteristics and competently demonstrate them to others.[385]

Self-Concept Development

A self-concept doesn't develop overnight or change in response to a particular event. It develops over time, slowly, over the course of a person's lifetime. It is a function of an individual's biological makeup, upbringing, and social environment.

Our sets of ideas about who we are don't change with our moods but are relatively stable over time.

The self-concept can change, though generally only in response to developmental changes and significant life events. For example, a person's self-concept can improve when they achieve a certain social marker, such as buying a fancy house or landing a powerful job. These markers can help the person feel like they are more important or somehow better than before, which can improve the self-concept. On the other hand, a successful professional arrested and imprisoned for a period of time and enduring public shame and humiliation will likely see a dive in his or her self-concept.

Inaccurate (Unhealthy) Self-Concepts
Sometimes a person's self-perceptions are unreasonably positive. I'm sure you know people with unrealistic perceptions about their attributes, abilities, and/or place in society. Consider the street brawler who takes on a well-trained fighter, sure he can win, oblivious that he's severely outclassed. Another example is the average-educated man who believes he is smarter and more entitled than all women, finding himself in the social company of a woman he is expected to address as "doctor" or "Your Honor." We generally consider these people as having an inflated sense of self, egotistical, or overly confident—they're not as great as they would like to think they are.

People's self-perceptions can also be unreasonably negative. Consider the truly talented individual with little confidence in her abilities, or the over-achieving perfectionist who constantly feels the need to prove himself well beyond others' satisfaction. People with low self-concepts tend to respond to constructive criticism or disagreement with harsh self-criticism.

Healthy Self-Concepts
A healthy self-concept is flexible and subject to change with evolving life circumstances. In general, however, most people's self-concepts don't change much over the course of their lives. A self-concept can be improved with extensive therapy, or with working through the paces of improving your self-esteem, as presented in Chapter 9.

Self-Concept and Self-Esteem

Low self-concepts are related to low self-esteem. Self-esteem is the *value* you place on yourself. It is the assessment of your self-image as positive or negative. Self-esteem is dynamic and can change in response to life circumstances.[401]

People with high self-esteem tend to be more outgoing and willing to communicate, and more comfortable initiating relationships. They're more likely to believe that expressions of love and kindness from a relational partner are genuine. When their relationships have problems, they're more likely to seek out new relationships. They tend to perform better academically and professionally, and are more shielded from stress.

Conversely, those with low self-esteem tend to behave aggressively toward others and have an affinity for substance abuse. Low self-esteem is often blamed for criminal and antisocial behaviors. Those with high self-esteem are generally happier with their lives than those with low self-esteem.[381]

Our degree of self-esteem doesn't just affect us—it affects our communications with others. Self-esteem interacts with three important interpersonal needs that affect how we communicate with others. These are the needs for control, inclusion, and affection.[53]

Our need for control motivates us to achieve and maintain some level of influence in our relationships. We need to have some say in what happens in our lives, including where others are involved.

Our need for inclusion is our need to belong. We need to have positive human contact and be included in the activities of others. When our need for inclusion is not met, people can experience mental and physical distress.

Our need for affection motivates us to have people in our lives who love and appreciate us and express their affection toward us. We also need to give love and intimacy to others. The more affection people give and receive, the healthier and happier they are.

All of these needs are fundamental and necessary to us as humans. People with high self-esteem tend to be more successful at getting these needs met through their communications with others.

Low self-esteem interacts with these needs by making these needs stronger. People with low self-esteem have greater needs for control, inclusion, and affection—

"control freaks", "whiners" about being left out, and "clingy" people. People with healthy self-esteem get these needs met without imposing on others.[53,402]

In sum: **Check your own level of self-esteem and the ways you get your needs for control, inclusion, and affection met. Be sure your needs are not excessive and you're not imposing on others.**

Aggressive Communication

A discussion of communicating in ways that are socially intelligent would not be complete without a segment on avoiding aggressive communication. This hearkens back to the material presented in Chapter 3 of this book.

Aggressive Versus Argumentative Communication

Aggressive communication is offset against argumentative communication based on the singular criterion of where the locus of attack falls. If you're attacking the person's self-concept in any way, through insults, whether veiled or direct, ridicule, mocking, most teasing, contempt, criticism, condescension, attacking family members and life choices, bringing up past errors, or any other way that gets at the person's sense of self and is aimed to get them to feel badly about themselves, which can also be as subtle as a tone of voice or an eye roll, this is considered aggressive communication. Hostile communication is a subset of aggressive communication and is used to express irritability, negativity, resentment and suspicion in various forms. None of these behaviors can be considered to be socially intelligent or representative of a competent communicator. All cause harm.[122]

On the other hand is argumentative communication. This might seem undesirable, as people often consider "argumentativeness" an undesirable trait in people. But when offset against aggressive communication, argumentativeness is desirable indeed. Argumentative communication sticks to the issue and does not leech into attacking the person's self-concept. Argumentative communication can become passionate and frustrating to deal with, but it's still better than the alternative, aggressive communication, because argumentative communication by this definition sticks to the ideas under discussion without attacking the speaker or the speaker's self-concept in any way. Assertiveness falls into argumentative communication because it focuses on issues rather than attacking people's personal characteristics and life choices.[122]

No one likes to be on the receiving end of aggressive or hostile communication. No one. No one likes to be the butt of a joke, or ridiculed or mocked for their life choices. Gentle teasing can be positive for the relationship, but aggressive teasing, such as veiled insults and assaults, are definitely aggressive. No one likes to be teased to the point of feeling bad. No one likes to be shamed by others, or have their tender spots poked, or have their personal weaknesses attacked or exploited. These can be done explicitly or implicitly, veiled with humor or as subtle as a tone of voice, but all are aggressive communication behaviors. When you engage in them, you are wielding words and nonverbal cues as personal weapons against the other person in an imagined battlefield of "it's either you or me." This is destructive and not on the path to social intelligence.[122]

Choose Assertiveness

Instead of resorting to hostility and verbal aggressiveness by giving the impression that you intend to harm the other person in some way, choose a route of assertiveness. In assertive communication, you are still interpersonally dominant and forceful and you use your communication to achieve your personal goals, but the difference is that you do this while instilling positive feelings in others. Assertiveness is considered a constructive communication trait because while you use verbal and nonverbal symbols to exert control and obtain justified rewards, you avoid violating the rights of others in this process. You may use symbols aggressively, but you also use them socially appropriately.[122]

Defining Assertiveness

In assertiveness, you stand up for your rights and express your thoughts feelings and beliefs in "direct, honest, and appropriate ways which do not violate another person's rights" (p. 7).[403] Additional assertiveness characteristics include openness, refusal of unreasonable requests, absence of interpersonal anxiety, initiation of requests, spontaneous expressions of one's feelings, refusal to be intimidated, outgoingness, willingness to take initiative, and active rather than passive disagreement.[404]

Assertiveness can be clustered into four dimensions. The first is directiveness, which is taking charge of situations. The second dimension is social assertiveness, which means feeling comfortable around people and having an ability to initiate conversations with variety of people, including strangers. The third is a defense of rights and interests, or standing up for one's rights, such as being able to confront others who are taking advantage of you. Finally, independence is the ability to maintain one's own personal convictions or position even when receiving pressure from others to conform.[405] Each of these behaviors is assertive, and in practicing them all you can be considered an assertive person. Again, the goal is to do all of this while instilling positive feelings in others.

It's fine to argue your point, and to argue it fully and well, with all of the evidence you can muster and all of the supports you can develop. You can argue it loudly and vehemently if you like. As long as you stick to the issue and don't attack the other person, you're practicing argumentative communication[122]—and social intelligence. Well, as long as you're also following the other steps for social intelligence you'll still be practicing social intelligence, that is. To be assertive, stand up for yourself while instilling positive feelings in others.

In sum: **Avoid aggressive communication behaviors. Practice assertive communication behaviors. (Don't attack others in any way; always stick to the issues.)**

Summary

Each of these 10 areas requires its own specific focus for improvement, and most of them will require daily attention. So, I have created a chart for you for easy reference.

ELEMENTS OF SOCIAL INTELLIGENCE

COMMUNICATION COMPETENCE
Communicate in ways that always protect the other person's needs to be deemed competent, autonomous, and socially adept. Be courteous.

LISTENING
Reduce poor listening practices; increase attentive listening.

LANGUAGE
Language is ambiguous and inexact, so don't get offended when you don't understand or aren't understood clearly. It's powerful, so use it consciously and responsibly. Try to avoid but.

POLLITENESS
Communicate in ways that always protect the other person's needs to be deemed competent, autonomous, and socially adept. Be courteous.

CO-CULTURAL DIFFERENCES
Have patience in interacting with others, as they've had different life experiences and see the world differently. Their perspectives are equally valid and valuable, even if (and sometimes especially if) they're different than our own.

CONFLICT
Watch yourself when you're in the middle of conflict: Avoid criticism, contempt, defensiveness, and stonewalling; and go for the win-win in seeking a resolution.

NONVERBAL MESSAGING
Use nonverbal cues intentionally. Be aware of what you're doing with your nonverbal cues. Match your nonverbal cues with your verbal cues so you don't send mixed messages.

SHOW VALUE
Always send confirming messages (recognition, acknowledgement, endorsement). Avoid sending disconfirming messages.

SELF-CONCEPT
Check your own level of self-esteem and the ways you get your needs for control, inclusion, and affection met. Be sure your needs are not excessive and you're not imposing on others.

AGGRESSIVE COMMUNICATION
Avoid aggressive communication behaviors. Practice assertive communication behaviors. (Don't attack others in any way; always stick to the issues.)

Conclusion

This chapter has presented key features of communication competence, also known as social intelligence or interpersonal competence. If you incorporate these behaviors into your habitual interactions with others, your relationships will vastly improve. Happier relationships means a happier life for you and for those with whom you share your life.

For your own mental well-being, put yourself in a healthy communication environment—one with the features of this chapter. This might mean cutting some current relationships, maybe even a lot of them. It might mean getting a new job and taking some serious distance from certain family members. It might put a new crunch on your marriage. Healing from trauma demands that you be in a safe environment. I'm not saying you need a new lover in order to heal from PTSD, but I am saying when you want to heal from a fear of being attacked, it helps if you're not actually attacked on a daily basis. If your life isn't really a safe place because the people in it constantly attack you, it's difficult to believe that life can be safe at all. When you have PTSD, you are missing precisely that sense of safety. The anxiety we experience around others helps protect us by forecasting those attacks and preparing us for them. If these attacks are real, the anxiety is warranted, and the PTSD will have every right to want to keep hanging around. If you want to get rid of the PTSD and its associated anxiety, it helps to actually put yourself in a safe environment. This means an environment of healthy communication, at minimum.

This list of 10 areas of focus is relatively short considering the world of possibilities that go into our communications, but work in these areas will get you to social intelligence. This is enough. There are only 10 areas here, and if you take them to heart and follow them carefully, your social intelligence will dramatically improve. Most of what is needed to master at least some of these requires only a small internal adjustment in your thinking and your approach to communicating with others.

Social intelligence holds more importance today than ever given the dynamics of contemporary life in a world seemingly smaller by the minute. As society progresses and our human population continues to grow at an exponential rate, this skill will gain even more importance. With more socially intelligent people in the world, it becomes a little easier for us all to live and work together in harmony and peace.

11.   The Intellect

We have arrived at the final chapter, the final segment of the self-wheel: the intellect. This dimension is different from all of the others. This is our consciousness. This is the most powerful tool we have. Without this component of the self-wheel, there would be no discussion at all, about anything.

Humans have evolved through our consciousness.

Its Role

Through the intellect, we can do whatever we want. We can learn languages both human and artificial, send satellites into orbit and rockets to Mars. We can cure sickness, plant gardens, learn and grow. We can become better people. We can heal.

Without going too far down this philosophical road, one of the elements that distinguishes *Homo sapiens* from other species is the evolution of our intellect.

Some may argue that our intellect is our greatest downfall. We use it to destroy each other in very sophisticated ways. In the animal kingdom a lot of species just butt heads, literally, until one of the two combatants capitulates for one reason or another, and the problem is solved. In the human world, we blow each other up from faraway continents with dead-on drones, and savvy advertising manipulates at levels beneath our consciousness multiple times a day. We are our own worst enemy. Yet we could achieve none of this without the intellect.

The point of entry into anything intentional is the intellect. We learn about things and solve our own problems. We set our minds to something and make it happen. We sense messages from the other dimensions of the self-wheel as they enter our field of awareness and we decide a course of action, all through the intellect. The intellect is the processor. It is the engine. We behave in accordance with what our intellect tells us to do. Someone knocks on your door, the little voice inside says, "ask who it is before opening the door," so that is exactly what you do.

The intellect is unlike any other of the primary dimensions of the human experience. In the first place, the intellect enables this discussion, and all other discussions, to occur. We could not talk about the spiritual realm or physical dimension or anything else without the intellect. I could not have written this book and you could not be reading it without the intellect. If we omit one of the other categories discussed here, a human being can still function and succeed in society—and so many of us do! But we cannot function without the intellect.

In the second place, sure the intellect can be harmed by a stressful childhood, but it can also remain very strong despite severe trauma, unlike any of the other dimensions discussed here. In some ways, the intellect is divorced from, separate from the other realms. The good news about this is that we can use the intellect to solve our problems even when those problems occur in those other spheres of our own existence. The bad news about this is, as we have seen in brilliant criminal minds over time, that highly intelligent and bat-guano crazy can easily coexist.

The two brain hemispheres
The brain has two hemispheres, each with its own specializations. Indeed, certain skills are housed in different hemispheres of the brain. The diagram below illustrates these differences.

The Human Brain Functions and Locations

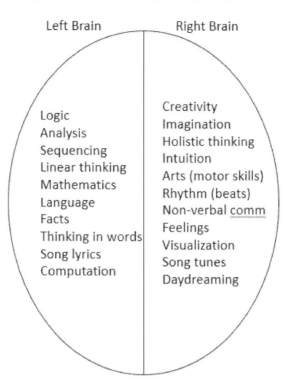

As you can see, characteristics of the left brain hemisphere include calculations, logic, and rationality, while those of the right brain include feeling, sensing, and creativity.

The Corpus Callosum

The left and right brain hemispheres were designed to work together. Everything has a linear and holistic existence simultaneously. Life is both rational and sensed. Songs have both lyrics and tunes.

In grad school I was a teaching assistant in a linguistics course one quarter. We saw a film clip about a man whose corpus callosum had been severed through an accident. This happenstance provided science with a rare opportunity to observe what happens when the left and right brain hemispheres no longer work together. Among the several tasks they asked this man to perform, the one that sticks with me involved viewing a drawing of a woman's head made up of individual pieces of fruit. When this man covered his left eye and looked through his right eye, using his left brain hemisphere and linear thought, he saw only a bunch of individual pieces of fruit. He did not see a woman's head. When he looked through his left eye only, accessing only his right brain hemisphere and holistic thought, this man saw only a woman's head—he saw no pieces of fruit. I found this a fascinating illustration of the linear versus holistic thinking that occurs in our respective brain hemispheres, yet we have no idea our brain is processing complex stimuli so seamlessly.

We need both hemispheres of our brains to work together so that we can see the whole picture and fully engage with whatever is before us.

Right brain hemisphere

Material presented in Section I said the right brain suffers harm in infancy, a very critical stage of development, when the baby lives in a stressful environment. Additionally, those of us in the industrialized world tend to preference left brain attributes over right brain attributes—we value facts over emotions, numbers over intuitions, math over art and music, and words actually vocalized despite the 93% of each message encoded in the nonverbal cues. This is the cultural value system that helps shape how we think.

Numerous online tests can help you identify whether your mental processing privileges either hemisphere or balances the two. In other words, are you more left-brained or right-brained? Most of us in the northern hemisphere and our powerful friends down under are more left-brained. As left-brain dominant individuals, our brain work is to strengthen our right brain. If we are processing all input with 70% off of one hemisphere and only 30% off of the other for example, don't you think we're missing out on using our brains to the fullest capacity available to us? The two hemispheres were designed to work together—so don't you think they should be balanced? I'm not saying weaken the 70%, I'm saying strengthen the 30% to a level that it matches the other side's previous 70%, with a relative 50-50 result.

Further, if our right brains actually did suffer harm during development, doesn't it make sense to focus a little on the specializations of the right brain to strengthen those attributes?

I think it's important to be able to use our whole brains as much as possible, and I think we tend to neglect some of those innate skills. Do you sing? Or are you one of those people who says "I can't sing" so you never do? Do you draw? Or do you say, "I can't draw" so you never do? Do you dance? Do you play a musical instrument? Do you listen to your intuition? None of these is something you must do well in order to do at all. I am not an Olympic walker but that does not mean I don't walk. Each of these activities is an important part of the human experience, and it is important that we humans partake in these activities so that we can exercise the parts of our right brains that house these activities. This chapter will provide some greater detail about approaches to exercising many specializations of the right brain hemisphere.

This chapter is short, light, and easy to read. There's no deep science here or any science really except for the commonly known work which identifies which attributes each brain hemisphere holds. In my search for relevant science to support and direct right brain hemispheric intellectual strengthening, I found a lot of science that focused on building certain areas, usually damaged due to a stroke, and of course Amen's work on targeting certain brain areas to obtain desired results in your life,[368] but I didn't really find anything that I could clearly relate to more general right-brain hemispheric development. In science's work to illuminate the specific, sometimes more general perspectives do not receive much attention. So, I offer here insights and logic instead.

Right Brain Focus
The brain is one complete organ with two parts that work together. For a well-rounded human being, it makes sense to have both brain hemispheres fully developed. That means many of us could use some dedicated focus in the areas of our lives governed by the brain's right hemisphere. We can create greater balance by focusing on the attributes housed in the right brain.

Creative arts
Spend time in creative activities. Get out the paints and some paper, or pens, or whatever floats your boat. Don't worry that you're no good at painting—it's not about being any good at it. I'm not a good surfer but I still get into the water and have fun with it. It's about the exercise, not the skill level. There are a lot of artistic media you can play with. I found a love for ceramics a few years ago.

Take a class, or just go buy some clay and shape it. There is mosaic, glass blowing, metal working, wood working, of course mixed media, and more. There are also hand crafts—knitting, crocheting, cross-stitching, sewing, needlepoint, embroidery, rug hooking, and more. It doesn't matter what creative activity you do. Just do something. Do a bunch of them. Try a few until you find something you like. Join a friend in his or her activity to see if you like it. The point is to get your hands busy in some creative activity—any creative activity, or a few of them.

Music

Spend some time making music. If you can play an instrument, great. Do that. If you can't, pull out a pot and beat it like a drum along to some of your favorite tunes. Don't worry that you might sound like a fool or that you can't keep the beat. Who cares! You're developing the skills of your right brain.

Also, dance! Again, it's not about being any good at it, and for sure, the more you do anything the better you'll get at it, if that's what you're concerned about. But it's about just doing it. It's about exercising your right brain and giving it some attention.

Hum the tune of your favorite song or any song. Just work with music in any and every way that you like. Take a class if you want. Learn an instrument. Learn to salsa or tango. Get music actively into your life!

Imagination creativity

Actively use your imagination. Make up stories either alone or with friends. Get creative with your humor. Get creative with your clothes. Activate your creativity and your imagination. Develop wild ideas. Let your mind go. Put yourself in situations where you're comfortable getting creative, around people who won't ridicule you for it but instead will appreciate you for it and support you. Be silly! Take some creative risks!

Emotional sensitivity

Pay more attention to your feelings. Don't tamp them down, especially you men out there (I'm sorry you were conditioned to do this). Don't pretend you don't have them. Your feelings are part of what make you human! And they are housed predominantly in your right brain. They are an integral part of your whole being and of who you are.

Express them. Feel them. Indulge in them! Never be afraid of them. If you're not used to expressing your feelings and then you start to, they might come as a waterfall as the dam first breaks, but don't worry—soon this will scale back to a normal trickle, just like everyone else.

Intuition

Activate your intuition. Practice it. Do intuition-building exercises. Close your eyes and sense what's happening around you. Try to "see" your environment and what those in it are doing without using your physical senses. You can solicit the help of a partner in this if you like—close your eyes and have them make a face at you, with (pretend) emotion behind it, and try to sense the sentiment they are sending to you. Close your eyes and have them look at you for a while then look away, and try to sense when they are looking at you and when they're not. Put out your feelers when you're around others—what do you sense? What do you pick up? If you have kids, try to sense what they're doing, feeling, and experiencing before asking them about it, then check with them for accuracy. Over time, you will be surprised at how much more accurate these assessments become! There are also lots of books available on building your intuition, and the visualization kind of meditation I mentioned earlier helps with this as well, particularly the chakra clearing and grounding meditations, plenty of which are readily available on Youtube.

One simple intuition exercise you can employ when making a decision. It works like this: Close your eyes. Relax by taking a few deep relaxing breaths. Try to clear your mind. Now focus intently on one of your options, and pay attention to your body. Be sure to think about this option objectively, not with any desire for it to be the accepted or rejected option. Just relax, and keep breathing and focusing on your option. Do you get sort of a sick, tight feeling in your gut? Or do you get sort of a soothing, relaxing, gentle feeling in your heart? As you can figure out, the former, gut-wrenching response is a "no" while the latter, heart-soothing response is a "yes". Go through each of your options and see how it feels in your body. If you don't feel anything, don't dismay. The sense is very gentle and if you're thinking too much, you won't feel anything. You have to relax. Take a few deep relaxing breaths and try it again. Be patient. If it still doesn't work, try it at a different time of day, when you're more relaxed. I use this to help me find parking spaces in crowded places.

Another simple intuition exercise you can do with food. Use your left hand (the left side of the body is controlled by the right brain and vice versa) and touch something you know to be bad for you. Maybe you're allergic to it, or if you don't have anything like that, use a household cleaner or gasoline. Imagine ingesting this thing. What is the sensation in your body? Do you feel a tightness in your gut? Do you feel a little ill? Is there somewhere deep within you screaming "No!" or "Ew!"? Now put your left hand on something you know to be good for you—like organic broccoli or carrots. Close your eyes, breathe slowly and deeply, and imagine ingesting it. How does your body feel? Maybe you will feel nothing at all, or maybe you will feel a gentle and welcoming "yes" rising from deep within you. In any case, you shouldn't feel the same sensation as you feel with the thing that you know will make you sick. Your body will tell you what it wants if you will just listen. This is a great, free, and effective way to determine your food allergies! It is also how people eat "intuitively".

Daydream
Moving on from developing your intuition, spend some time daydreaming, visualizing something—anything! If you have a hammock, lie in it. And let it take you away to some foreign exotic place. If you don't have a hammock, just find some place comfortable. Spend some time in your mind, letting it take you far away. Don't worry that you're wasting time—you're not! You're activating and exercising your right brain!

Holistic perspective-taking
Lastly, think about processes or situations and as you do, think about the whole picture. Don't think about the individual components, but rather, think about how each component contributes to the whole. You might consider the running of your household or your workplace for example. It runs like a well-oiled machine. Think about this process as a whole, look at it as a whole entity, with each step being a part of a synchronistic whole rather than an end in itself, and appreciate that.

I love being around artists, because their right-brains are usually more activated than most other people's which gives them different perspectives. One time while looking at the port activity, unloading containers and loading trains, I asked an artist friend of mine what his favorite part of the container-ship-train process was, and his response was, "all of it." His viewpoint encompasses the entire process, in full recognition that each individual piece plays a vital role, but there is no whole without each composite part doing its job. My favorite part was the trains.

Conclusion
You can focus on right-brain development in all of the ways listed above and more—using your creativity and imagination, of course—until you test at 50-50, left brain-right brain. I neglect to suggest how to strengthen left brain hemispheric skills here simply because most of us don't seem to have that problem. If you do happen to test with more right-brain dominant results, then certainly, play some sudoku at minimum and take a math, language, or computer class. Read about

science, since reading as well as the linear logic of scientific thinking are left-brain tasks. Learn information. Do calculations by hand.

After all, you have two hemispheres to your brain. Why would you want to reduce the power of either side? Why would you want to limit your potential in any way?

Pay specific attention to all of the attributes and capabilities of your brain. Activate all of your tools. Use your own intellect to branch out from the material in this book and further investigate certain trajectories for yourself. Forge your own path through the woods of your own healing by pulling from influences that draw you. Indeed, use the attributes of both hemispheres, the right activating intuition to choose a path and the left responsible for following it, in determining your personal course of action.

Conclusion

So there you have it—a complete explanation of what a stressful childhood environment looks like, what happens to us as a result of developing in a stressful environment, and tools for moving past the harm that environment brings. Our brains didn't develop properly in stressful environments, and we have some deficiencies that we need to strengthen as a result.

Even if our mother was just emotionally unavailable—even just that alone—means our brains didn't form properly and we weren't given the appropriate tools, or maybe even any tools at all, to manage life's stressors. If she was also mean, we've got some wicked internal models to deconstruct and we've got to check the coping mechanisms we've developed. In fact, we need to check all of our behaviors and ways of thinking against the various lists of characteristics provided in this book and be sure we're using the healthy options. If we want out of the hole dug for us as a launch into adult life, we have to fight against the forces we were taught and be bold enough to step outside of those norms to find the path of mental wellness.

Healing
Recipients of childhood mistreatment can follow the steps outlined in Section II in order to have a healthy, or at least healthier, life. If we're avoiding engaging in these healthy behaviors, we're skipping out. We're not healing. By our inaction, we're voluntarily keeping ourselves in the hole dug for us. If we want out of the pain that having a stressful upbringing gave us, we have to fight for it. It's worth fighting for.

The conditions reported here are dire and severe. But they don't have to be permanent. For you poker players out there, consider a game of 5-card draw: You get dealt a hand, go around the table, and decide if you want to trade some of the cards you were dealt in hopes to get some better ones so you can more easily win the pot. Trying to win the pot with a poor hand means you have to fake it all the way. You bluff because you don't actually hold the goods. Being raised in a stressful environment and/or with childhood trauma means we were dealt a poor hand and are bluffing it through life. We are trying to give impressions of confidence and competencies that we actually lack. This book gives you a deck of cards to draw from to improve the hand you were dealt. But unlike the game of 5-card draw where you get only 1 or maximum 2 chances to improve your hand, in this game of real life, you can replace as many cards as you want, working up to a powerful winning hand. And, even though there may be some adjustment periods with some of these ideas since they are new to you and your life, you are guaranteed to trade up in the quality of your hand with every draw. Poker never promises that!

Give yourself the gifts that a better life offers. The steps here are not that hard to adopt and they're presented here individually and clearly laid out for you. Exchange a couple of cards in your hand with a couple from the deck of options I offer you here. Choose a starting place—it doesn't matter where and for goodness sake, please do not go through these in order! Do each step as it calls to you. Tackle one at a time from the variety of choices presented. There's plenty to think about here and plenty to keep you busy for a long time if you decide to embrace this healing journey. Remember, I didn't make this stuff up; I've pulled from all kinds of authorities in putting this toolkit together for you. I just combined this wonderful information in a way that made sense to me. And since I found the trail to peace and happiness, I wanted to illuminate it in case anyone else wants to take it.

Recap

In Section I, I talked about what mentally unwell behavior looks like and what it does to us. I talked a lot about the consequences of this kind of stressful upbringing on our brains and consequently, on our adult lives—the distortions, anxiety, relationship struggles, even physiological pain and suffering that ensue.

I then brought in a lot of emotional manipulation techniques because they are so confusing, so hard to identify, and really really mess us up when we are raised by a person who practices these techniques in her daily interactions. I also presented aggressive communication tactics because they also do us a great deal of harm. This sort of setting is not good for anyone, particularly a developing child. Mental and emotional mistreatment is very confusing and hard to identify—part of its inherent insidiousness and ability to inflict harm and one of the main reasons it's so effective—so it's helpful to have a list of characteristics against which we can gauge the behaviors of our parent(s) as well as others in our lives. If we can understand the traits that harm us, we can protect ourselves from them. Also, if we are delivering harm without being aware of this, hopefully we can recognize that.

After fully illustrating the stressful childhood home environment and the problems it brings to us as adults, I went through healing in six dimensions of the human experience.

Together, this information will help you understand what happened to you, why you are the way you are in many respects and why you make the kinds of poor decisions you sometimes make, and how to heal from all of that.

The Problem
In Section I, I went through what happens to us neurologically, physiologically, and psychologically when we are raised in a mentally unwell environment. I personally found those implications absolutely astounding. It is such a relief to better understand what happens to you during development when you're raised by a mentally unwell person, especially a mother because of her role as your primary caregiver. I found it astonishing to learn that trauma can begin even before birth if the woman carrying you is super anxious, and also astounding to learn the actual neurodevelopmental problems that can result from being raised in a stressful environment. It's not just that we have problems with interacting well with others as a result of this mother-child relationship—our brains didn't even actually form properly and we didn't learn how to manage our emotions or indeed, cope with life's stressors at all, predisposing us to a lifetime of anxiety.

Further, those problems are just the beginning. We saw how being raised in a stressful environment creates all sorts of distortions in our perceptions, thinking, feeling and behaving; generates unhealthy coping techniques; and leads to real problems finding and maintaining healthy, fulfilling relationships. No wonder we feel like we're a mess sometimes—we kind of are.

The Solution
Section II shows the way out, however. This toolkit provides rich and effective strategies to straighten out the wonkiness that results from being raised in a stressful environment. This self-straightening requires time and a fair amount of effort, but most of it involves adjusting your ways of perceiving, thinking, feeling and behaving, primarily about your self, slowly but surely moving the needle on the anxiety gauge to the healthy zone. Indeed, there are actually things most of you can do to straighten yourself out from this kind of developmental damage and live a happy, healthy life despite where you came from and what happened to you as a kid. You do not have to live your entire life with the pain and struggles instilled in you as a small child. You can see that with this toolkit, that way of life becomes a choice—

you can stay where you were raised and placed, or you can take the steps to get out of that living hell and make your own way of peace.

The toolkit section, Section II, provided strategies for improving in every major area of your life that was subjected to distortions due to your twisted upbringing. There are six primary planes of existence, and six chapters in this section. The section begins with adopting a spiritual practice. Meditation quells the anxiety within and sets a serene internal landscape for the other work you have to do. It's all a lot easier if you're not a ball of anxiety to begin with—less to struggle against. Also, a mindfulness practice in its own right has been found to work wonders in healing mental and even physical ailments: It cannot be overrated.

Discussions of attending to your physical body come next, with perspectives on diet, rest, exercise, hygiene and posture. Our physical plane is not only the most visible to ourselves and others, but in some ways it's the hardest to attend to because it demands certain intentional behaviors to address—we need to take excellent care of ourselves in terms of what we eat, how much we sleep, how much we exercise, and for some of us, even our hygiene. These are physical behaviors. The best way to motivate yourself to do these things to take care of yourself in these ways is to do them from a place of loving yourself. You love yourself so you will take care of your body in these ways, thus honoring your self and treating yourself with love, dignity and respect—just like you would treat anyone you love.

A chapter on emotional intelligence comes next. This is a relatively short chapter because it's not a complex topic and, if you develop a dedicated mindfulness practice, emotional intelligence will take care of itself. Developing your emotional intelligence basically means you manage the expression of your emotions responsibly. Most of our emotions are not too difficult to manage, but those in the anxious category and sometimes also the sad category generally require some dedicated focus and also some patience with ourselves to manage appropriately in social interactions.

Following emotional intelligence comes the very important chapter on psychological development. This chapter contains some simple characteristics of what mental health looks like in order to articulate a destination for where you're headed with all of this work. It talks about how to adjust your way of thinking to re-view your traumas and other difficult experiences, and presents some healing tools from psychologists. This chapter also focuses on ways to build your self-esteem. Kids raised in unhealthy environments don't come out of them with healthy self-esteem, so we need to do some work in this area. This chapter makes self-esteem develop-ment simple and straightforward, and not at all painful or difficult. It closes with a brief discussion and outline of ethics, again to provide a set of guidelines for appro-priate behavior.

The social intelligence techniques come next. This chapter is hugely important be-cause coming out of stressful childhood homes, we developed internal models of relationships as explosive, cruel, and/or painful. We take these expectations—and behaviors of our own—into our future relationships: small wonder we can't find healthy and satisfying ones. This chapter offers areas of focus within relationships to help you better understand relational dynamics and more intentionally behave within those relationships. Our relational skills took a deep hit in our stressful child-hood homes, so this chapter is absolutely essential for smoothing out your way of being on all planes.

The final chapter addresses the intellect and strengthening the skills of our right brain hemisphere. Not only is our right brain hugely underrated in our culture, but as infants with mentally unwell mothers, our right brain didn't even develop properly in the first place. The right brain governs intuition, emotion, creativity, music and art. To balance our selves, it is useful to spend some time exercising and expanding the skills of our right brains. We can do this simply by exercising the skills that the right brain houses. We all have a right brain, and we all have the capabili-ties the right brain offers. Let us not allow those capabilities to atrophy from un-deruse but instead, let us amplify and celebrate those capabilities, bringing them up to the skill level of our left-brain consciousness. In this way, we become more well-rounded and better-balanced individuals.

We suffered damage on each of these planes of our selves, so healing requires ded-icated attention to strengthening and improving each of these planes separately. The growth offered by following these strategies is best achieved by working through them one small piece at a time, slowly adding a new piece when you feel ready.

Strategizing
There is no appropriate timeframe for working through, adopting, and internalizing these ways of thinking and being—we all work at our own pace, and we have the rest of our lives to figure this stuff out.

At the same time, stopping the pain is an immediate goal for most of us, so I would direct you to the chapters on spirituality (Chapter 6), the tapping portion of Chapter 8, and psychology (Chapter 9) for some immediate relief.

Importantly, please take your time overall and allow these new ways of thinking and perceiving to sink in slowly. These changes should not occur overnight but rather, take a lot of time to fully internalize and integrate into your life. There is no rush. You're not going anywhere until you hit the grave so you've got time.

I hope that this book has provided insights to you and illuminated the complex dynamics of how a stressful environment interacts with a developing child, helping you to better understand your self and your personal struggles. As you can see, the anxieties you bear are not your own fault—you didn't create them. But of course, those struggles are entirely yours now, and all your responsibility to work through and put to rest. I hope that you find this guidance for straightening yourself out useful and very helpful. The journey can be long and arduous, I'm not going to lie, but arriving at the promised land of mental health, ease, and well-being is definitely worth every step. Besides—our only task on this planet is to fill our time here. What could be a better way to spend that time than to focus on being a better person and making tomorrow so much better and easier than today, for our selves and for those in our lives.

Please approach these techniques in any way that calls to you, and by no means in the exact order as presented in this book. Choose one technique at a time and work on incorporating that one, then another technique, perhaps in the same dimension or perhaps for a different one. It's okay to map out your healing route holistically rather than linearly—and so very right-brained of you to do so! Try to take a baby step every single day. Maybe give yourself a focus for the day or for the week such as, "I'm going to work on my listening skills today" and then "I'm going to pay attention to my emotions rising today" and "I'm going to behave with absolute integrity in all of my interactions and behaviors today." One step at a time, one focus at a time, one day at a time—you'll get there.

Revisit attributes from time to time, as they could probably use fine-tuning. Then take a break sometimes and recognize and appreciate how far you've come. Honor yourself for the growth you're making. Be proud of yourself. You are showing yourself love and you are healing. Kudos to you!!

In Your Future

I hope you hold on to this book and refer to it from time to time. I realize you probably read pretty much straight through this book, as we tend to do, and I also hope you see that these are not techniques that you can employ instantly or even all at the same time.

These concepts take time to develop within you and fully internalize, and that development and internalization requires that you revisit the source occasionally to remind yourself where you're going. It's easy to fall off track when we're blazing new terrain, as we're not sure exactly where we're going or what that looks like, and everyone comfortable with our old version of our selves wants to keep us on the old path so we tend to get some resistance to our growth, making it even that much harder.

Blazing those trails in our psyche is not an exception—it's still absolutely new to us, these ways of perceiving, thinking, and behaving—and occasionally consulting a road map along the way can help immensely to ensure we're still headed in the right direction. I am sure that along your journey, you will find some beautiful surprises in your new realizations—so very exciting!

Onward and Upward!

Be excited! A whole new you is emerging! And that person is absolutely stunningly beautiful! There's a little work to do to get there, but that work is oh so very worth it for the tremendous beauty and bounty your life will reveal. I promise you, it is worth every single step.

References

1.	Hart SN, Brassard MR. A major threat to children's mental health: Psychological maltreatment. *American Psychologist.* 1987;42:160-165.
2.	Cloitre M, Scarvalone P, Difede J. Posttraumatic stress disorder, self-and interpersonal dysfunction among sexually retraumatized women. *Journal of Traumatic Stress.* 1997;10:437-452.
3.	Cloitre M, Tardiff K, Marzuk PM, Leon AC, Portera L. Childhood abuse and subsequent sexual assault among female inpatients. *Journal of Traumatic Stress.* 1996;9:473-482.
4.	Merrill LL, Newell CE, Thomsen CJ, et al. Childhood abuse and sexual revictimization in a female navy recruit sample. *Journal of Traumatic Stress.* 1999;12:211-225.
5.	Schaaf KK, McCanne TR. Relationship of childhood sexual, physical, and combined sexual and physical abuse to adult victimization and posttraumatic stress disorder. *Child Abuse & Neglect.* 1998;22:1119-1133.
6.	Kilpatrick DG, Acierno R, Saunders B, Resnick HS, Best CL, Schnurr PP. Risk factors for adolescent substance abuse and dependence: data from a national sample. *Journal of Consulting and Clinical Psychology.* 2000;68:19-30.
7.	Dunn GE, Ryan JJ, Dunn CE. Trauma symptoms in substance abusers with and without histories of childhood abuse. *Journal of Psychoactive Drugs.* 1994;26(4):357-360.
8.	Eliason JW, Ross CA, Sainton K, Mayran LW. 60. *1.* 1996;39-51.
9.	Van der Kolk BA, Fisler RE. Childhood abuse and neglect and loss of self-regulation. *Bulletin of the Menninger Clinic.* 1994;58(2):145-168.
10.	Khantzian EJ. The self-medication hypothesis of addictive disorders: Focus on heroin and cocaine dependence. *American Journal of Psychiatry.* 1985;142:1259-1264.
11.	Conger JJ. Reinforcement theory and the dynamics of alcoholism. *Quarterly Journal of Studies on Alcohol.* 1956;17:296-305.
12.	Afifi T, Boman J, Fleisher W, Sareen J. The relationship between child abuse, parental divorce, and lifetime mental disorders and suicidality in a nationally representative adult sample. *Child Abuse & Neglect.* 2009;33:139-147.
13.	Finkelhor D, Browne A. The traumatic impact of child sexual abuse: A conceptualization. *American Journal of Orthopsychiatry.* 1985;55(4):530-541.
14.	Smiljanich K, Briere J. Sexual abuse history and trauma symptoms in a university sample. . Conference of the American Psychological Association; 1993; Toronto, Canada.
15.	Spertus I, L., Yehuda R, Wong CM, Halligan S, Seremetis SV. Childhood emotional abuse and neglect as predictors of psychological and physical symptoms in

women presenting to a primary care practice. *Child Abuse & Neglect.* 2003;27:1247-1258.

16. Felitti VJ, Anda RF, Nordemberg D, et al. Relationship of childhood abuse to many of the leading causes of death in adults: the adverse childhood experiences (ACE) study. *American Journal of Preventative Medicine.* 1998;14(4):245-258.

17. Perry BD. The neuro-developmental impact of violence in childhood. In: Schetky D, Benedek E, eds. *Textbook of child and adolescent forensic psychiatry.* Washington DC: American Psychiatric Press, Inc.; 2001:221-238.

18. Shonkoff J, Phillips D, eds. *From neurons to neighborhoods: The science of early childhood development.* Washington DC: National Academy Press; 2000.

19. Greenough WT, Black JE, Wallace CS. Experience and brain development. *Child Development.* 1978;58:539-559.

20. Matthews KA, Rakaczky CJ, Stoney CM, al. e. Are cardiovascular responses to behavioral stressors a stable individual difference variable in childhood? *Psychophysiology.* 1987;24:464-473.

21. Perry BD. Neurobiological Sequelae of Childhood Trauma: Post traumatic Stress Disorders in Children. In: Murburg M, ed. *Catecholamine Function in Post Traumatic Stress Disorder: Emerging Concepts.* Washington DC: American Psychiatric Press; 1994.

22. Schofferman J, Anderson D, Hines R. Childhood psychological trauma and chronic refractory low-back pain. *Clinical Journal of Pain.* 1993;9:260-265.

23. Heim C, Newport DJ, Wagner D, Wilcox MM, Miller AH, Nemeroff CB. The role of early adverse experience and adulthood stress in the prediction of neuroendocrine stress reactivity in women: A multiple regression analysis. *Depression and Anxiety.* 2002;15:117-125.

24. Smith GD, Ben-Shlomo Y, Beswick A, Yarnell J, Lightman S, Elwood P. Cortisol, testosterone, and coronary heart disease: Prospective evidence from the Caerphilly study. *Circulation.* 2005;112:332-340.

25. Walker ED, Keegan D, Gardner G, Sullivan M, Bernstein D, Katon WJ. Psychosocial Factors in Fibromyalgia Compared With Rheumatoid Arthritis: II. Sexual, Physical, and Emotional Abuse and Neglect. *Psychosomatic Medicine.* 1997;59:572-577.

26. Schürks M, Rist PM, Bigal ME, Buring JE, Lipton RB, Kurth T. Migraine and cardiovascular disease: Systematic review and meta-analysis. *BMJ.* 2009:339-b3914.

27. Lanktree CB, Briere J, Zaidi LY. Incidence and impacts of sexual abuse in a child outpatient sample: The role of direct inquiry. *Child Abuse & Neglect* 1991;15:447-453.

28. Kolko DJ, Moser JT, Weldy SR. Behavioral/emotional indications of sexual abuse in child psychiatric inpatients: A controlled comparison with physical abuse. *Child Abuse and Neglect* 1988;12:529-542.

29. Saunders BE, Villeponteaux LA, Lipovsky JA. Child sexual assault as a risk factor for mental disorders among women: A community survey. *Journal of Interpersonal Violence* 1992;7:189-204.

30. Stein JA, Golding JM, Siegel JM. Long-term psychological sequelae of child sexual abuse: The Los Angeles epidemiological catchment area study. In: Wyatt GE, Powell GJ, eds. *The lasting effects of child sexual abuse.* Newbury Park, CA: Sage; 1988.

31. Ford JD. Disorders of extreme stress following war-zone military trauma: associated features of posttraumatic stress disorder or comorbid but distinct syndromes? . *Journal of Consulting and Clinical Psychology.* 1999;67:3-12.

32. Herman JL. *Trauma and recovery: the aftermath of violence-from domestic abuse to political terror.* New York: Basic Books; 1997.

33. Roth S, Newman E, Pelcovitz D, van der Kolk B, Mandel FS. Complex PTSD in victims exposed to sexual and physical abuse: results from the DSM-IV Field Trial for Posttraumatic Stress Disorder. *Journal of Traumatic Stress.* 1997;IO:539-555.

34. Van der Kolk BA, Roth SH, Pelcovitz D, Sunday S, Spinazzola J. Disorders of extreme stress: The empirical foundation of complex adaptation to trauma. *Journal of Traumatic Stress.* 2005;18:389-399.

35. Carmen EJ, Rieker PP, Mills T. Victims of violence and psychiatric illness. *American Journal of Psychiatry* 1984;141:378-383.

36. Stukas-Davis C. The influence of childhood sexual abuse and male sex role socialization on adult sexual functioning. . In. California School of Professional Psychology: Los Angeles, CA; 1990.

37. Egeland B. A longitudinal study of high risk families: Issues and findings. Research Forum on Issues in the Longitudinal Study of Child Maltreatment; October, 1989; Toronto.

38. Bateman A, Fonagy P. *Mentalization based treatment for borderline personality disorder: A practical guide.* Oxford: Oxford University Press; 2006.

39. Schore AN. *Affect regulation and the origin of the self: The neurobiology of emotional development.* Mahwah, NJ: Erlbaum; 1994.

40. Siegel D. *The developing mind: How relationships and the brain interact to shape who we are.* New York: Guilford Press; 1999.

41. Taylor GJ, Bagby RM, Parker JDA. *Disorders of affect regulation: alexithymia in medical and psychiatric illness.* Cambridge: Cambridge University Press; 1997.

42. Bremner JD, Southwick SM, Johnson DR, Yehuda R, Charney DS. Childhood psysical abuse and combat-related posttraumatic stress disorder in Vietnam veterans. *American Journal of Psychiatry.* 1993;150(2):235-239.

43. Graham DP, Savas L, White D, et al. Irritable bowel syndrome symptoms and health related quality of life in female veterans. *Alimentary Pharmacology & Therapeutics.* 2010;31(2):261-273.

279

44.   Cole PM, Putnam FW. Effect of incest on self and social functioning: developmental psychopathology perspective. *Journal of Consulting and Clinical Psychology.* 1992;60(2):174-184.

45.   McCauley J, Kem D, Kolodner K, et al. Clinical characteristics of women with a history of child abuse: Unhealed wounds. *Journal of the American Medical Association.* 1997;277:1362-1368.

46.   Poulsny M, Follette V. Theory and review of the empirical literature. *Applied & Preventative Psychology.* 1995;4:143-166.

47.   Putnam FW. Childhood maltreatment adverse outcomes. 152nd Annual Meeting of the American Psychiatric Association; 1999; Washington, D.C.

48.   van der Kolk BA, Perry C, Herman JL. Childhood origins of self-destructive behavior. *American Journal of Psychiatry.* 1991;148:1665-1671.

49.   Kilpatrick DG, Resnick HS, Freedy JR, et al. Posttraumatic stress disorder field trial: Evaluation of the PTSD construct – Criteria A through E. . In: Widiger TA, Frances AJ, Pincus H, et al., eds. *DSM-IV Sourcebook* Vol 4. 4 ed. Washington DC: American Psychiatric Association Press; 1998.

50.   Ruchkin V, Henrich CC, Jones SM, Vermeiren R, Schwab-Stone M. Violence exposure and psychopathology in urban youth: the mediating role of posttraumatic stress. *Journal of Abnormal Child Psychology.* 2007;35:578-593.

51.   Wasserman GA, McReynolds LS. Contributors to traumatic exposure and posttraumatic stress disorder in juvenile justice youths. *Journal of Traumatic Stress.* 2011;24:422-429.

52.   Putnam FW. *Dissociation in children and adolescents: a developmental perspective.* New York: The Guilford Press; 1997.

53.   Floyd K. *Interpersonal Communication: The whole story.* New York: McGraw Hill; 2009.

54.   Fonagy P, P. L. A developmental, mentalization-based approach to the understanding and treatment of borderline personality disorder. *Development and Psychopathology.* 2009;21:1355-1381.

55.   Bryer J, Nelson B, Miller JB, Krol PA. Childhood sexual and physical factors in adult psychiatric illness. *American Journal of Psychiatry.* 1987;144:1426-1430.

56.   Fleming J, Mullen PE, Sibthrope B, Bammer G. The long term impact of childhood sexual abuse in Australian women. *Child Abuse and Neglect.* 1999;23:145-159.

57.   Widom CS, Czaja SJ, Dutton MA. Childhood victimization and lifetime revictimization. *Child Abuse and Neglect.* 2008;32(8):785-796.

58.   Bernard ML, Bernard JL. Violent intimacy: The family as a model for love relationships. *Family Relations.* 1983;32:283-286.

59.   Riggs DS, O'Leary KD. Aggression between heterosexual dating partners: An examination of a causal model of courtship aggression. *Journal of Interpersonal Violence.* 1996;11(4):519-540.

60.   Tjaden P, Thoennes N. *Full Report of the Prevalence, Incidence, and Consequences of Violence Against Women: Findings from the National Violence*

Against Women Survey. Washington, D.C.: National Institute of Justice and the Centers for Disease Control and Prevention;2000.

61.   Morrill AC, Kasten L, Urato M, Larson MJ. Abuse, addiction, and depression as pathways to sexual risk in women and men with a history of substance abuse. *Journal of Substance Abuse.* 2001;13:169-184.

62.   Van der Kolk B, Greenburg MS, Orr S. Pain perception and engogenous opioids in post-traumatic stress disorder. *Psychopharmacol Bulletin.* 1989;25.

63.   Perry BD. Childhood Trauma, the Neurobiology of Adaptation, and "Use-dependent" Development of the Brain: How "States" Become "Traits". *Infant Mental Health Journal.* 1995;16(4):271-272.

64.   Miczek KA, Thompson ML, Tornatzky W. Subordinate animals: Behavioral and physiological adaptations and opioid tolerance. In: Brown MR, Koob GF, Rivier C, eds. *Stress: Neurobiology and Neuroendocrinology.* New York: Marcek Dekker; 1990:323-357.

65.   Lyons-Ruth K. Rapproachment or approchement: Mahler's theory reconsidered from the vantage point of recent research in early attachment relationships. *Psychoanalytic Psychology.* 1991;8:1-23.

66.   Main M, Hesse E. Parents' unresolved traumatic experiences are related to infant disorganized attachment status: Is frightened/frightening parental behavior the linking mechanism? . In: Greenberg MT, Cicchetti D, Cummings EM, eds. *Attachment in the Preschool Years: Theory, Research, and Intervention.* Chicago, IL: University of Chicago Press; 1990:161-182.

67.   Bradshaw GA, Schore AN, Brown JL, Poole JL, Moss CJ. Elephant breakdown. *Nature.* 2005;433(7028):807.

68.   James J, Meyerding J. Early sexual experiences as a factor in prostitution. *Archives of Sexual Behavior.* 1977;7:31-42.

69.   Bowlby J. *Attachment and loss.* Vol 2: Separation. New York: Basic Books; 1973.

70.   Courtois C. Complex trauma, complex reactions: Assessment and treatment. *Psychotherapy: Theory, Research, Practice, Training, .* 2004;41(4):412-425.

71.   van der Kolk BA, Roth SH, Pelcovitz D, Mandel F. *Complex PTSD: Results of the PTSD field trials for DSM-IV.* Washington, DC: American Psychiatric Association;1993.

72.   Taft CT, Watkins LE, Stafford J, Street AE, Monson CM. Posttraumatic stress disorder and intimate relationship problems: A meta-analysis. *Journal of Consulting and Clinical Psychology.* 2011;79(1):22-33.

73.   Taft CT, Kaloupek DG, Schumm JA, et al. Posttraumatic stress disorder symptoms, physiological reactivity, alcohol problems, and aggression among military veterans. *Journal of Abnormal Psychology.* 2007;116:498-507.

74.   Taft CT, Schumm JA, Marshall AD, Panuzio J, Holtzworth-Munroe A. Family-of-origin maltreatment, PTSD symptoms, social information processing deficits, and

relationship abuse perpetration. *Journal of Abnormal Psychology.* 2008;117:637-646.

75.   Taft CT, Street AE, Marshall AD, Dowdall DJ, Riggs DS. Posttraumatic stress disorder, anger, and partner abuse among Vietnam combat veterans. *Journal of Family Psychology.* 2007;21:270-277.

76.   Ford JD, Fisher P, Larson L. Object relations as a predictor of treatment outcome withchronic posttraumatic stress disorder. *Journal of Consulting and Clinical Psychology.* 1997;65(4):547-559.

77.   Lewis CS, Jospitre T, Griffing S, Chu M, Sage RE, Madry L. Childhood maltreatment, familial violence, and retraumatization: assessing inner-city battered women. *Journal of Emotional Abuse.* 2006;6(9):47-67.

78.   Wortmann JH, Park CL, Edmondson D. Trauma and PTSD symptoms: Does spiritual struggle mediate the link? *Psychological Trauma: Theory, Research, Practice, and Policy.* 2011;3(4):442.

79.   Crittenden PM. Distorted patterns of relationship in maltreating families: The role of internal representational models. *Journal of Reproductive and Infant Psychology.* 1988;6:183-199.

80.   Luxenberg T, Spinazzola J, Hidalgo J, Hunt C, van der Kolk BA. Complex trauma and disorders of extreme stress (DESNOS) part two: treatment. *Directions in Psychiatry.* 2001;21:395-414.

81.   Zweig-Frank H, Paris J. Parents' Emotional Neglect and Overprotection According to the Recollections of Patients With Borderline Personality Disorder. *American Journal of Psychiatry.* 1991;148(5):648-651.

82.   AmericanPsychiatricAssociation. *Diagnostic and statistical manual of mental disorders (DSM-5®).* American Psychiatric Pub; 2013.

83.   Mayo Clinic Staff. Mental illness. Mayo Clinic. Patient Care & Health Information, Diseases & Conditions Web site. https://www.mayoclinic.org/diseases-conditions/mental-illness/diagnosis-treatment/drc-20374974. Accessed May 28, 2020.

84.   Mayo Clinic Staff. Personality disorders. Mayo Clinic. Patient Care & Health Information, Diseases & Conditions Web site. https://www.mayoclinic.org/diseases-conditions/personality-disorders/symptoms-causes/syc-20354463. Published 2016. Accessed May 28, 2020.

85.   Hollis C. Depression, family environment, and adolescent suicidal behavior. . *Journal of the American Academy of Child and Adolescent Psychiatry.* 1996;35:622-630.

86.   Alexopoulos GS, Bruce ML, Hull J, Sirey JA, Kakuma T. Clinical determinants of suicidal ideation and behavior in geriatric depression. *Archives of General Psychiatry.* 1999;56:1048-1053.

87.   Garrison CZ, McKeown RE, Valois RF, Vincent ML. Aggression, substance use, and suicidal behaviors in high school students. *American Journal of Public Health.* 1993;83:179-184.

88.   Beautrais AL, Joyce PR, Mulder RT. Risk factors for serious suicide attempts among youths aged 13 through 24 years. *Journal of the American Academy of Child and Adolescent Psychiatry.* 1996;35:1174-1182.

89.   Dinwiddie S, Heath AC, Dunne MP. Early sexual abuse and lifetime psychopathology: a co-twin-control study. *Psychological Medicine.* 1990;30:41-52.

90.   Briere J, Runtz M. Multivariate correlates of childhood psychological and physical maltreatment among university women. *Child Abuse & Neglect.* 1988;12:437-452.

91.   Mullen PE, Martin JL, Anderson JC, Romans SE, Herbison GP. The long-term impact of the physical, emotional, and sexual abuse of children: A community study. *Child Abuse & Neglect.* 1996;20:7-21.

92.   Rich DJ, Gingerich KJ, Rosen LA. Childhood emotional abuse and associated psychopathy in college students. *Journal of College Student Psychotherapy.* 1997;11:13-28.

93.   Sackett LA, Saunders DG. The impact of different forms of psychological abuse on battered women. *Violence and Victims.* 1999;14:105-117.

94.   Johnson JG, Cohen P, Smailes EM, Skodol AE, Brown J, Oldham JM. Childhood verbal abuse and risk for personality disorders during adolescence and early adulthood. *Comprehensive Psychiatry.* 2001;42:16-23.

95.   Pitzner JK, Drummond PD. The reliability and validity of empirically scaled measures of psychological/verbal control and physical/sexual abuse: Relationship between current negative mood and a history of abuse independent of other negative life events. *Journal of Psychosomatic Research.* 1997;43:125-142.

96.   Meston CM, Heiman JR, Trapnell PD. The relation between early abuse and adult sexuality. *Journal of Sex Research.* 1999;36:385-395.

97.   Deering C, Glover S, Ready D, Eddleman H, Alarcon R. Unique patterns of comorbidity in posttraumatic stress disorder from different sources of trauma. *Comprehensive Psychiatry.* 1996;37:336-346.

98.   Shalev A. Measuring outcome in posttraumatic stress disorder. *Journal of Clinical Psychiatry.* 2000;61:33-39.

99.   Kessler R, Sonnega A, Bromet E, Hughes M, Nelson C. Posttraumatic stress disorder in the national comorbidity survey. *Archives of General Psychiatry.* 1995;52:1048-1060.

100.   Creamer M, Burgess PM, McFarlance AC. Posttraumatic stress disorder: Findings from the Australian National Survey of Mental Health and Well-Being. *Psychological Medicine.* 2001;31(7):1237-1247.

101. Kosten TR, Mason JW, Giller EL. Sustained urinary norepinephrine and epinephrine elevation in post-traumatic stress disorder. *Psychoneuroendocrinology* 1986.

102. Hollon SD, Garber J. Cognitive therapy. In: Abramson LY, ed. *Social cognition and clinical psychology: A synthesis* New York: Guilford Press; 1988:204-253.

103. McCann L, Pearlman LA. *Psychological trauma and the adult survivor: Theory, therapy, and transformation.* New York: Brunner/Mazel; 1990.

104. Piaget J. *Possibility and necessity.* Vol 2. Minneapolis: University of Minnesota Press; 1987.

105. Resick PA, Schnicke MK. *Cognitive processing therapy for rape victims: A treatment manual.* Newbury Park, CA: Sage; 1993.

106. Beck AT. *Depression; Causes and Treatment.* Philadelphia: University of Pennsylvania Press; 1972.

107. Martin RC, Dahlen ER. Cognitive emotion regulation in the prediction of depression, anxiety, stress, and anger. *Personality and Individual Differences* 2005;39(7):1249-1260.

108. Bailey HN, Moran G, Pederson DR. Childhood maltreatment, complex trauma symptoms, and unresolved attachment in an at-risk sample of adolescent mothers *Attachment and Human Development.* 2007;9:139-161.

109. George Simon J. *In Sheep's Clothing: Understanding and dealing with manipulative people.* Revised ed. Little Rock: Parkhurst Brothers, Inc.; 1996, 2010.

110. Stein A. *Prologue to violence : child abuse, dissociation, and crime.* Mahwah, New Jersey: Analytic Press; 2006.

111. Blackman J. *How the Mind Shields Itself.* Virginia: Taylor & Francis; 2003.

112. Horowitz MJ, Becker SS. The compulsion to repeat trauma: Experimental study of intrusive thinking after stress. *The Journal of Nervous and Mental Disease.* 1971;153(1):32-40.

113. Nolen-Hoeksema S. The role of rumination in depressive disorders and mixed anxiety/depressive symptoms. *Journal of Abnormal Psychology.* 2000;109:504-511.

114. Conway M, Mendelson M, Giannopoulos C, Csank PAR, Holm SL. Childhood and adult sexual abuse, rumination on sadness, and dysphoria. *Child Abuse & Neglect.* 2004;28:393-410.

115. Mikulincer M. Attachment style and the mental representation of the self. *Journal of Personality and Social Psychology.* 1995;69:1203-1215.

116. Mikulincer M, Florian V. The relationship between adult attachment styles and emotional and cognitive reactions to stressful events. In: Simpson J, Rholes S, eds. *Attachment theory and close relationships.* New York: Guilford; 1998:143-165.

117.   van der Kolk BA, Fisler RE. Dissociation and the fragmentary nature of traumatic memories: overview and explanatory study. *Journal of Traumatic Stress.* 1995;8(4):505-525.

118.   Stein PT, Kendall J. *Psychological Trauma and the Developing Brain: Neurologically based Interventions for Troubled Children.* New York: Haworth Maltreatment and Trauma Press; 2004.

119.   Chu JA. *Rebuilding shattered lives: The responsible treatment of complex posttraumatic stress and dissociative disorders* 2ed. Hoboken, NJ: Wiley; 2011.

120.   George Simon J. *Character Disturbance: the phenomenon of our age.* Chicago: Parkhurst Brothers, Inc.; 2011.

121.   Infante DA. Aggressiveness. In: McCroskey JC, Daly JA, eds. *Personality and interpersonal communication.* Newbury Park, CA: Sage; 1987:157-192.

122.   Rancer AS, Avtgis TA. *Argumentative and Aggressive Communication: Theory, research and application.* Thousand Oaks: Sage; 2006.

123.   Berkowitz L. Aggressive personalities. In: Barone D, Hersen FM, VanHasselt VB, eds. *Advanced Personality.* New York: Plenum Press; 1998:263-285.

124.   Infante DA, Wigley CJ. Verbal aggressiveness: An interpersonal model and measure. *Communication Monographs.* 1986;53:61-69.

125.   DeBellis MD, Keshavan MS, Clark DB, et al. Developmental traumatology part II: Brain development. *Biological Psychiatry.* 1999;45:1271-1247.

126.   Leckman J, March I. Developomental neuroscience comes of age. *Annual Research Review issue.* 2011;52(4):333-338.

127.   Schore A, McIntosh J. Family law and the neuroscience of attachment, part I. *Family Court Review* 2011;49(3):501-512.

128.   Chiron C, Jambaque I, Nabbout R, Lounes R, Syrota A, Dulac O. The right brain hemisphere is dominant in human infants. *Brain.* 1997;120:1057-1065.

129.   Schore JS, Schore AN. Modern Attachment Theory: The Central Role of Affect Regulation in Development and Treatment. . *Clinical Social Work Journal.* 2008;36:9-20.

130.   Schore AN. Dysregulation of the right brain: a fundamental mechanism of traumatic attachment and the psychopathogenesis of posttraumatic stress disorder. *Australian and New Zealand Journal of Psychiatry.* 2002;36(1):9-30.

131.   Teicher MH, Andersen SL, Polcari A, Anderson CM, Navalta CP, Kim DM. The neurobiological consequences of early stress and childhood maltreatment. *Neuroscience and Biobehavioral Reviews.* 2003;27:33-44.

132.   Kalivas PW, P. D. Similar effects of daily cocaine and stress on mesocorticolimbic dopamine neurotransmission in the rat. *Biological Psychiatry.* 1989;25:913-928.

133.   Perry BD, Southwick SM, Giller EJ. Adrenergic receptors in posttraumatic stress disorder. In: E.L. G, ed. *Biological Assessment and Treatment of Post traumatic Stress Disorder.* Washington, DC: American Psychiatric Press; 1990:87-115.

134.   Gabbard GO. Mind, brain, and personality disorders. *American Journal of Psychiatry.* 2005;162(4):648-655.

135.   Lauder JM. Neurotransmitters as morphogens. *Progress in Brain Research.* 1988;73:365-388.

136.   Teicher MH, Andersen SL, Polcari A, Anderson CM, Navalta CP. Developmental neurobiology of childhood stress and trauma. *Psychiatric Clinics of North America.* 2002;25(2):397-426.

137.   Teicher MH, Feldman R, Polcari A, et al. Early adverse experience and the neurobiology of borderline personality disorder: gender differences and implications for treatment. In: Pearson KH, Sonswalla SB, Rosenbaum JF, eds. *Women's Health and Psychiatry.* New York: Lipincott/Williams & Wilkins; 2002:9-26.

138.   Deutch AY, Tam SY, Roth RH. Footshock and conditioned stress increase 3,4-dihydroxyphenylacetic acid (DOPAC) in the ventral tegmental area but not substantia nigra. *Brain Research.* 1985;333(1):143-146.

139.   Knorr AM, Deutch AY, Roth RH. The anxiogenic beta-carboline FG-7142 increases in vivo and in vitro tyrosine hydroxylation in the prefrontal cortex. *Brain Research.* 1989;495(2):355-361.

140.   Reinhard Jr JF, Bannon MJ, Roth RH. Acceleration by stress of dopamine synthesis and metabolism in prefrontal cortex: antagonism by diazepam. *Naunyn Schmiedebergs Archives of Pharmacology.* 1982;318(4):374-377.

141.   Arnsten AFT. The biology of being frazzled. *Science* 1998;280:1711-1712.

142.   Teicher MH, Ito Y, Glod CA, Schiffer F, Gelbard HA. Neurophysiological mechanisms of stress response in children. In: Pfeffer C, ed. *Severe stress and mental disturbance in children.* Washington DC: American Psychiatric Association Press; 1996:59-84.

143.   LeDoux JE. Emotion circuits in the brain. *Annual Review Neuroscience.* 2000;23:155-184.

144.   Pinchus JH, Tucker GJ. *Behavioral neurology.* New York: Oxford; 1978.

145.   Lee GP, Bechara A, Adolphs R, et al. Clinical and physiological effects of stereotaxic bilateral amygdalotomy for intractable aggression. *Journal of Neuropsychiatry and Clinical Neurosciences.* 1998;10(4):413-420.

146.   Bogdon R, Williamson DE, Hariri AR. Mineralocorticoid receptor iso/Val (rs5522) Genotype Moderates the Association Between Previous Childhood emotional Neglect and Amygdala reactivity. *American Journal of Psychiatry.* 2012;169(5):515-522.

147.   Maheu FS, Mazzone L, Merke DP, et al. Altered amygdala and hippocampus function in adolescents with hypercortisolemia: a functional magnetic resonance imaging study of Cushing syndrome. *Development and Psychopathology.* 2008;20:1177-1189.

148.   Lupien SJ, McEwen BS, Gunnar MR, Heim C. Effects of stress throughout the lifespan on the brain, behaviour and cognition. *National Review of Neuroscience.* 2009;10:434-445.

149.   McCrory E, De Brita SA, Viding E. Research review: the neurobiology and genetics of maltreatment and adversity. *Annual Research Review issue.* 2010;51:1079-1095.

150.   Yehuda R. Post-traumatic stress disorder. *New England Journal of Medicine.* 2002;346:108-114.

151.   Grillon C, Southwick SM, Charney DS. The psychobiological basis of posttraumatic stress disorder. *Molecular Psychiatry.* 1996;1(4):278-297.

152.   Rauch SL, Van der Kolk B, Fisler RE, et al. A symptom provocation study of posttraumatic stress disorder using positron emission tomography and script-driven imagery. *Archives of General Psychiatry.* 1996;53(5):380-387.

153.   Rauch SL, Whalen PJ, Shin LM, et al. Exaggerated amygdala response to masked facial stimuli in posttraumatic stress disorder: a functional MRI study. *Biological Psychiatry.* 2000;47(9):769-776.

154.   Shin LM, Kosslyn SM, McNally RJ, et al. Visual imagery and perception in posttraumatic stress disorder. A positron emission tomographic investigation. *Archives of General Psychiatry.* 1997;54:233-241.

155.   Villarreal G, King CY. Brain imaging in posttraumatic stress disorder. *Seminars in Clinical Neuropsychiatry.* 2001;6(2):131-145.

156.   Drevets WC, Price JL, Bardgett ME, Reich T, Todd RD, Raichle ME. Glucose metabolism in the amygdala in depression: relationship to diagnostic subtype and plasma cortisol levels. *Pharmacology Biochemistry & Behavior.* 2002;7(3):431-447.

157.   Heim C, Mletzko T, Purselle D, Musselman DL, Nemeroff CB. The dexamethasone/corticotropin-releasing factor test in men with major depression: role of childhood trauma. *Biological Psychiatry.* 2008;63:398-405.

158.   Meaney MJ. Maternal care, gene expression, and the transmission of individual differences in stress reactivity across generations. *Annual Review Neuroscience.* 2001;24:1161-1192.

159.   Hairiri AR. The Neurobiology of individual differences in complex behavioral traits. *Annual Review Neuroscience.* 2009;32:225-247.

160.   Siegle GJ, Steinhauer SR, Thase ME, Stenger VA, Carter CS. Can't shake that feeling: event-related fMRI assessment of sustained amygdala activity in response to emotional information in depressed individuals. *Biological Psychiatry.* 2002;51:693-707.

161.   Maheu FS, Dozier M, Guyer AE, et al. A preliminary study of medial temporal lobe function in youths with a history of caregiver deprivation and emotional neglect. *Cognitive, Affective, & Behavioral Neuroscience.* 2010;10:34-49.

162. Tottenham N, Hare TA, Millner A, Gilhooly T, Zevin JD, Casey BJ. Elevated amygdala response to faces following early deprivation. *Developmental Science.* 2011;14:190-204.

163. White MG, Bogdan R, Fisher PM, Muñoz KE, Williamson DE, Hariri AR. FKBP5 and emotional neglect interact to predict individual differences in amygdala reactivity. *Genes, Brain and Behavior.* 2012;11:869-878.

164. Gianaros PJ, Horenstein JA, Hariri AR, et al. Potential neural embedding of parental social standing. *Social Cognitive and Affective Neuroscience.* 2008;3:91-96.

165. Mehta MA, Golembro NI, Nosarti C, et al. Amygdala, hippocampal and corpus callosum size following severe early institutional deprivation: the English and Romanian adoptees study pilot. *Annual Research Review issue.* 2009;50:943-951.

166. Tottenham N, Hare TA, Quinn BT, et al. Prolonged institutional rearing is associated with atypically large amygdala volume and difficulties in emotion regulation. *Developmental Science.* 2010;13:46-61.

167. Desgranges B, Baron JC, Eustache F. The functional neuroanatomy of episodic memory: the role of the frontal lobes, the hippocampal formation, and other areas. *Neuroimage.* 1998;8(2):198-213.

168. Bancaud J, Brunet-Bourgin F, Chauvel P, Halgren E. Anatomical origin of deja vu and vivid memories in human temporal lobe epilepsy. *Brain.* 1994;17(Pt 1):71-90.

169. Mesulam MM. Dissociative states with abnormal temporal lobe EEG. Multiple personality and the illusion of possession. *Archives of Neurology.* 1981;38(3):176-181.

170. Gray JA. A theory of anxiety: the role of the limbic system. *Encephale.* 1983;9(4):161B-166B.

171. Reiman EM, Raichle ME, Robins E, et al. The application of positron emission tomography to the study of panic disorder. *American Journal of Psychiatry.* 1986;143(4):469-477.

172. Teicher MH. Biology of anxiety. In: Frazier S, ed. *Medical clinics of North America.* Philadelphia: G. Harcourt; 1988:791-814.

173. Gould E, Tanapat P. Stress and hippocampal neurogenesis. *Biological Psychiatry.* 1999;46(11):1472-1479.

174. Sapolsky RM, Uno H, Rebert CS, Finch CE. Hippocampal damage associated with prolonged glucocorticoid exposure in primates. *Journal of Neuroscience.* 1990;10:2897-2902.

175. Stein MB. Hippocampal volume in women victimized by childhood sexual abuse. *Psychological Medicine.* 1997;27(4):951-959.

176. Cowan WM, Fawcett JW, O'Leary DD, Stanfield BB. Regressive events in neurogenesis. *Science.* 1984;225(4668):1258-1265.

177. Purves D, Lichtman JW. Elimination of synapses in the developing nervous system. *Science.* 1980;210(4466):153-157.

178. Rakic P, Bourgeois JP, Eckenhoff MF, Zecevic N, Goldman-Rakic PS. Concurrent overproduction of synapses in diverse regions of the primate cerebral cortex. *Science*. 1986;232(4747):232-235.

179. Bremner JD, Randall P, Vermetten E, et al. Magnetic resonance imaging-based measurement of hippocampal volume in posttraumatic stress disorder related to childhood physical and sexual abuse—a preliminary report. *Biological Psychiatry*. 1997;41(1):23-32.

180. Borod JC. Interhemispheric and intrahemispheric control of emotion: a focus on unilateral brain damage. *Journal of Consulting and Clinical Psychology*. 1992;60:339-348.

181. Hirschman RS, Safer MA. Hemisphere differences in perceiving positive and negative emotions. *Cortex*. 1982;18(4):569-580.

182. Ross ED, Thompson RD, Yenkosky J. Lateralization of affective prosody in brain and the callosal integration of hemispheric language functions. *Brain Language*. 1997;56(1):27-54.

183. Silberman EK, Weingartner H. Hemispheric lateralization of functions related to emotion. *Brain Cognition*. 1986;5(3):322-353.

184. Tomarken AJ, Davidson RJ, Wheeler RE, Doss RC. Individual differences in anterior brain asymmetry and fundamental dimensions of emotion. *Journal of Personality and Social Psychology*. 1992;62(4):676-687.

185. Jones GH, Hernandez TD, Kendall DA, Marsden CA, Robbins TW. Dopaminergic and serotonergic function following isolation rearing in rats: study of behavioural responses and postmortem and in vivo neurochemistry. *Pharmacology Biochemistry & Behavior*. 1992;43(1):17-35.

186. Anderson SL, Lyss PJ, Dumont NL, Teicher MH. Enduring neurochemical effects of early maternal separation on limbic structures. *Annals of the New York Academy of Science*. 1999;877:756-759.

187. Schiffer F, Teicher MH, Papanicolaou AC. Evoked potential evidence for right brain activity during the recall of traumatic memories. *Journal of Neuropsychiatry and Clinical Neurosciences*. 1995;7:169-175.

188. Teicher MH, Ito Y, Glod CA, Schiffer F, Gelbard HA. Early abuse, limbic system dysfunction, and borderline personality disorder. In: Silk K, ed. *Biological and neurobehavioral studies of borderline personality disorder* Washington DC: American Psychiatric Association Press; 1994:177-207.

189. Andersen P. The dopamine uptake inhibitor GBR 12909: selectivity and molecular mechanism of action. *European Journal of Pharmacology*. 1989;166:493-504.

190. Ito Y, Teicher MH, Glod CA, Ackerman E. Preliminary evidence for aberrant cortical development in abused children: a quantitative EEG study. *Journal of Neuropsychiatry and Clinical Neurosciences*. 1998;10:298-307.

191. Teicher MH, Ito Y, Glod CA, Andersen SL, Dumont N, Ackerman E. Preliminary evidence for abnormal cortical development in physically and sexually abused

children using EEG coherence and MRI. *Annals of the New York Academy of Science.* 1997;82(1):60-75.

192.   Yazgan MY, Wexler BE, Kinsbourne M, Peterson B, Leckman JF. Functional significance of individual variations in callosal area. *Neuropsychologia.* 1995;33(6):769-779.

193.   Teicher MH, Andersen SL, Dumont NL, et al. Childhood neglect attentuates development of the corpus callosum. *Society for Neuroscience Abstracts.* 2000;26:549.

194.   Williams RW, Herrup K. The control of neuron number. *Annual Review Neuroscience.* 1988;11:423-453.

195.   Allen G, Buxton RB, Wong EC, Courchesne E. Attentional activation of the cerebellum independent of motor involvement. *Science.* 1997;275(5308):1940-1943.

196.   Riva D, Giorgi C. The contribution of the cerebellum to mental and social functions in developmental age. *Fiziologiia Cheloveka.* 2000;26(1):27-31.

197.   Schmahmann JD. An emerging concept. The cerebellar contribution to higher function. *Archives of Neurology.* 1991;48(11):1178-1187.

198.   Schmahmann JD. Cerebellum—the true thinking machine. In: Zigmond MB, Landis S, Roberts J, Squire L, eds. *Fundamental neuroscience.* San Diego: Academic Press; 1998.

199.   Schmahmann JD. A new role for the cerebellum: the modulation of cognition and affect. In: Joseph A, ed. *Movement disorders.* 2 ed. Boston: Blackwell Science; 1999.

200.   Schmahmann JD. The role of the cerebellum in affect and psychosis. *Journal of Neurolinguistics.* 2000;13:189-214.

201.   Andreasen NC, Paradiso S, O'Leary DS. Cognitive dysmetria as an integrative theory of schizophrenia: a dysfunction in corticalsubcortical-cerebellar circuitry? *Schizophrenia Bulletin.* 1998;24(2):203-218.

202.   Riva D. The cerebellar contribution to language and sequential functions: evidence from a child with cerebellitis. *Cortex.* 1998;34(2):279-287.

203.   Reis DJ, Golanov EV. Autonomic and vasomotor regulation. *International Review of Neurobiology.* 1997;41:121-149.

204.   Snider RS, Maiti A, Snider SR. Cerebellar pathways to ventral midbrain and nigra. *Experimental Neurology.* 1976;53(3):714-728.

205.   Snider SR, Snider RS. Structural and functional relationships between cerebellum and catecholamine systems: an overview. *Experimental Brain Research.* 1982;Suppl(6):6.

206.   Del Bo A, Ross CA, Pardal JF, Saavedra JM, Reis DJ. Fastigial stimulation in rats releases adrenomedullary catecholamines. *American Journal of Physiology.* 1983;244(6):R801-809.

207. Del Bo A, Sved AF, Reis DJ. Fastigial stimulation releases vasopressin in amounts that elevate arterial pressure. *American Journal of Physiology.* 1983;244(5):H687-694.

208. Dietrichs E, Haines DE, Roste GK, Roste LS. Hypothalamocerebellar and cerebellohypothalamic projections—circuits for regulating nonsomatic cerebellar activity? *Histology and Histopathology.* 1994;9(3):603-614.

209. Riklan M, Cullinan T, Cooper IS. Tension reduction and alerting in man following chronic cerebellar stimulation for the relief of spasticity or intractable seizures. *Journal of Nervous and Mental Disease.* 1977;164(3):176-181.

210. Ichimiya T, Okubo Y, Suhara T, Sudo Y. Reduced volume of the cerebellar vermis in neuroleptic-naive schizophrenia. *Biological Psychiatry.* 2001;49(1):20-27.

211. Jacobsen LK, Giedd JN, Berquin PC, et al. Quantitative morphology of the cerebellum and fourth ventricle in childhood-onset schizophrenia. *American Journal of Psychiatry.* 1997;54(12):1663-1669.

212. Levitt JJ, McCarley RW, Nestor PG, et al. Quantitative volumetric MRI study of the cerebellum and vermis in schizophrenia: clinical and cognitive correlates. *American Journal of Psychiatry.* 1999;156(7):1105-1107.

213. Loeber RT, Cintron CM, Yurgelun-Todd DA. Morphometry of individual cerebellar lobules in schizophrenia. *American Journal of Psychiatry.* 2001;158(6):952-954.

214. Snider SR. Cerebellar pathology in schizophrenia—cause or consequence? *Neuroscience & Biobehavioral Reviews.* 1982;6(1):47-53.

215. Volz H, Gaser C, Sauer H. Supporting evidence for the model of cognitive dysmetria in schizophrenia—a structural magnetic resonance imaging study using deformation-based morphometry. *Schizophrenia Research.* 2000;46(1):45-56.

216. Berquin PC, Giedd JN, Jacobsen LK, et al. Cerebellum in attention-deficit hyperactivity disorder: a morphometric MRI study. *Neurology.* 1998;50(4):1087-1093.

217. Castellanos FX, Giedd JN, Berquin PC, et al. Quantitative brain magnetic resonance imaging in girls with attention-deficit/hyperactivity disorder. *Archives of General Psychiatry.* 2001;58(3):289-295.

218. Mostofsky SH, Reiss AL, Lockhart P, Denckla MB. Evaluation of cerebellar size in attention-deficit hyperactivity disorder. *Journal of Child Neurology.* 1998;13(9):434-439.

219. Lauterbach EC. Bipolar disorders, dystonia, and compulsion after dysfunction of the cerebellum, dentatorubrothalamic tract, and substantia nigra. *Biological Psychiatry.* 1996;40(8):726-730.

220. Loeber RT, Sherwood AR, Renshaw PF, Cohen BM, Yurgelun-Todd DA. Differences in cerebellar blood volume in schizophrenia and bipolar disorder. *Schizophrenia Research.* 1999;37(1):81-89.

221. Sweeney JA, Strojwas MH, Mann JJ, Thase ME. Prefrontal and cerebellar abnormalities in major depression: evidence from oculomotor studies. *Biological Psychiatry.* 1998;43(8):584-594.

222. DeBellis MD. Posttraumatic stress disorder and acute stress disorder. In: Ammerman R, Hersen M, eds. *Handbook of Prevention and treatment with Children and Adolescents.* New York: John Wiley & Sons, Inc.; 1997:455-494.

223. Papez JW. A proposed mechanism of emotion. *Journal of Neuropsychiatry Clinical Neuroscience.* 1937;7(1):103-112.

224. Healy D. Lines of evidence on the risks of suicide with selective serotonin reuptake inhibitors. *Psychotherapy and Psychosomatics.* 2003;72:71-79.

225. Sullivan RM, Dufresne MM. Mesocortical dopamine and HPA axis regulation: Role of laterality and early environment. *Brain Research.* 2006;1076:49-59.

226. Gunnar MR. Early adversity and the development of stress reactivity and regulation. In: Nelson CA, ed. *The effects of adversity on neurobehavioral development:Minnesota symposium on child psychology.* Vol 31. Mahwah, NJ: Lawrence Erlbaum; 2000:163-200.

227. Yehuda R. Biology of posttraumatic stress disorder. *Journal of Clinical Psychiatry.* 2001;62(suppl 17):41-46.

228. Yehuda R, Giller EL, Southwick SM, Lowy MT, Mason JW. Hypothalamic-pituitary-adrenal dysfunction in posttraumatic stress disorder. *Biological Psychiatry.* 1991;30(10):1031-1048.

229. Schechter DS, Willheim E. Disturbances of attachment and parental psychopathology in early childhood. *Child and Adolescent Psychiatric Clinics of North America* 2009;18(3):665-686.

230. Schore AN. Early relational trauma, disorganized attachment, and the development of a predisposition to violence. . In: Solomon MF, Siegel DJ, eds. *Healing trauma: Attachment, mind, body, and brain.* New York: Norton; 2003.

231. Kirz J, Drescher K, Klein J, Gusman F, Schwartz M. MMPI-2 assessment of differential post-traumatic stress disorder patterns in combat veterans and sexual assault victims. *Journal of Interpersonal Violence.* 2001;16(619-639).

232. Miller MM, Resick PA. Internalizing and externalizing subtypes in female sexual assault survivors: Implications for the understanding of complex PTSD. *Behavior Therapy.* 2007;38:58-71.

233. Ainsworth MDS, Blehar MC, Waters E, Wall S. *Patterns of attachment.* Hillsdale, NJ: Erlbaum; 1978.

234. Bowlby J. *Attachment and loss.* Vol 3: Loss. New York: Basic Books; 1980.

235. Bowlby J. *A secure base: Parent-child attachment and healthy human development.* New York: Basic Books; 1988.

236. Main M, Kaplan K, Cassidy J. Security in infancy, childhood, and adulthood: A move to the level of representation. *Monographs of the Society for Research in Child Development,* . 1985;50(1-2).

237. Polan HJ, Hofer MAL. Psychobiological origins of infant attachment and its role in development. In: Cassidy J, Shaver PR, eds. *Handbook of Attachment: Theory, Research, and Clinical Applications.* 2 ed. New York: Guilford; 2008:158-172.

238. Sroufe LA, Waters E. Heart rate as a convergent measure in clinical and developmental research. *Merrill-Palmer Quarterly.* 1977;23:3-27.

239. Bretherton I. Attachment Theory: Retrospect and prospect. *Monographs of the Society for Research in Child Development,.* 1985;50(102 (serial no. 209)).

240. Ovtscharoff WJ, Braun K. Maternal separation and social isolation modulate the postnatal development of synaptic composition in the infralimbic cortex of *Octodon degus. Neuroscience.* 2001;104:33-40.

241. Falk D, Hildebolt C, Cheverud J, Vannier M, Helmkamp RC, Konigsberg L. Cortical asymmetries in frontal lobes of Rhesus monkeys (Macada mulatta). *Brain Research.* 1990;512:40-45.

242. Schore AN. Early organization of the nonlinear right brain and development of a predisposition to psychiatric disorders. *Development and Psychopathology.* 1997;9:595-631.

243. Henry JP. Psychological and physiological responses to stress: The right hemisphere and the hypothalamo-pituitary-adrenal axis, an inquiry into problems of human bonding. *Integrative Physiological and Behavioral Science.* 1993;28:369-387.

244. Neve RL, Bear MF. Visual experience regulates gene expression in the developing striate cortex. *Proceedings of the National Academy of Sciences of the Unites States of America.* 1989;86:4781-4784.

245. Thatcher RW. Cyclical cortical reorganization: Origins of human cognitive development. In: Dawson G, Fischer KW, eds. *Human behavior and the developing brain.* New York: Guilford; 1994:232-266.

246. Isen AM, Daubman KA, Nowicki GP. Positive affect facilitates creative problem solving. *Journal of Personality and Social Psychology.* 1987;52(6):1122-1131.

247. Fuendeling JM. Affect regulation as a stylistic process within adult attachment. *Journal of Social and Personal Relationships.* 1998;15:291-322.

248. Applegate JS, Shapiro JR. *Neurobiology for clinical social work: Theory and practice.* New York: Norton; 2005.

249. LeDoux JE. *The emotional brain.* London: Weidenfeld & Nicolson; 1998.

250. Brewin DR, Dalgleish T, Joseph S. A dual representation theory of posttraumatic stress disorder. *Psychological Review.* 1996;103:670-686.

251. Sander L. Infant and caretaking environment. In: Anthony EJ, ed. *Explorations in child psychiatry* New York: Plenum; 1975:129-165.

252. Sander L. Where are we going in the field of infant mental health? . *Infant Mental Health Journal.* 2000;21:1-18.

253. Herman JL. Complex PTSD: A syndrome in survivors of prolonged and repeated trauma. *Journal of Traumatic Stress.* 1992;5:377-392.

254. van der Kolk BA, ed *Psychological trauma.* Washington, DC: American Psychiatric Press; 1987.
255. Herman JL. *Trauma and recovery.* New York: Basic Books; 1992.
256. Herman JL, Cloitre M, Ford JD. Proposal for adding complex PTSD as a new diagnosis to DSM-V. 2009.
257. DeBellis MD, Soares JC, Gershon S. The neurobiology of posttraumatic stress disorder across the life cycle. In: *The handbook of medical psychiatry.* New York: Marcel Dekker Inc; 2003:449-466.
258. DeBellis MD. Developmental traumatology: The psychobiological development of maltreated children and its implications for research, treatment, and policy. *Development and Psychopathology.* 2001;13:537-561.
259. NationalCenterforPTSD. PTSD and DSM-5. U.S. Department of Veterans Affairs. Published 2017. Updated Feb 21, 2017. Accessed July 31, 2017.
260. AmericanPsychiatricAssociation. *Diagnostic and Statistical Manual of Mental Disorders.* Arlington, VA: American Psychiatric Publishing; 2013.
261. DeBellis MD, Hooper SR, Woolley DP, Shenk CE. Demographic, Maltreatment, and Neurobiological Correlates of PTSD Symptoms in Children and Adolescents. *Journal of Pediatric Psychology.* 2010;35(5):570-577.
262. Fjell AM, Walhovd KB, Reinvang I, et al. Age does not increase rate of forgetting over weeks—neuroanatomical volumes and visual memory across the adult life-span. *Journal of the International Neuropsychological Society.* 2005;11(1):2-15.
263. Schmidt D, Krause BJ, Weiss PH, et al. Visuospatial working memory and changes of the point of view in 3D space. *Neuroimage.* 2007;36(3):955-968.
264. Yago E, Ishai A. Recognition memory is modulated by visual similarity. *Neuroimage.* 2006;31(2):807-817.
265. DeBellis MD. Developmental traumatology: A contributory mechanism for alcohol and substance use disorders. *Psychoneuroendocrinology.* 2002;27:155-170.
266. DeBellis MD, Clark DB, Beers SR, et al. Hippocampal volume in adolescent onset alcohol use disorders. *American Journal of Psychiatry.* 2000;157:737-744.
267. Green BL, Korol M, Grace MC, et al. Children and disaster: Age, gender, and parental effects on PTSD symptoms. *Journal of the American Academy of Child and Adolescent Psychiatry.* 1991;30(6):945-951.
268. AmericanPsychiatricAssociation. *Diagnostic and Statistical Manual of Mental Disorders.* 4 ed. Washington DC2000.
269. Orth U, Wieland E. Anger, hostility, and posttraumatic stress disorder in trauma-exposed adults: A meta-analysis. *Journal of Consulting and Clinical Psychology.* 2006;74:698-706.
270. Whisman M. Marital dissatisfaction and psychiatric disorders: Results from the National Comorbidity Survey. *Journal of Abnormal Psychology.* 1999;108:701-706.

271. Whisman M, Uebelacker L. Comorbidity of relationship distress and mental and physical health problems. In: Snyder DK, Whisman M, eds. *Treating difficult couples: Helping clients with coexisting mental and relationship disorders.* New York: Guilford Press; 2003:3-26.

272. Bowen GL, Orthner DK. *The organization family: Work and family linkages in the US military.* New York: Praeger; 1989.

273. Pierce PF. Retention of Air Force women serving during Desert Shield and Desert Storm. *Military Psychology.* 1998;10(195-213).

274. Schumm W, Bell D, Resnick G. Recent research on family factors and readiness: Implications for military leaders. *Psychological Reports.* 2001;89:153-165.

275. Segal D, Rohall D, Jones J, Manos A. Meeting the missions of the 1990s with a downsized force: Human resource management lessons from the deployment of PATRIOT missile units to Korea. *Military Psychology.* 1999;11:149-167.

276. Pynoos RS, Steinberg AM, Wraith R. A developmental model of childhood traumatic stress. In: Cicchetti D, Cohen DJ, eds. *Developmental Psychopathology.* Vol 2. New York: John Wiley & Sons, Inc.; 1995:72-95.

277. Cicchetti D, Lyncy M. Failures in the expectable environment and their impact on individual development: the case of child maltreatment. In: Cicchetti D, Cohen DJ, eds. *Developmental Psychopathology.* Vol 2. New York: John Wiley & Sons, Inc.; 1995:32-71.

278. Council NR. *Understanding Child Abuse and Neglect.* Washington DC: National Academy Press; 1993.

279. Shields AM, Cicchetti D, Ryan R. The development of emotional and behavioral self-regulation and social competence among maltreated school-age children. *Development and Psychopathology.* 1994;6:57-75.

280. Kaplow JB, Widom CS. Age of onset of child maltreatment predicts long term mental health outcomes. *Journal of Abnormal Psychology.* 2007;116:176-187.

281. Herman JL, Perry JC, Kolk BAvd. Childhood trauma in borderline personality disorder. *American Journal of Psychiatry.* 1989;146(4):490-495.

282. Ogata SN, Silk KR, Goodrich S, Lohr NE, Westen D, Hill EM. Childhood sexual and physical abuse during childhood: Long-term health consequences for women. *Child Abuse & Neglect.* 1990;17:623-640.

283. Saxe GN, Chinman G, Berkowitz R, et al. Somatization in patients with dissociative disorders. *American Journal of Psychiatry.* 1994;151(9):1329-1334.

284. Kluft RP. Clinical presentaitons of multiple personality disorder. *Psychiatric Clinics of North America.* 1991;14(3):605-629.

285. Putnam FW. Pierre Janet and modern views of dissociation. *Journal of Traumatic Stress.* 1989;2(4):413-429.

286. Ross CA, Miller SD, Bjornson L, Reagor P, Fraser GA, Anderson G. Abuse histories in 102 cases of multiple personality disorder. *Canadian Journal of Psychiatry.* 1991;36(2):97-101.

287. Ross CA, Norton GR, Wozney K. Multiple personality disorder: an analysis of 236 cases. *Canadian Journal of Psychiatry.* 1989;34(5):53-59.
288. Saxe GN, van der Kolk BA, Berkowitz R, et al. Dissociative disorders in psychiatric inpatients. *American Journal of Psychiatry.* 1993;150(7):1037-1042.
289. DeGroot JM, Kennedy S, Rodin G, McVey G. Correlates of sexual abuse in women with anorexia nervosa and bulimia nervosa. *Canadian Journal of Psychiatry.* 1992;37(7):516-518.
290. Herzog DB, Staley JE, Carmody S, Robbins WM, van der Kolk BA. Chlidhood sexual abuse in anorexia nervosa and bulimia nervosa: a pilot study. *Journal of the American Academy of Child and Adolescent.* 1993;32(5):962-966.
291. McFarlane AC, McFarlane CM, Gilchrist PN. Posttraumatic bulimia and anorexia nervosa. *International Journal of Eating Disorders.* 1988;7(5):705-708.
292. van der Kolk BA, M.D. The Assessment and Treatment of Complex PTSD. In: Yehuda R, ed. *Traumatic Stress.* American Psychiatric Press; 2001.
293. Luthra R, R. A, Chemtob C. Relationship between type of trauma exposure and posttraumatic stress disorder among urban children and adolescents. *Journal Of Interpersonal Violence.* 2009;24(11):1919-1927.
294. Koenen KC, Widom CS. A prospective study of sex differences in the lifetime risk of posttraumatic stress disorder among abused and neglected children grown up. *Journal of Traumatic Stress.* 2009;22(6):566-574.
295. Carmichael A. Physical development and biological influences. In: Tonge B, Burrows GD, Werry JS, eds. *Handbook of Studies in Child Psychiatry.* Amsterdam: Elsevier; 1990.
296. Pfefferbaum A, Mathalon DH, Sullivan EV, Rawles JM, Zipursky RB, Lim KO. A quantitative magnetic resonance imaging study of changes in brain morphology from infancy to late adulthood. *Archives of Neurology.* 1994;34:71-75.
297. Frazier JA, Giedd JN, Hamburger SD. Brain anatomic magnetic resonance imaging in childhood-onset schizophrenia. *Archives of General Psychiatry.* 1996;53:617-624.
298. Weinberger DR, Wyatt RJ. Cerebral ventricular size: a biological marker for subtyping chronic schizophrenia. In: Esdin E, Handen J, eds. *Biological Markers in Psychiatry and Neurology.* Elmford, NJ: Pergamon Press; 1982:505-512.
299. Jernigan T. Anatomical and CT scan studies of psychiatric disorders. In: Berger P, Brodie HKH, eds. *American Handbook of Psychiatry.* Vol 8. New York: Basic Books; 1986:213-235.
300. Ron M. The alcoholic brain: CT scan and psychological findings. *Psychological Medicine Monograph.* 1986;Suppl 3:1-33.
301. Pearlson G, Garbacz D, Breakey W, Ahn H, DePaulo J. Lateral ventricular enlargement associated with persistend unemployment and negative symptoms in both schizophrenia and bipolar disease. *Psychiatry Research.* 1984;12:1-9.
302. Scott M, Golden C, Ruedrich S, Bishop R. Ventricular enlargement in major depression. *Psychiatry Research.* 1983;8:91-93.

303. Andreasen NC, Flaum M, Swayze II V, al e. Intelligence and brain structures in normal individuals. *American Journal of Psychiatry.* 1993;150:130-134.

304. Skills CfN. Frontal Lobes. Neuroskills.com. https://www.neuroskills.com/brain-injury/frontal-lobes.php. Published 2018. Accessed August 8, 2018.

305. Fuster JM. *The Prefrontal Cortex: Anatomy, Physiology, and Neuropsychology of the Frontal Lobe.* New York: Raven Press; 1980.

306. Goldman-Rakie PS. Working memory dysfunction in schizophrenia. *Journal of Neuropsychiatry Clinical Neuroscience.* 1994;6:348-357.

307. Weinberger DR. Implications of normal brain development for the pathogenesis of schizophrenia. *Archives of General Psychiatry.* 1987;44:660-669.

308. Knight RT, Grabowecky MF, Scabini D. Role of human prefrontal cortex in attention control. *Advances in Neurology.* 1995;66:21-34.

309. Jensen V, Rinholm JE, Johansen TJ, et al. N-methyl-D-aspartate receptor subunit dysfunction at hippocampal glutamatergic synapses in an animal model of attention-deficit/hyperactivity disorder. *Neuroscience.* 2009;158:353-364.

310. Diamond DM, Fleshner M, Ingersoll N, Rose GM. Psychological stress impairs spatial working memory: relevance to electrophysiological studies of hippocampal function. *Behavoral Neurosciences.* 1996;110:661-672.

311. Watanabe Y, Gould E, McEwen BS. Stress induces atrophy of apical dendrites of hippocampal CA3 pyramidal neurons. *Brain Research.* 1992;588:341-345.

312. Sapolsky RM. Glucocorticoids and hippocampal atrophy in neuropsychiatric disorders. *Archives of General Psychiatry.* 2000;57:925-935.

313. Tanapat P, Galea LA, Gould E. Stress inhibits the proliferation of granule cell precursors in the developing dentate gyrus. *Journal of Developmental Neuroscience.* 1998;16:235-239.

314. Bremner JD, Randall PR, Capelli S, Scott T, McCarthy G, Charney DS. Deficits in short-term memory in adult survivors of childhood abuse. *Psychiatry Research.* 1995;59:97-107.

315. Bremner JD, Vythilingam M, Vermetten E, et al. MRI and PET study of deficits in hippocampal structure and function in women with childhood sexual abuse and posttraumatic stress disorder. *American Journal of Psychiatry.* 2003;160(3):924-932.

316. Moradi AR, Doost HTN, Taghavi MR, Yule W, Dalgleish T. Everyday memory deficits in children and adolescents with PTSD: performance on the Rivermead Behavioral Memory test. *Annual Research Review issue.* 1999;40:357-361.

317. Moradi AR, Taghavi MR, Neshat-Doost HT, Yule W, Dalgleish T. Memory bias for emotional information in children and adolescents with posttraumatic stress disorder: A preliminary study. *Journal of Anxiety Disorders.* 2000;14:521-532.

318. Sullivan EV, Marsh L, Mathalon DH, Lim KO, Pfefferbaum A. Anterior hippocampal volume deficits in non-amnesiac, aging chronic alcoholics. *Alcoholism: Clinical and Experimental Research.* 1995;19:110-122.

319. Ramaekers G, Nijiokiktijen C. *The child's corpus callosum.* Vol 3. Amsterdam: Suyi Publications; 1991.
320. de Lacoste MC, Kirkpatrick JB, Ross ED. Topography of the human corpus callosum. *Journal of Neuropathology and Experimental Neurology.* 1985;44:578-591.
321. Lezak M. *Neuropsychological Assessment.* 3 ed. New York: Oxford; 1995.
322. Paloutzian RF, Ellison CW. Loneliness, spiritual well-being and the quality of life. In: Peplau LA, Perlman D, eds. *Loneliness: A sourcebook of current theory, research, and therapy* New York: Wiley-Interscience; 1982:224-237.
323. Campbell JD, Yoon DP, Johnstone B. Determining relationships between physical health and spiritual experience, religious practices, and congregational support in a heterogeneous medical sample. *Journal of Religion and Health.* 2010;49:3-17.
324. Meadows LA, Kaslow NJ, Thompson MP, Jurkovic GJ. Protective factors against suicide attempt risk among African American women experiencing intimate partner violence. *American Journal of Community Psychology.* 2005;36(109-121).
325. Nad S, Marcinko, D., Vuksan-Æusa B, Jakovljevic M, Jakovljevic G. Spiritual well-being, instrinsic religiosity, and suicidal behavior in predomi-nantly Catholic Croatian war veterans with chronic postraumatic stress disorder: A case control study. *Journal of Nervous and Mental Disease.* 2008;196:79-83.
326. Krejci M, Thompson KM, Simonich H, et al. Sexual trauma, spirituality, and psychopathology. *Journal of Child Sexual Abuse.* 2004;13(2):85-103.
327. Gall T, Basque V, Damasceno-Scott M, Vardy G. Spirituality and the current adjustment of adult survivors of childhood sexual abuse. *Journal for the Scientific Study of Religion.* 2007;46(1):101-107.
328. Garbarino J, Bedard C. Spiritual challenges to children facing violent trauma. *Childhood.* 1996;3:467-478.
329. Ryan PL. Spirituality among adult survivors of childhood violence: A literature review. *Journal of Transpersonal Psychology* 1998;30:39-51.
330. Tedeschi RG, Calhoun LG. Posttraumatic growth: Conceptual foundations and empirical evidence. *Psychological Inquiry* 2004;15:1-18.
331. Cahn BR, Polich J. Meditation states and traits: EEG, ERP, and neuroimaging studies. *Psychological bulletin.* 2006;132(2):180.
332. Chiesa A, Serretti A. A systematic review of neurobiological and clinical features of mindfulness meditations. *Psychological medicine.* 2010;40(8):1239-1252.
333. Pagnoni G, Cekic M. Age effects on gray matter volume and attentional performance in Zen meditation. *Neurobiology of Aging.* 2007;28:1623-1627.
334. Greeson JM. Mindfulness research update: 2008. *Complementary health practice review.* 2009;14(1):10-18.
335. Jain S, Shapiro SL, Swanick S, et al. A randomized controlled trial of mindfulness meditation versus relaxation training: effects on distress, positive states of mind, rumination, and distraction. *Annals of behavioral medicine.* 2007;33(1):11-21.

336.   Ramel W, Goldin PR, Carmona PE, McQuaid JR. The effects of mindfulness meditation on cognitive processes and affect in patients with past depression. *Cognitive therapy and research.* 2004;28(4):433-455.

337.   Sephton SE, Salmon P, Weissbecker I, et al. Mindfulness meditation alleviates depressive symptoms in women with fibromyalgia: results of a randomized clinical trial. *Arthritis Care & Research.* 2007;57(1):77-85.

338.   Zylowska L, Ackerman DL, Yang MH, et al. Mindfulness meditation training in adults and adolescents with ADHD: a feasibility study. *Journal of Attention Disorders.* 2008;11(6):737-746.

339.   Bowen S, Witkiewitz K, Dillworth TM, et al. Mindfulness meditation and substance use in an incarcerated population. *Psychology of addictive behaviors.* 2006;20(3):343.

340.   Ortner CN, Kilner SJ, Zelazo PD. Mindfulness meditation and reduced emotional interference on a cognitive task. *Motivation and emotion.* 2007;31(4):271-283.

341.   Beauchemin J, Hutchins TL, Patterson F. Mindfulness meditation may lessen anxiety, promote social skills, and improve academic performance among adolescents with learning disabilities. *Complementary Health Practice Review.* 2008;13(1):34-45.

342.   Goldin P, Ramel W, Gross J. Mindfulness meditation training and self-referential processing in social anxiety disorder: Behavioral and neural effects. *Journal of Cognitive Psychotherapy.* 2009;23(3):242.

343.   Astin JA. Stress reduction through mindfulness meditation. Effects on psychological symptomatology, sense of control, and spiritual experiences. *Psychotherapy and Psychosomatics.* 1997;66:97-106.

344.   Jain S, Shapiro S, Swanick S, et al. A randomized controlled trial of mindfulness meditation versus relaxation training: effects on distress, positive states of mind, rumination, and distraction. *Annals of Behavioral Medicine.* 2007;33:11-21.

345.   Shapiro S, Astin J, Bishop S, Cordova M. Mindfulness-based stress reduction for health care professionals : results from a randomized trials. *International Journal of Stress Management.* 2005;12:164-176.

346.   Shapiro S, Brown K, Biegel G. Teaching self-care to care-givers : effects of mindfulness-based stress reduction on the mental health of therapists in training. *Training and Education in Professional Psychology.* 2007;1:105-115.

347.   Chambers R, Lo B, Allen N. The impact of intensive mindfulness training on attentional control, cognitive style and affect. *Cognitive Therapy and Research.* 2008;32:303-322.

348.   Jha A, Krompinger J, Baime M. Mindfulness training modifies subsystems of attention. *Cognitive, Affective and Behavioral Neuroscience.* 2007;7:109-119.

349.   Valentine ER, Sweet PLG. Meditation and attention: a comparison of the effects of concentrative versus mindfulness meditation on sustained attention. *Mental Health, Religion and Culture.* 1999;2:59-70.

350.   Desbordes G, Negi LT, Pace TW, Wallace BA, Raison CL, Schwartz EL. Effects of mindful-attention and compassion meditation training on amygdala response to emotional stimuli in an ordinary, non-meditative state. *Frontiers in human neuroscience.* 2012;6.

351.   Carlson LE, Ursuliak Z, Goodey E, Angen M, Speca M. The effects of a mindfulness meditation-based stress reduction program on mood and symptoms of stress in cancer outpatients: 6-month follow-up. *Supportive care in Cancer.* 2001;9(2):112-123.

352.   Speca M, Carlson LE, Goodey E, Angen M. A randomized, wait-list controlled clinical trial: the effect of a mindfulness meditation-based stress reduction program on mood and symptoms of stress in cancer outpatients. *Psychosomatic medicine.* 2000;62(5):613-622.

353.   Kabat-Zinn J, Wheeler E, Light T, et al. Influence of a mindfulness meditation-based stress reduction intervention on rates of skin clearing in patients with moderate to severe psoriasis undergoing photo therapy (UVB) and photochemotherapy (PUVA). *Psychosomatic medicine.* 1998;60(5):625-632.

354.   Miller JJ, Fletcher K, Kabat-Zinn J. Three-year follow-up and clinical implications of a mindfulness meditation-based stress reduction intervention in the treatment of anxiety disorders. *General hospital psychiatry.* 1995;17(3):192-200.

355.   Zeidan F, Johnson SK, Diamond BJ, David Z, Goolkasian P. Mindfulness meditation improves cognition: Evidence of brief mental training. *Consciousness and cognition.* 2010;19(2):597-605.

356.   Tang Y-Y, Ma Y, Wang J, et al. Short-term meditation training improves attention and self-regulation. *Proceedings of the National Academy of Sciences.* 2007;104(43):17152-17156.

357.   Zeidan F, Martucci KT, Kraft RA, Gordon NS, McHaffie JG, Coghill RC. Brain mechanisms supporting the modulation of pain by mindfulness meditation. *Journal of Neuroscience.* 2011;31(14):5540-5548.

358.   Morone NE, Greco CM, Weiner DK. Mindfulness meditation for the treatment of chronic low back pain in older adults: a randomized controlled pilot study. *Pain.* 2008;134(3):310-319.

359.   Rosenzweig S, Greeson JM, Reibel DK, Green JS, Jasser SA, Beasley D. Mindfulness-based stress reduction for chronic pain conditions: variation in treatment outcomes and role of home meditation practice. *Journal of psychosomatic research.* 2010;68(1):29-36.

360.   Davidson RJ, Kabat-Zinn J, Schumacher J, et al. Alterations in brain and immune function produced by mindfulness meditation. *Psychosomatic medicine.* 2003;65(4):564-570.

361.   Fox KC, Nijeboer S, Dixon ML, et al. Is meditation associated with altered brain structure? A systematic review and meta-analysis of morphometric neuroimaging in meditation practitioners. *Neuroscience & Biobehavioral Reviews.* 2014;43:48-73.

362. Lazar SW, Kerr CE, Wasserman RH, et al. Meditation experience is associated with increased cortical thickness. *Neuroreport.* 2005;16(17):1893.

363. Hölzel BK, Ott U, Gard T, et al. Investigation of mindfulness meditation practitioners with voxel-based morphometry. *Social cognitive and affective neuroscience.* 2007;3(1):55-61.

364. Hölzel BK, Lazar SW, Gard T, Schuman-Olivier Z, Vago DR, Ott U. How does mindfulness meditation work? Proposing mechanisms of action from a conceptual and neural perspective. *Perspectives on psychological science.* 2011;6(6):537-559.

365. Luders E, Kurth F, Mayer EA, Toga AW, Narr KL, Gaser C. The unique brain anatomy of meditation practitioners: alterations in cortical gyrification. *Frontiers in human neuroscience.* 2012;6.

366. Vestergaard-Poulsen P, van Beek M, Skewes J, et al. Long-term meditation is associated with increased gray matter density in the brain stem. *Neuroreport.* 2009;20(2):170-174.

367. University WS. Nutrition Basics. Washington State University. myNutrition Web site. https://mynutrition.wsu.edu/nutrition-basics#protein. Published 2019. Accessed October 1, 2019.

368. Amen DG. *Change your brain, change your life: The breakthrough program for conquering anxiety, depression, obsessiveness, lack of focus, anger, and memory problems.* 2 ed. New York: Harmony; 2015.

369. Koebnick C, Garcia AL, Dagnelie PC, et al. Long-Term Consumption of a Raw Food Diet Is Associated with Favorable Serum LDL Cholesterol and Triglycerides but Also with Elevated Plasma Homocysteine and Low Serum HDL Cholesterol in Humans. *The Journal of Nutrition.* 2005;135(10):2372-2378.

370. Almeida OP, al e. Successful mental health aging: results from a longitudinal study of older Australian men. *American Journal of Geriatric Psychiatry.* 2006;14:27-35.

371. Lytle ME, al. e. Exercise level and cognitive decline: the MoVIES project. *Alzheimer Disease & Associated Disorders.* 2004;18:57-63.

372. Weuve J, al. e. Physical activity including walking and cognitive function in older women. *Journal of the American Medical Association.* 2004;292:1454-1461.

373. Yaffe K, al. e. A prospective study of physical activity and cognitive decline in elderly women. *Archives of Internal Medicine.* 2001;161:1703-1708.

374. Larson EB, al. e. Exercise is associated with reduced risk for incident dementia among persons 65 years of age or older. *Annals of Internal Medicine.* 2006;144:73-81.

375. Kramer AF, Erickson KI. Capitalizing on cortical plasticity: influence of physical activity on cognition and brain function. *TRENDS in Cognitive Sciences.* 2007;11(8):342-348.

376. Colombe SJ, al e. Cardiovascular fitness, cortical plasticity, and aging. *Proceedings of the National Academy of Sciences.* 2004;101:3316-3321.

377. Goleman D. *Emotional intelligence: Why it can matter more than IQ.* New York: Bantam Books; 1995.

378. Goleman D. *Working with emotional intelligence.* New York: Bantam Books; 1998.

379. Branden N. *How to Raise Your Self-Esteem: The Proven Action-Oriented Approach to Greater Self-Respect and Self-Confidence* New York: Bantam; 1987.

380. Josephson M. Teaching ethical decision making and principled reasoning. *Ethics: Easier Said Than Done.* 1988;Winter:28-29.

381. Adler RB, Rosenfeld LB, Russell F. Proctor I. *Interplay: The process of interpersonal communication.* 10 ed. New York: Oxford University Press; 2007.

382. Buhrmester D, Furman W, Wittenberg MT, Reis HT. Five domains of interpersonal competence in peer relations. *Journal of Personality and Social Psychology.* 1988;55:991 – 1008.

383. Bavelas JB, Coates L, Johnson T. Listener responses as a collaborative process: The role of gaze. *Journal of Communication.* 2002;52:566-580.

384. Arundale RB. Face as relational and interactional: A communication framework for research on face, facework, and politeness. *Journal of Politeness Research Language, Behaviour, Culture.* 2006;2(2):193-216.

385. Goffman E. *The presentation of the self in everyday life.* New York: Doubleday; 1959.

386. Goffman E. *Interaction ritual: Essays on face-to-face behavior.* New York: Doubleday Anchor; 1967.

387. Francis CA. The Mediating Force of "Face": Supervisor Character and Status Related to Perceived Organizational Support and Work Outcomes. *Journal of Leadership & Organizational Studies.* 2012;19(1):58-67.

388. Mao LR. Beyond politeness theory: 'Face' revisited and renewed. *Journal of Pragmatics.* 1994;21(5):451-486.

389. Vilkki L. Politeness, face and facework: Current issues. *A Man of Measure Festschrift in honour of Fred Karlsson in his 60th birthday SKY Journal of Linguistics.* 2006;19(special supplement):322-332.

390. Baumeister RF, Leary MR. The need to belong: The desire for interpersonal attachments as a fundamental human motivation. *Psychological Bulletin.* 1995;117:497-529.

391. Blum-Kulka S. Indirectness and politeness in requests: Same or different? *Journal of Pragmatics.* 1987;11(2):131-146.

392. Bousfield D, Locher MA, eds. *Impoliteness in Language: Studies on its interplay with power in theory and practice.* Berlin: Mouton DeGruyter; 2008.

393. Brown P, Levinson SC. Universals in language usage: Politeness phenomenon. In: Goody EN, ed. *Questions and politeness.* Cambridge: Cambridge University Press; 1978:56-289.

394.   Holmes J. Politeness Strategies as Linguistic Variables. In: Editor-in-Chief: Keith B, ed. *Encyclopedia of Language & Linguistics (Second Edition).* Oxford: Elsevier; 2006:684-697.

395.   Post L, Senning DP. *Emily Post's Etiquette: Manners for today.* Vol 19. New York: Harper Collins; 2017.

396.   Brito R, Waldzus S, Sekerdej M, Schubert T. The contexts and structures of relating to others: How memberships in different types of groups shape the construction of interpersonal relationships. *Journal of Social and Personal Relationships.* 2011;28(3):406-432.

397.   Gottman JM. *What predicts divorce? The relationship between marital processes and marital outcomes.* Hillsdale, NJ: Lawrence Erlbaum Associates; 1994.

398.   Burgoon JK, Koper RJ. Nonverbal and relational communication associated with reticence. *Human Communication Research.* 1984;10:601-626.

399.   Chapman AJ. Eye contact, physical proximity and laughter: A re-examination of the equilibrium model of social intimacy. *Social Behavior and Personality.* 1975;3:143-155.

400.   Floyd K. *Communicating affection: Interpersonal behavior and social context.* Cambridge, England: Cambridge University Press; 2006.

401.   Judge TA, Erez A, Bono JE, Thoresen CJ. Are measures of self-esteem, neuroticism, locus of control, and generalized self-efficacy indicators of a common core construct? *Journal of Personality and Social Psychology.* 2002;83:693-710.

402.   Campbell JD, Lavallee LF. Who am I? The role of self-concept confusion in understanding the behavior of people with low self-esteem. In: Baumeister RF, ed. *Self-esteem: the puzzle of low self regard.* New York: Plenum press; 1993:3-20.

403.   Lange AJ, Jakubowski P. *Responsible assertive behavior.* Champaign, IL: Research Press; 1976.

404.   Norton R, Warnick B. Assertiveness as a communication construct. *Human Communication Research.* 1976;3:62-66.

405.   Infante DA, Rancer AS, Womack DF. *Building communication theory.* 4 ed. Prospect Heights, IL: Waveland Press; 2003.

Index

About the Author

Michele Poff earned her Bachelor of Arts in English literature from University of California at Berkeley, her Master of Arts in linguistics from Portland State University, and Doctor of Philosophy in communication at University of Washington: two of these are among the world's top ten universities and top three public universities, so any shortcomings in this book are not owing to her background. She is from the United States west coast and currently lives an imperfectly cruelty-free life predominantly in Central and South America, searching for warm serene beaches and surfable waves—atmospheres conducive to deep listening of self and other as well as pointed intellectual work. Michele has also lived in Germany and Italy for some years, and she speaks several European languages. She owns and runs Accomplish, a strategic communication consulting company, where she helps businesses and individuals with their writing, research, and instructional design needs.

Notes

Made in the USA
Columbia, SC
20 September 2020

21225212R00198